Teaching Fear

Nicole E. Rader

TEACHING FEAR

How We Learn to Fear Crime and Why It Matters

TEMPLE UNIVERSITY PRESS
Philadelphia • Rome • Tokyo

TEMPLE UNIVERSITY PRESS
Philadelphia, Pennsylvania 19122
tupress.temple.edu

Copyright © 2023 by Temple University—Of The Commonwealth System
   of Higher Education
All rights reserved
Published 2023

Library of Congress Cataloging-in-Publication Data

Names: Rader, Nicole E., author.
Title: Teaching fear : how we learn to fear crime and why it matters /
   Nicole E. Rader.
Description: Philadelphia : Temple University Press, 2023. | Includes
   bibliographical references and index. | Summary: "This book covers the
   myths we learn about crime and how we learn them and teach them. It
   covers cultural, educational, and familial sources and the harmful
   behaviors and beliefs that follow. It also details how we might teach
   future generations more accurately about safety"—Provided by
   publisher.
Identifiers: LCCN 2022024965 (print) | LCCN 2022024966 (ebook) | ISBN
   9781439921029 (cloth) | ISBN 9781439921036 (paperback) | ISBN
   9781439921043 (pdf)
Subjects: LCSH: Fear of crime—United States. | Crime—United
   States—Public opinion. | Women—United States—Attitudes. |
   Women—Crimes against—Prevention. | Children—Crimes
   against—Prevention.
Classification: LCC HV6250.3.U5 R33 2023 (print) | LCC HV6250.3.U5
   (ebook) | DDC 362.880973—dc23/eng/20220831
LC record available at https://lccn.loc.gov/2022024965
LC ebook record available at https://lccn.loc.gov/2022024966

♾ The paper used in this publication meets the requirements of the American National
Standard for Information Sciences—Permanence of Paper for Printed Library Materials,
ANSI Z39.48-1992

Printed in the United States of America

9 8 7 6 5 4 3 2 1

This book is dedicated to three fearless women in my life: my daughter, Kate; my sister, Sarah; and my mother, Pam.

Contents

	Acknowledgments	ix
1	**Gendered Crime Myths**	1
	Why Gender Matters	2
	Crime Myths	6
2	**Learning Myths**	18
	Learning from Loved Ones—Parents	18
	Learning from Authority Figures at School	33
	Learning from Strangers—the Media	39
3	**Living Out Crime Myths**	49
	Action-Based Precautionary Behaviors	50
	Avoidance-Oriented Crime Prevention Strategies	60
	Adaptation	68
	Consequences	77

4	**Raising Gen Z Children with Gen X Safety Values**	80
	Instilling Safety Values	84
	Using Safety Lessons from the Past	85
	Teaching Fear with an Eye to the Future	94
5	**What Kids Hear and What Kids Fear**	108
	What Kids Hear Parents Say	109
	Translating What Kids Hear from Parents to What Kids Fear	112
	Kids at School	116
	Other Things Learned from Kids	121
	Kids Teaching Other Kids	128
6	**How to Teach Fear Better**	132
	What Society Can Do	133
	What We Can Do	138
	Conclusions	147
	Appendix: Research Studies	149
	Notes	155
	References	183
	Index	199

Acknowledgments

Teaching Fear has been a long time coming; it has been in the forefront of my mind for most of my academic career. It has only recently come to the surface because of the support and encouragement of many people.

My husband, Cody, and children, Lucas and Kate, were the best coaches and cheerleaders for me while I wrote this book. Thank you to all of you for your dinner time conversations that made me feel I could keep moving forward with this project. Thank you for being a sounding board when I needed it, for pushing me when I wanted to give up, and for being so genuinely happy for me at the conclusion of this book. You gave me the confidence to do this. I am so thankful for all of you, and I love you all.

My extended family were also great listeners and encouraged me during the time I wrote this book. To my dad, Jim, for his weekly calls inquiring about my book, to my mom, Pam, who always knows how to make me feel like I can do anything, to my brother, Jason; my stepdad, Tom; my stepmom, Paige; and my step-siblings, Jody, Kelly, David, and Brett: I am so thankful for your support during this time! My sister, Sarah, battled cancer during the time that I wrote *Teaching Fear*. I am grateful that I was able to spend time with her while she got well, and I thank her for all her advice on this book! Finally, Di and Byron, my wonderful in-laws, have been supportive of me and my career over the years, and I am grateful for them! My family has always been the most important thing in my life, and I thank all of you for your amazing support of me now and always.

I have been lucky to live in a community where I have an incredible support system; as they say, it takes a village. Thank you to all my friends who were there for me during this time when work and life were both very intense. Thank you especially to Rowan Haug, Megan Bean, Florencia Meyer, Michelle Anderson, and Polly Fulford for helping me with kids, doing girls' nights when I needed them, and listening to me talk about this book; you all are the best!

My work community of friends and colleagues was also extremely helpful during this time. Maggie Hagerman was a huge help to me from the time I conceptualized this book until I finished it. Thank you for reading chapters and talking through concepts and the organization of *Teaching Fear* with me and for your friendship! Tommy Anderson was a great listener during this time—thank you for encouraging me to keep moving forward! Thank you also to Raymond Barranco for your advice reading chapters and thank you to Kimberly Kelly, my longtime friend and colleague, for also being supportive of me while I wrote this book.

Special thanks to Courtney Heath, who served as my research assistant while I wrote this book, and to Paula Jones, Mary Ann Dean, Stacey Wilkinson, Jeanett Mallett, and the Department of Sociology at Mississippi State University. The staff in the main office have listened to me talk about this book more than anyone else besides my husband and children. Thank you for your encouragement during this project. The Mississippi State University Department of Sociology has been my home for 16 years and I am fortunate to have (and have had) amazing colleagues, bosses, students, and staff to work with over the years. I want to thank all of you for believing in me and making my workplace a fun and happy place each day.

Thank you to the staff in the Mississippi State University College of Arts and Sciences dean's office who were supportive of me writing this book while I was an associate dean. *Teaching Fear* likely would not have gotten started if you all were not in my lives in just the right moment! Thank you to Rick Travis for his reassurance that I could write a book while also serving as an administrator. Rick has been one of my biggest advocates and I am thankful to him for taking a chance on me and supporting me over the past six years.

I'd also like to thank all of the faculty who have mentored me over the years at Southern Illinois University Carbondale, Drury University, and Central Methodist University. Special thanks to Michelle Hughes Miller.

Thank you to the reviewers, to the Temple University Press Board, and to the editorial team at Temple University Press for making this book better and helping me tell the best story. Special thanks to Ryan Mulligan for his belief in my project.

Finally, thank you to my participants, who have taken time out of their lives to participate in my projects and who have shared their lives with me. It is only because of you that *Teaching Fear* is possible.

Teaching Fear

1
Gendered Crime Myths

Madeleine McCann, a British 4-year-old girl, disappeared from an apartment bed while on vacation with her family in Portugal in 2007. Her disappearance remains unsolved despite her case being described by the *Daily Telegraph* as the "most heavily reported missing-person case in modern history."[1] In 2005, Natalee Holloway, an 18-year-old girl from Alabama, went missing during a high school graduation trip to Aruba. Her remains were never found and her murder was never solved. Elizabeth Smart, a 14-year-old girl, disappeared from her Utah bedroom in 2002. One year later, she was found alive, having endured a horrific experience, held hostage by two fanatical religious individuals who repeatedly drugged, sexually assaulted, and tortured her.[2] Finally, JonBenet Ramsey, a 6-year-old girl, was found dead in her home in 1990, and the crime remains unsolved.[3] As a frequent beauty pageant contestant, many videos of the pageants circulated to the general public, providing constant media images of JonBenet. Whether it be Madeleine McCann, Natalee Holloway, Elizabeth Smart, or JonBenet Ramsey, most readers can picture their faces. These cases capture viewer attention because of the horrific nature of each crime and because these victims are seen as vulnerable (young white girls).

Sensationalized kidnapping cases influence what we think about crime and what scares us; they also affect the steps we take to prevent victimization. You probably heard about kidnapping prevention strategies growing up, all of which emphasized the dangers associated with strangers. For example, you may recall being told never take candy from a stranger or never go with a stranger no matter what they say to you. If you are a parent, you likely teach your children similar things about stranger danger that you were taught growing up. While a common practice, you may be surprised to know that many of the core safety beliefs we hold and teach to others are based on crime myths that distinctively apply to women.[4]

Statistically speaking, most people (both men and women) are never going to experience victimization. For example, a 2018 Bureau of Justice Statistics report found that only 21 out of every 1,000 people in the United States were victims of violent crime.[5] Put another way, there is a 2.1 percent chance of experiencing personal victimization. When crime does happen, most offenses reported to the police are committed *against* men *by* men. The National Crime Victimization Survey consistently finds that men are more likely than women to be victims of a crime—except for the crime of sexual assault, where women are more likely to be victims. Further, women of color are more likely to be crime victims, including of sexual assault, than white women.[6] So while we frequently see young, white women as victims through the media, statistics paint a much different picture.[7]

Although women (especially white women) are unlikely to become victims of crime, women are more likely to fear crime than men. This finding is so prominent in the research that it has been called the gender-fear paradox.[8] Women's fear of crime is paradoxical because it is not rooted in actual victimization odds. As we shall see, this paradox is partially explained through gendered safety myths.[9] For women, especially white women, gendered safety myths that dictate fear of crime are out of line with the reality of their victimization chances.

Why Gender Matters

Stanford Sociologist Cecilia Ridgeway argues that gender is one of our primary frames for organizing relations in society.[10] Society has different expectations for girls and boys that ultimately create what Ridgeway calls "the rules of gender." There are unspoken rules that women follow because these things are just things that women *should do*.[11] These daily and subtle taken-for-granted actions are an essential part of a gendered upbringing, one that may not always be conscious.[12] Society likely influences gender roles, gendered attitudes, and gendered behavior much more than we may realize. Such gendered rules pressure people to conform to the more traditional gender roles and behaviors they perform each day.[13] As Ridgeway says, gender is like a frame for a photograph or the rose-colored glasses we sometimes wear when we see something through a lens.

There are several examples of gender rules we learn through childhood. In University of California, Berkeley, sociology professor Barrie Thorne's classic work *Gender Play*, she spent hours observing elementary school–aged children on the playground, in the classroom, and in the lunchroom.[14] Not surprisingly, she found that gender boundaries were already apparent. Her work found that gender play was sex-segregated on multiple levels. Boys defended their identity by picking on girls and defended the boundary within their group of friends, and boys and girls segregated into gendered activities. Such gendered cultures in elementary school ultimately set the stage for gender dynamics in later years.

Another example comes from research on gendered speech patterns among boys and girls. Researchers have found that boys are more likely than girls to use assertive speech and assertive strategies (i.e., confrontation, physical aggression) to mitigate conflict. In contrast, girls are more likely to use "affiliative strategies" (collaborative solutions, seeking to change the topic) to reduce conflict.[15] While subtle, gender rules surrounding such speech patterns can inhibit girls' confidence and assertiveness in making decisions.

The media further supply gender rules for young girls and women.[16] For example, the media often portray only those women who meet idealized beauty standards (e.g., those who have thinner body sizes than average women in America) and treat them as sex objects.[17] The media also present women in stereotypical gender roles, such as mother, girlfriend, or wife, and in gender-traditional occupations that emphasize nurturing characteristics.[18] The impact of these gendered stereotypes is often severe, especially for young girls and teens, who are taught from a young age that women are objects and only fit in traditional gendered boxes.[19]

For example, University of Colorado, Boulder, psychology professor Elizabeth Daniels and her colleagues found that more than half of stories in teen magazines focused on physical appearance more than anything else, and nearly three-quarters of advertising in these magazines did as well.[20] These findings show the importance of the idealized body image sold to teens who ultimately become adult consumers. In another study focusing on television, researchers Alexander Sink and Dana Mastro from the University of California, Santa Barbara, examined projections of women and men on TV.[21] They concluded that "many empirical studies demonstrate that media use, particularly television viewing, exerts a small but significant influence on gender role attitudes and gendered behavior."[22] Women and girls may see other women in magazines or on television who do not necessarily act or look like them and may strive to achieve such idealized notions of femininity.

Finally, paid work and the division of labor in the household are other arenas where gender rules create expectations for women.[23] For example, women struggle with work-life balance issues, since women are responsible for more housework and childcare than men, even when both partners in the household have full-time jobs.[24] Thus, even though today's men do more at home and as fathers than men did in the 1950s, gaps persist between women's and men's unpaid labor in the domestic sphere. These differences ultimately reinforce gender stereotypes about ideal types of women, such as excellent mothers who put their families before their jobs. Such gender stereotypes even persist in high-earning dual-career families. Jill Yavorsky and her colleagues at the Ohio State University researched high-earning dual-career couples who had just become parents.[25] Using surveys and time journals with the participants, they found some critical insights about the division of labor. While paid work hours stayed the same for both men and women once they became parents, women did two hours more housework per day in the home after having a child, whereas men did 40 minutes of housework more per day. Thus, even between dual-earning couples, we still see a gap in the division of labor. So, even in households with the resources to share work in more gender-equal ways, we still see traditional gender norms surrounding the family and work.

The rules of gender are clear-cut for most areas of social life. However, it is essential to note that gender is also more than just a fixed, permanent role.[26] Put another way; you are not simply a sponge that sucks up learning without any ability to decide who you are or what you do. Gender is something you *do*, not something you *are*. University of California, Santa Cruz, sociologist Candace West and University of California, Santa Barbara, sociologist Don Zimmerman came up with the term "doing gender" to describe this very process.[27] Women learn the rules of gender, which teach appropriate femininity stemming from established gender norms. However, we have a choice in how we live out gendered lives. The key is that if we choose to violate these rules, it may mean that we will be punished or have consequences. It is also crucial that we understand that social forces are at work and typically push most ideas on us. For example, you may not even realize your daughter owns gendered toys because every toy in the "girl" aisle is pink, traditionally feminine, and exemplifies nurturing qualities (e.g., dolls). Women "accomplish" femininity, then, through a combination of social forces, accountability to the norms, and their own actions. Whether through dress, language, occupation, the management of conflicts, or the division of labor in the household, we accomplish gender each day.[28]

Gendered Safety Beliefs

You might be surprised to hear that what we learn, believe in, and value about safety is gendered. I'd argue that gendered safety beliefs are more antiquated than beliefs about some other areas of social life. For example, women learn that they are supposed to be afraid of crime (and men are not). Women also learn that they should fear strangers (stranger danger centers around men) and under what circumstances (when in public locations and when alone). Finally, many preventive measures women rely on to avoid potential victimization require total avoidance of certain spaces or reliance on others for protection. As we shall see, these gendered safety beliefs are very much a part of the white woman crime victim myth.

We can see facets of gendered safety messages emerge in childhood. For example, research shows that parents supervise girls at greater levels than boys. Parents more closely monitor girls' behaviors by keeping their daughters closer than sons and within sight range. Boys, on the other hand, are allowed to run free and without much supervision.[29] In other words, behaviors of boys and girls are judged using different standards.[30] Different expectations for the behaviors of sons versus daughters lead to differential consequences for misbehavior.[31] Research has found that when boys do not live up to parental expectations, the consequences are less harsh than for girls who engage in similar behaviors. By having different expectations and levels of supervision for girls and boys, we create gendered safety beliefs.

Researcher Saskia De Groof reinforces these points in her study with Flemish adolescents.[32] The study found gender differences in fear of crime among these adolescents, with girls fearing at much higher levels than boys. Parents of the youth participants were also surveyed in the study. De Groof found that parents restricted girls' free time, whereas parents allowed boys more free time in public spaces (e.g., outdoors). De Groof discussed the importance of socialization and the implications of the study, stating, "during childhood and adolescence, youngsters are taught not only what to fear but what not to fear, and sometimes not to show fear at all . . . girls are socialized to be vulnerable, to need protection, to [avoid] risk . . . , to be cautious, to care, and so on. Boys are socialized to protect, to take risks, and to be aware of their physical strength. . . . girls are allowed to fear, but boys are not. Women—as the symbolic paradigm suggest—are culturally coded to be vulnerable and helpless, men to be fearless or even aggressive."[33] De Groof's research also ties to research with adults that has found that women fear more than men. While the reasons for these gendered differences will certainly vary as we age, the importance of social learning in this process cannot be understated.[34]

Safety guidelines during childhood, then, teach girls to be more afraid of crime and to fear strangers and public spaces, and that boys are better able to protect themselves from harm.[35] While the difference in safety advice between girls and boys is not always this clean-cut, researchers have shown that gendered safety lessons and guidelines carry over to adulthood and may help explain women's higher fear of crime levels.

My research with married and divorced women found that women "do gendered fear." There are many safety behaviors women engage in and many places they are expected to avoid because they are women. For example, women are expected to act fearful—we anticipate that women in society fear crime because we've taught women that this is what women should do. However, women also have agency (although restricted agency) in how they react to expectations of gendered behavior. For instance, when talking to recently divorced women, I found many had relied on husbands to be in charge of safety precautions in the home. However, once the women became divorced, they had to develop new ways to meet their own safety needs. Thus, the ways that divorced women did gendered fear was noticeably different post-divorce.

Whether it be from parents, schools, friends, or the media, women are taught gendered safety images in ways that give women little choice but to buy into gendered safety practices.[36] It makes sense, then, that women fear crime more than men. Women are taught from a young age to believe they are the most likely crime victims. They also come to rely on the gendered myth that women should fear unknown men in public spaces. The reliance on this crime myth can have profound implications. Women may believe they have a higher likelihood of criminal victimization than is warranted and may restrict their activities based on these beliefs.

Crime Myths

There are three key gendered safety myths that most influence women's fear of crime and are the focus of this book. These include the "stranger danger myth," the idea that criminals are always unknown people (typically men), the "white woman crime victim myth," the idea that white women are the most likely crime victims, and the "victim-centered crime prevention myth," the idea that through individual precautionary efforts, potential victims can prevent victimization. These crime myths translate into how women learn and teach fear to others, thus recirculating gendered crime myths from generation to generation and making them a staple of our society.

The Stranger Danger Myth

Most people are familiar with the phrase "stranger danger." Stranger danger suggests that all strangers have the capability to hurt people.[37] However, statistics show that a fear of strangers is unwarranted since most crime victims know their attacker. It is important to know that your chances of being victimized by a stranger are very low. For example, data from the National

Incident-Based Reporting System found that less than 12 percent of all crimes were committed by strangers.[38] So, statistically speaking, the chance of being victimized at all is low, but if victimization does occur, the possibility of being victimized by a stranger is even lower.

Knowing the chances of stranger-induced victimization are low, how does the stranger danger myth live on in society? Historically, stranger danger became a fabric of our culture in the 1970s, when surveys with Americans started to reveal a pattern of mistrust of other people, especially among those living in urban areas.[39] Even these days, when looking at the General Social Survey (GSS), a national survey conducted each year, we see some interesting results.[40] In 2018, 64 percent of Americans said that "you can't be too careful" when asked the question, "generally speaking, would you say that most people can be trusted or that you can't be too careful in dealing with people." Americans, then, lack trust toward others. In the same survey, 33 percent of Americans said they were afraid to walk in their neighborhoods at night, indicating a fear of strangers in public places. The two GSS questions were highly related—those who did not trust others were also more afraid of crime. The combination of trust, fear, and misinformation about the likelihood of stranger-induced victimization helps solidify the stranger danger myth.

The stranger danger myth is so taken for granted, so much a part of our lives, that we don't even notice we primarily fear strangers. As M.A. Stokes notes, "The stranger is the modern embodiment of the 'wicked witch' or 'bogeyman.' We fear more for those who we think cannot protect themselves from the bogeyman and those who are seen as more physically vulnerable (e.g., women, the elderly, and children). To avoid interactions and violence by strangers, we teach 'stranger danger' to our children along with an armory of possible prevention techniques. Thus, strangers produce the most fear of crime among people but especially among women."[41]

Thinking back to your childhood, do you remember learning about ways to stay safe from strangers? In my research over the years, I've found that when people are asked to recollect what they remember about crime growing up, they talk about the same images with fascinating consistency. Childhood images consistently focus on stranger danger and ways to prevent victimization at the hands of strangers.

The personal characteristics of strangers are also part of the stranger danger myth. If I say the word "stranger" to you, what do you envision? More than likely, you envision a crime when hear the word "stranger," and the stranger you see is probably an unknown man.[42] The unspoken vivid image of male strangers is hardwired into the brains of every fourth grader learning about stranger danger through educational programs like McGruff the Crime Dog.[43] In fact, in my research spanning 20 years on the topic of women's fear of crime, not one respondent has ever mentioned, described, or even used a female pronoun (she, her, hers) when describing or discussing a threatening stranger. It is pretty powerful to think about this taken-for-granted element—*strangers are always male*. Thus, the fundamental premise that male strangers are to be avoided and feared is vital for our mental picture of crime and influences how we teach safety lessons to others.

Mythical Beliefs and Stranger-Induced Crimes
Kidnapping and sexual assault are two horrific crimes that cause a lot of fear of crime. While both crimes are horrible, they are rarely committed by strangers to the victim. Nevertheless, people continually rank these two crimes high on the list of things they fear happening to them or their loved ones, in part because they are *perceived as* typical.[44] Another reason these two crimes rank high on the list is that they involve two groups often perceived as vulnerable to victimization—women and children.[45] The impact of the stranger danger myth, then, is that women are fearful, and parents fear for children.[46]

When it comes to kidnapping, only 1 percent of all missing children in the United States are abducted by a stranger. Yet parents and people in general spend an incredible amount of time worrying about, fearing, and taking action against the possibility of this extremely rare crime. According to researcher Joel Best, fear of kidnapping became a national phenomenon in the mid-1980s.[47] A fear of children going missing was not considered worthy of public concern until 1981, when the term "missing children" was coined. The timetable defining and labeling missing children as a social problem does not mean that children did not go missing before 1981. It only suggests that Americans saw missing children kidnapped by a stranger after 1981 as a social problem that they should worry about. As Best goes on to explain, "Americans saw photographs of missing children on milk cartons and grocery bags, billboards and televised service messages. Toy stores and fast-food restaurants distributed abduction-prevention tips for both parents and children. Parents could have their children fingerprinted or videotaped to make identification easier. . . . In short, ordinary citizens may have encountered explicit reminders of missing children more often than reminders of any other social problem."[48]

Kidnapping messages were particularly relevant for the Generation X (often called Gen X) birth cohort (born between 1965 and 1980).[49] Gen Xers, then, would have been in their elementary or middle school years when kidnapping campaigns were at their height (the mid-1980s) and would have a distinctive connection to kidnapping as visualized through this lens (at the hands of strangers). When Gen Xers grew up, they began to have children of their own, and their childhood fears of kidnapping translated into how they viewed safety and risk for their children. Gen Z children (born between 1997 and 2012), who often have Gen X parents, learned safety values and what to fear from their parents, who relied on their 1980s childhoods to help make sense of crime.[50] In my research, Gen X parents and Gen Z children talk about stranger-perpetrated kidnapping with concern. Parents mention kidnapping as a fear-producing crime, but they also implement numerous precautions to keep their children safe from abduction. Children rely heavily on parental messages of kidnapping when they talk about their fear of crime as well. Thus, while only 1 percent of missing children are taken by a stranger, kidnapping fears typify the stranger danger crime myth.

In terms of sexual assault, stranger-perpetrated sexual assault is also mythical. Crime statistics suggest that only 14 percent of sexual assault victims who report to the police are assaulted by an unknown person. Put another way: sexual assault victims have an 86 percent chance of being sexually victimized by someone *other than a stranger*.[51] Yet we teach and expect women to fear strangers and abide by safety precautions that prevent stranger-induced sexual victimization. It is easy to see how sexual assault becomes part of the stranger danger myth.

Criminology professor Hannah Scott studied this very notion: how likely is stranger danger for women, and what do women do about it?[52] Using survey data with 12,300 Canadian women, she found that women overwhelmingly feared strangers. Scott explains, "What this suggests is that experience with male strangers plays a stronger formative role in fear production in the lives of women than how old they are, whether they are single, what their financial resources may be, and to a less extent what educational achievement they may have made over their lives."[53] Scott also found that women who were the most afraid of crime avoided places or situations where strangers lurked. Women also took various precautions, including carrying a weapon, avoiding walking by boys or men in public spaces, avoiding walking alone after dark, avoiding using public transportation alone after dark, checking the back seat of the car, and avoiding parking garages when alone after dark. These behaviors provided women options to avoid or protect themselves from strangers.

The stranger-induced sexual assault myth, then, has some significant consequences for women. First, it means that women fear the wrong types of people. Because women are taught from a young age to fear only unknown men sexually assaulting them, they often worry less about the potential likelihood of being sexually assaulted by a known man, such as a date, boyfriend, or male friend, each of whom is more likely to be the perpetrator of sexual assault. Women are rarely taught to fear known attackers, thus providing the wrong message to women about sexual assault prevention.

Further, the stranger-induced sexual assault myth focuses on unknown elements of sexual assault for women (i.e., an unknown male attacker in an undisclosed location). With so many unknowns, many women fear all crime because they believe any can turn into a sexual assault. For example, a home invasion may turn into a sexual assault, a robbery may turn into a sexual assault, or a harassing encounter on the street may turn into a sexual assault. Ferraro used the term the "shadow of sexual assault" to explain how fear of sexual assault seeps over to a fear of all crime.[54] Since the mid-1990s, the shadow of sexual assault theory has been tested by many researchers and is a primary cause of women's fear.[55]

Whether through kidnapping or sexual assault, societal fears of stranger danger reinforce gendered crime myths and simultaneously steer precautions taken to protect "vulnerable groups" from these crimes. Stranger danger myths (especially those surrounding kidnapping and sexual assault) supersede other reasons one might fear crime, such as other personal characteristics (race, class, age) and even one's previous experience with direct victimization (being a victim) or indirect victimization (knowing or hearing about a victimization experience).

The White Woman Crime Victim Myth

White women are less likely than women of color to be crime victims.[56] However, while white women have low levels of victimization risk, there is a societal perception that white women are more likely than other types of people to be crime victims.[57] Therefore, it is essential to understand where the white woman crime victim myth comes from and why it persists. The process of convincing women of this myth begins in childhood, where parents give children guidance and rules on acting appropriately for a person's gender.

Projecting Racialized Images

It is clear that crime myths are gendered and almost exclusively apply to women, but what is it about being a *white* woman that is connected to crime myths? First, it is important to note that because of societal norms and historical factors, white women have benefitted from chivalry, mobilization, and opportunity compared to other groups of women.[58] In addition, compared to different groups of women, white women similarly benefit from the racialized/gendered privilege attached to perceptions of and treatment of crime victims.[59]

As New York University researcher Kristen Day explains, "Women's fear stems in part from race privilege and from race prejudice. White women, for instance, frequently fear men of color, who are demonized as aggressive and hypersexualized in relation to 'vulnerable' White women."[60] White women, then, are viewed by society as "vulnerable" when it comes to potential victimization. We know that part of the reason society sees white women *as* vulnerable is that they are *perceived* as vulnerable. Even though women of color are more likely than white women to be crime victims, women of color are rarely considered "vulnerable" to victimization.

Society is influenced heavily by something Syracuse University communications researcher Carol Liebler calls the "missing white woman syndrome" when deciding who is a likely crime victim.[61] The missing white woman syndrome is defined as "The national media's selective coverage of pretty, young kidnapping, sexual assault, and murder victims and the exclusion of girls and women of color who have met the same fate."[62] We can see how being white is just as important here as being a woman. We do not think of women of color when we think of kidnapping victims because the media rarely pick up the stories of women of color.[63] Because of these sensationalized media stories that paint white women as the most likely crime victims, the missing white woman syndrome persists. The consequences of the missing white woman syndrome are significant for non-white women and also for white women. Both reinforce racialized and gendered ideologies and ultimately reproduce crime myths.

While white women benefit from the privilege of societal focus on their possible vulnerability and their victimhood experiences, such a focus is a smoke-and-mirrors trick, as is the focus on chivalry, vulnerability, and being viewed as in need of protection. White women ultimately need to modify their daily lives to fit in and live up to these expectations. For example, white women are expected to avoid public spaces after dark or when alone at all costs with little rationale for why they should do so. Such behavioral modifications reduce freedom of mobility and routine activities.

Sociology researcher Kristine De Welde's work on fear of crime is an excellent example of the additive effect of race and gender for white women.[64] She spent three and a half years with white middle-class women who took self-defense classes. De Welde first explains why being a white woman matters. Self-defense classes did make women feel empowered, but constant exposure "[reifies] the public/private split by encouraging women to remain 'safe' in their homes, away from the dangers of crime-ridden streets."[65] The effect of the public/private split for white women is an increased fear of strangers and a restriction in public space. Thus, for De Welde, while being a white woman comes with privilege in many ways, these overblown and unrealistic safety concerns are likely unique to white women's lived experience.

A second point that becomes very important in constructing the white woman as a crime victim is the myth that Black men hurt white women. Again, the combination of race and gender here (Black man, white woman) make the myth so pervasive. The history of racism in America greatly contributes to the prominence and apprehension of this racialized image. The "Black man as offender" construction and the "white woman as victim" construction both have a long and ugly history in the United States. Before and during the Civil War, Black men who were slaves were accused of and convicted of raping white women married to white slave owners. Researchers have since found that male slave owners promoted the paranoia of a relationship between their wives and enslaved men to keep women and slaves alike in a position of powerlessness. The majority of rapes during this period more likely occurred when white men slave owners victimized Black women slaves, while most relationships between Black men slaves and white women were more likely to be consensual. After Reconstruction, fear of relationships between Black men and white women in the South continued on, as explained by New York University historian Martha Hodes: "the shift away from white toleration for sex between white women and black men accompanied the political transformations that came with the demise of racial slavery. The separation of blacks and whites was essential to Southern whites who were determined to retain supremacy after the Civil War. . . . Because it was the men among the former slave population who gained suffrage rights and a measure of political power—and who therefore had the potential to destroy the racial caste system—whites focused on the taboo of sex between white women and black men with a new urgency."[66]

The post–Civil War anxiety about Black men was also exacerbated by Ku Klux Klansmen, who focused on protecting white women from Black men. As Hodes goes on to explain, "Klansmen took offense when a black man acted in a manner they judged even mildly insulting to a white woman. In the minds of Klansmen and their sympathizers, the rape of white women was the logical extreme to which black men would go without the institution of slavery to restrain them."[67] What we can learn from historians, then, is that the image of the white woman as crime victim and the Black man as rapist has long been rooted in American culture.

Although inaccurate, these myths and images gained staying power and continued to fuel myths about victimization, offending, and perceptions of risk. As researchers have noted, many Americans see only Black men in their minds' eyes when they think about offenders.[68] Some have argued that racial stereotyping of Black men by the criminal justice system is so commonplace that "race and crime are already so deeply connected that it is unnecessary to speak directly of race, because talking about crime is talking about race."[69] False images of Black men offenders perpetrating crimes on white women victims provide incorrect information.[70] Black men have the highest rate of victimization of all groups of people.

Further, most crime is intraracial, so when Black men are offenders, they are likely to hurt other Black men. When Black women are victimized, they are hurt by Black men, and when white women are victimized, they are hurt by white men. Thus, the white woman as victim and Black man as perpetrator stereotype is indeed a myth.[71] Although not based in reality, such beliefs are a powerful indication of the construction of and belief in the white woman crime victim myth. Because fear of crime and societal coverage of victims are tied to white women, we can see how the white woman crime victim myth perseveres in society.

The white woman crime victim myth is enhanced by the fact that there are very few studies on the experiences of women of color and what women of color learn through childhood and within the family about safety and fear of crime.

Because existing research is mainly focused on white experiences, we do not know as much as we should about Black and Latinx individuals' fear of crime. Black and Latina women have remained virtually invisible when considering fear of crime and victimization risks by the general public, the media, and researchers alike. Michigan State University criminologist Jennifer Cobbina and her colleagues provide an exception in their study of disadvantaged urban African American youth.[72] They found that African American women in their study took various precautions to prevent victimization, indicating similarities to white women. African American women's specific behaviors included avoiding public spaces, especially where men dominated the space. Future research needs to determine what women of color fear, how they try to prevent victimization, and how accurate these prevention efforts are in crime reduction. Further, as an extension of this book, I plan to examine how safety beliefs and fear are discussed and negotiated in Black families.[73] These critical parts of racial socialization and how they differentially affect various race and ethnic identities likely play into crime myths more than we are accounting for in the research.

Another reason this research is important is that we also do not know much about how women of color perceive white women's victimization odds. In a study with Black, white, and Latinx women in New York and New Jersey, sociologist Esther Madriz found that non-white women also believed white women were the most likely crime victims.[74] The respondents of her study, regardless of racial identity, saw white women as "innocent" and in need of protection. As she notes, "Consistent with my hypothesis, white middle-class women fit the image of the innocent victim that prevails in mainstream society's ideology of crime."[75] In other words, it is not only white women who believe that they are more likely to be crime victims. Even women who have much higher chances of becoming crime victims, like Black or Latina women, also think that white women are more likely to experience victimization.

As a result, both women of color and white women are placed in categories that do not help prevent victimization. A more accurate picture of what women should fear and teach others about fear is needed.

The Victim-Centered Crime Prevention Myth

A final myth about crime that women are taught throughout their lifetime is that potential victims are responsible for victim prevention.[76] This myth emphasizes victim responsibility rather than societal responsibility for victimization prevention. When we think of victimization prevention advice, education, or programming, we mostly think about advice to potential victims. An alternative victimization prevention campaign seems illogical. For example, what would a campaign look like that taught offenders how not to be offenders? Or taught ways that all people (both victims and those who will never be victims) can reduce victimization in society as a whole? Because the focus is on *victim-centered* crime prevention, a variety of responsibilities fall on the shoulders of potential victims, and we sidestep/miss out on the opportunity to focus on the societal reasons victimization against women occurs, such as the reinforcement of societal rape myths.[77]

To see this victim-focused prevention myth, one only has to look at any victim prevention literature. This literature tells women to avoid going out late at night, avoid going out alone, always take a buddy, watch how much they drink, watch what they wear, and always have an exit strategy. While some of these precautions may be good advice, they rarely protect women from being sexually assaulted.[78]

Sociologist Alex Campbell studied how the victim prevention myth is perpetuated in society.[79] Campbell found that victim-centered sexual assault prevention advice is available on college campuses, at police stations, from ads on television, from women's magazines, on television shows, and on the internet. Further, Campbell found that prevention advice across these sources had similarities. For example, in all areas, women were the market group for prevention literature that provided guidance on safekeeping strategies. Prevention advice further highlighted stranger danger and sexual assault victimization. All of these lend themselves to fear of stranger-induced crime and victim-centered prevention.

A victim prevention document produced for police officers by the U.S. Department of Justice shows another example of victim-centered prevention efforts.[80] The document highlights self-protection information, ways to report a crime, how to locate a police station, locations of dangerous areas, and information regarding neighborhood watch programs and sex offender registries. However, there is no guidance on ways to inform and educate potential victims of interpersonal crimes or how to prevent such crimes. Thus, while not the primary motivation of prevention training, police officers are trained to reinforce the victim-centered prevention myth.

Finally, even the media significantly contribute to the victim-centered crime prevention myth. For example, in an NBC news story, the book *The New Super Power for Women* is discussed.[81] Newswriter Steve Kardian discusses "the seven-second rule: how to avoid being an easy target." In the NBC article, we see a picture of a woman walking late at night, grabbing her purse tightly as she is approached by a person we assume is a man (he is larger than the woman) with a black hoodie. The woman is clearly afraid. The article says, "it can take a seasoned criminal less than seven seconds to size you up. To decide whether you would be easy to rob, assault, kidnap, or whatever else is on his mind. Count to seven now: One. Two. Three. Four. Five. Six. Seven." The article goes on to say, "Remember to be a STAAR; Stride: Take forceful, confident steps with a gait that is neither too short nor too long. Tall: Shoulders back, chin up. Arms: Let them bend naturally at the elbow and swing them as you walk. Awareness: Take a look around as you walk, noticing people and things that might seem out of place. Relax: Above all, stay calm, cool, and collected."[82]

As the STAAR campaign showcases, stranger danger and victim-centered prevention techniques are deemed necessary in preventing victimization. Another element of potential victimization prevention involves the physical body. Most safety advice women receive focuses on the possibility of being overpowered by a physically stronger male stranger. Women learn they cannot physically break free from male stranger attackers, but they are still required to be responsible for victim prevention.[83] Women's choice for crime prevention, then, is limited to avoiding public spaces and other places where strangers lurk. Many women may feel that they will never physically measure up to a possible attacker, and, therefore, they do not try to occupy spaces where they believe attackers may exist. My research with my colleagues Lynne Cossman and Jeremy Porter examined the relationship between perceptions of physical vulnerability and fear of victimization.[84] When women believe they are more vulnerable to victimization, they are more afraid of crime.

Further, in the interview research I've done over the years, one key difference between men and women is that women fear *all* men who are strangers in a public space. In contrast, men tend to fear other men who are strangers in a public space based on the attacker's size. The men I have interviewed tell me this is because they are sizing up their ability to win in a physical attack. Women, on the other hand, feel vulnerable around strange men in public spaces no matter what.

The outcome of victim-centered prevention efforts is that women are expected to stay on high alert and take many precautions each day to avoid potential victimization, even though these prevention efforts are for a situation that will likely never occur.[85] As discussed, sexual assault by a stranger is a significant fear for women, yet most sexual assaults occur between people who know each other and in private dwellings. Thus, avoiding public spaces will not reduce victimization likelihood most of the time. Much research has also been done to show that sexual assault is not a matter of sexual excitement for offenders but is about enforcing power dynamics and taking power away from a victim. So, what a woman wears, drinks, or does will rarely prevent a sexual assault from occurring. These misconceptions about victims coupled with victim-centered prevention strategies create an unattainable "perfect" victim.[86] Victims are not supposed to know their attacker and should never be in perceived dangerous places. Victims also are expected to minimize expressions of sexuality (i.e., revealing clothes, a voluptuous body type, and any sexual history) and to exert appropriate feminine characteristics. Unfortunately, victims rarely attain such idealized notions of "perfect" victimhood.[87]

A consequence of not achieving perfect victim status is that women are held responsible for the crimes committed against them. Victim blame occurs when we hold a victim accountable for their victimization.[88] For example, if a woman is sexually assaulted by a boyfriend or husband or friend (rather than a stranger), people may say that she should have known better than to go out with/marry/be friends with that person. Likewise, people may comment on the blameworthiness of a sexual assault victim who was drinking or wearing specific clothing. In other words, most victims are viewed as having characteristics that make them imperfect. Since most victims know their attacker, or drink something alcoholic, or wear something that someone might consider sexually provocative, others think the victim is unworthy of attaining the perfect victim status.[89]

While the perfect victim status is a myth, people may start to believe that women who are sexually assaulted or victimized (at least under certain conditions) get what they deserve because of the focus on victim responsibility. This idea is sometimes called the "just world hypothesis." Good people get good things, and bad people get what they deserve.[90] Thus, victims feel shame, as if they should have done something differently to prevent their victimization. Victim blame is one of the primary reasons victims of sexual assault have such a low rate of reporting the crime to police. Given the high stakes of being held responsible for victimization, it makes sense that women do everything they can to adhere to the safety "rules," even if the rules are based on gendered crime myths and do little to prevent actual victimization.

At first glance, women's fear of crime seems really out of line with the reality of crime. However, through very subtle everyday interactions, women are taught myths about crime that fully explain this fear. Women (particularly white women) are taught to fear crime through the stranger danger myth and to rely on traditional gendered safety norms and behaviors, like relying on others for protection and avoiding strangers at all costs. Women who do not follow these gendered safety rules may be held responsible for their victimization should they ever become crime victims. White women are left to wonder how they can protect themselves from crime but are also taught they don't have the physical strength or ability to defend themselves. As De Welde summarizes: "the impending threat of violence, whether real or perceived, serves to reproduce women's dependency on male protectors.... White women have little pragmatic power in discourses that propagate their vulnerability and perpetual victim status."[91] Thus, it isn't all that surprising that white women fear crime independent of the reality of crime. Because women are also bombarded through the media with images of white women victims, all women have misperceptions of their chances of victimization and the victimization and fear of victimization among women of color are overlooked. Next, we turn to how women learn gendered crime myths through parents, school officials, and the media.

2

Learning Myths

> *I remember playing games with my friend April in third grade where we would—we lived in kind of a rural area—and we would hang out by a highway, hiding in the bushes and we would count the number of kidnapper vans. . . . Those were the vans with no windows, and we would pretend that [we were hiding]. We'd get down really low because we'd see the kidnapper van coming and like "(gasp) the kidnapper van's gonna get us!" We would just be totally stupid like that, and I don't know if that was specific for the time or if that happened all the time, but I just remember that pretty vividly.*
>
> —Katie,* a Midwestern woman

Katie's story exemplifies the power of crime myths. Her story is recollected after 20 years with vivid detail and highlights a fear of strangers. Specifically, Katie, who would have been about eight years old during this story, is afraid of people who snatch children off the street in a van without windows. In this chapter, we discuss how these types of tales from our childhoods crystalize for adult women. The stranger danger myth, the white woman crime victim myth, and the victim-centered crime prevention myth are taught to us by our parents, schools, and media.

Learning from Loved Ones—Parents

Longstanding research shows that how you parent is usually based on how your parents raised you.[1] As one could imagine, there are a variety of parenting types or styles.[2] Parenting style is defined as "a constellation of attitudes towards the child that are communicated to the child and that, taken together, create an emotional climate in which the parent's behaviors are expressed."[3] Psychologists tell us there are four main categories of parenting styles. "Authoritative" parents are those who combine support and warmth along with flexible disciplinary practices. "Authoritarian" parents are those who restrict children's autonomy and value their obedience. "Permissive" parents are those who are responsive to the needs of their children but also do not set boundaries regarding discipline. Finally, "neglectful" parents are those who do not respond to their children's needs and are generally detached.⁴ It should also be noted that a critique of these particular styles is that they may not apply to all types of families. Other types of families (e.g., single-parent families) have not been given enough attention by the literature to know if the same typology applies or if there are additional/different categories. These categories seem to apply best to white families, families with higher income levels, or families with two parents in the household.⁵

Such parenting styles are not only something academics research but are also the source of much discussion among the general public. The term "helicopter parenting" is a popular term used in the general public. "Helicopter parenting refers to a style of parents who are overly focused on their children," according to a *Parents* magazine article. The article explains there are four reasons why well-intentioned parents helicopter their children. These include (1) parents are afraid that their children will fail at something, (2) parents try to overcompensate for issues from their childhood, (3) parents have feelings of anxiety about something terrible happening to their children, and (4) parents feel peer pressure by other parents to helicopter children. The outcomes of helicoptering for children can be low self-esteem, lack of confidence, lack of coping skills, higher levels of anxiety, underdeveloped life skills, and a sense of entitlement.⁶

Most parents have also heard the term "free-range parenting" (which likely aligns with permissive parenting). This term appears in popular magazines and newspaper outlets. For example, the popular magazine *Good Housekeeping* ran a story called "Everything You Need to Know about the Free-Range Parenting Methods." The article defines free-range parenting as a style of parenting that "aims to foster independence in children by giving them greater autonomy and less adult supervision."⁷ For example, a parent might allow a child to walk to a location without supervision. However, free-range parenting methods have been controversial since this type of parenting could be viewed as neglectful or, at the very least, as not matching up with societal norms about what parents should do.

As these two examples suggest, there is a range of parenting styles with both pros and cons. These parenting styles influence what children learn and what they grow up to value themselves.

Do Parenting Styles Influence Fear of Crime Socialization?

When considering fear of crime research and safety myths, research on parenting styles is sparse. So, knowing what we know about parenting styles, we can ask: what type of parent might be more likely to talk to children about safety, and how might these lessons impact what children learn about safety growing up?

We can see how there is a spectrum of parenting styles. At the one end of the spectrum, parents over-supervise, over-message, and model safety concerns in traditional ways, whereas at the other end of the spectrum, parents under-supervise, under-message, and perhaps provide no model for understanding safety concerns. While these are examples of more extreme types of parents, there are likely many parenting styles in the middle of the spectrum.

We can make some inferences about how parent's styles might impact fear of crime. Based on the research, both authoritarian and neglectful parenting styles may inflate fear of crime levels among children. On the other hand, we might see the permissive, combination, and authoritative parenting styles decrease fear of crime levels among children. Therefore, based on the research, parenting styles may have a curvilinear relationship with fear of crime.[8] While more research is needed on this topic for a clearer sense of how parenting styles impact children's fear of crime, it is interesting to think about. What parenting style did you grow up with? How do you think parenting styles influenced your fear of crime as an adult?

Without question, parents represent the most powerful socialization agent in children's lives, including how they view crime. De Groof explains it like this, "Many studies show strong similarities between parents and children regarding values, practices, norms, and so forth. Parental fears can likewise be passed on to children; this congruence can be induced by role modeling."[9] De Groof found that children often have the same safety concerns and fears as their parents, likely passed on through parental modeling. De Groof's study also considered some factors related to parenting styles and examined four ways parenting styles might affect their adolescent children's fear of crime levels. These factors included (1) a consideration of supervision levels, (2) stimulation (the degree to which parents organize leisure and free time activities), (3) autonomy (the extent to which parents allow children to discover and try new things), and (4) freedom (how often parents let their children spend time freely).

Interestingly, De Groof found the only factor that directly influenced fear of crime was amount of supervision. Parents who fell in the high supervision category were most likely to have children who were afraid of crime. Children from families with high levels of parental supervision also had restrictions on activities, free time, and autonomy, but these restrictions did not directly influence their fear of crime.

How attached children are to their parents is another factor considered in fear of crime research. In other words, do children who have close relationships with their parents fear crime differently than those children who are less close with their parents? Criminology researchers Lisa Wallace and David May considered this very question.[10] The researchers asked how close adolescents were to their parents and determined their fear of crime levels. The study found that adolescent boys with lower levels of parental attachment were more afraid of crime than boys with higher levels of parental attachment. Parental attachment had no impact on adolescent girls' fear of crime levels. While these findings are interesting, they also leave a lot of questions for future research.

Another study by psychology researchers at the University of Basque Country in Spain brings this point home.[11] Laura Vomediano and her colleagues surveyed parents with young children and found that parents were very likely to fear for their children, especially those parents (both men and women) with daughters. Having a daughter was the strongest predictor of fear for children. Knowing that parents fear for their children (especially daughters) and teach children safety lessons based on myths, we can see how influential parents can be in how we learn to fear crime. Based on the findings of the study, one could speculate that parental attachment may be a more critical element in fear of crime for boys. In contrast, for girls, supervision may be a more important element in determining fear of crime. Such differences tie into gendered safety beliefs.

Gendered specific safety lessons are also evident in a study by Australian researchers Sarah Foster and her colleagues at the University of Western Australia and the University of Melbourne. They examined how parents' fear of strangers affected children's independent mobility.[12] They found parents with higher fear of strangers were more likely to restrict children's mobility, and mobility restriction was gendered. Girls were more likely to be restricted than boys. In other words, parents told female children that they should not leave spaces, were more likely to make corrections when they did not listen, and held girls to a higher standard of behavior. Foster and colleagues had the following to say about their findings: "Although well-intentioned, this almost zero-tolerance approach to risk unintentionally but adversely inhibits children's social, emotional, and physical development."[13]

Learning specific safety myths from parents is also evident in my studies. When asked, most people easily recall a story from childhood when their parents taught them to fear strangers in public places. Such stories are a vital feature of the interviews I've conducted in my research. Melissa, a Midwestern woman, explains the significance of learning about crime from loved ones:

> I remember when I was ten, somebody went around like taking kids from schools and stuff and so they [my parents] sat down and talked to me about "you can't go to strangers" and we had to make up like a code word and then I think there was even a question to go with

the code word in case someone strange picked you up from school, they had to know it.

Although kidnapping of children by a stranger is extremely rare, asked about what Melissa learned growing up, she first recalls strangers as bad, dangerous boogiemen who steal young children.[14] Like Katie at the beginning of this chapter, Melissa easily recalls these images. When asked where she learned about kidnapping, Melissa remembers that her parents were the first to ingrain concerns about kidnapping happening to her.

Mothers and Fathers

Knowing that parents fear for their children and that parents influence children's fear of crime, the question becomes: are safety myths and lessons taught differently by mothers and fathers?

Some researchers argue that mothers' and fathers' fear for their children is not all that different. For example, University of Texas at Austin sociologists Mark Warr and Christopher Ellison examined how mothers and fathers may differ in their fear for children.[15] This research suspected women were more likely to be responsible for childcare. They reasoned, then, that mothers would be more fearful for their children than fathers. Using data from a sample of Texas residents, they didn't quite find what they expected. Mothers were only slightly more likely to fear for children than fathers. Warr and Ellison argued that the finding might be more a function of fathers' protector role in the family than of mothers' childrearing role. In other words, while mothers were responsible for more childrearing, fathers felt pressure to serve as guardians of the family, leading to more fear for their children and spouses. Both mothers and fathers felt a sense of responsibility for the safety of children.

Other studies have found that fear of crime for children differs in type if not in intensity between mothers and fathers. For example, University of Haifa researchers Gustavo Mesch and Gideon Fishman studied mothers' and fathers' fear for children in Israel and found that 11 percent of men were afraid for their children compared to 38 percent of women.[16] Based on these findings, Mesch conducted a follow-up study where he interviewed 300 mothers with young children in Israel about their personal fear of crime and their fear of crime for their children.[17] Mesch argued that because women tend to be "connected to and interdependent with others, and in their thinking as focusing on care," women were more likely to fear for children in unique ways.[18] This study found that mothers were more afraid for their children than themselves and were concerned about stranger-induced victimization.

University of Seattle Pacific Sociologist Karen Snedker also studied the importance of gender roles in formulating fear for others.[19] As she points out (and as should not be forgotten), women are often responsible for what sociologists call "emotion work" or emotional labor.[20] Emotion work means that women must express emotions in expected ways (and men must suppress certain emotions). In other words, women's fear of crime is yet another way that women express their emotional labor. Snedker found that empathy is a part of emotion work for women, and "as women are the primary providers of emotion work, cultivating empathetic feelings, they may also be disproportionately fearful for others under their care. Moreover, women as mothers and the primary caretakers of children link their children's vulnerability to their own well-being."[21] So, we can see how both positive and negative emotions and gendered expectations would influence fear of crime for women, particularly mothers' fear of crime for their children.

How might our mothers' fear for us as children influence our fear of crime as adults? First, we know that parents often model behavior for their children.[22] Thus, if mothers are more afraid for children than for themselves and are more vocal about this fear, children will likely pick up on this fear. Children will then absorb that fear of crime into their own identity and future selves. Second, mothers subconsciously feel societal pressure to fear for their children and may unknowingly bequeath unrealistic fears of crime to children through safety myths.[23] For example, by emphasizing the stranger danger myth, parents (especially mothers) teach us to fear strangers. Girls, especially white girls, may also discover that safety is a gendered and raced phenomenon.

Studies I've conducted look at the influence of mothers on their children's fear of crime. Jenna, a Southern woman, tells me about her mother, whom she sees as overly and unnecessarily fearful. She recalls what her mother told her and what she saw as a child watching her mother.

JENNA: Any time that I wasn't really with her, if I went in the neighborhood, riding on my bike, anything like that. Anytime I wasn't by her hip, she would give me warnings.
NICOLE: And how did that affect how you think or feel about crime?
JENNA: In two ways. In some ways, it put this kind of innate fear in me because I started thinking about that worst-case scenario. And then, in some ways, I just joked about it. It's almost kind of like, whatever, Mom. I'm okay, and so I almost didn't take it as seriously as I should have, you know? It was almost so much that it didn't seem real, if that makes sense. But at the same time, when I am by myself, now grown up, if my husband is on a trip or something, I'm not saying that I spend a hundred percent of

the time worrying, but there will be some moments where suddenly a fear comes in, and that would be really scary.

Jenna highlights a few essential points regarding mothers and how we learn to fear crime from them. First, she recalls that her mother was highly fearful of crime. Jenna talks about seeing this firsthand from her mother and can articulate that her mother was always thinking about the worst-case scenario. She also sees how this affected her own fear of crime as an adult. In some cases, Jenna sees that her mother's fear level was over the top or not based on reality, but even so, it still causes her to worry more than she would have had she not watched her mother fear crime. While Jenna can often push the fear to the side, recognizing it is an unrealistic fear, when Jenna feels unprotected or in an environment that induces fear in most women (being home alone), her fears inch back in.

Although Maya lives across the Atlantic Ocean in southern Sweden, she also shows how learning fear from mothers works. For example, she easily recalls her mother's lessons about crime and begins telling me the precautions her mother wanted her to take as a child.

It was really important that you should always lock your bike, so nobody came and took it from you, stole it from you and that also, I feel that my mother is very much, almost like that she expects that people want to hurt her that she sees crime everywhere.

Maya learned another lesson about crime that is subtle in childhood but becomes powerful in adulthood for most women. That is, she saw her mother as someone who "saw crime everywhere" and saw people as generally bad. In addition, Maya saw her mother as someone who was always on the defensive with strangers. This lesson strengthens her adult commitment to stranger danger myths.

We can also see how parenting styles and supervision levels influence how we act as adults. For example, Paula, a woman from the U.S. South, explains to me the ways that supervision increased for her once her parents got divorced:

So I'm wondering if that [her mother getting divorced] has something to do with it as well, because, you know, my mom worked two jobs, and I'd go with her to her second job and sit and wait while she worked at night or I went to day care or the Boys and Girls Club. So, you know, it took her a long time to let me stay at home by myself. When I was able to stay at home by myself, I knew what to do and what not to do.

In this case, when Paula thinks about safety behaviors and safety values, she recalls that her mother was strict with her supervision after her parents' divorce. Such strictness taught Paula how to act when she was finally allowed to spend time alone, thus showing a prominent example of the power of learning from our parents.

Learning from Mothers as Adults

While we might expect that adult women only recall lessons learned from mothers as children, my research has found that mothers continue to play a role in safety lessons for their adult daughters. Such findings seem to apply only to adult children who are women—not men. Whereas parents tend to stop worrying about crime happening to sons after they move out, parents continue to fear for their daughters well into adulthood.[24] Such a notion plays into the patriarchal desire to "protect" girls from the world, a desire that can last long into their adulthood.[25]

In one of my studies, where I interviewed both recently married and divorced women, adult respondents' mothers were discussed as a significant source of information about crime. The mother's influence was especially noticeable in the participants who were divorced. While divorce may not seem like something that would affect adult women respondents' fear of crime, divorced women have a more acute awareness of their safety than when they were married. I talk about this elsewhere as "fear work transference" in romantic relationships.[26] Put another way, when women are married, they often noticeably shift concerns about their safety and safety behaviors to their husbands. For example, women may rely on husbands to check on strange noises at night. Fear work transference from wives to husbands happens regardless of the gendered equity of the household or the gendered attitudes of participants. In other words, even the most progressive, egalitarian-minded wives still seem to transfer "fear work" to their husbands upon marriage.

While this fear work transference is only subtly visible to married women, divorced women see the absence of the household "safety manager" very clearly. Divorced women have to pick back up some of the fear work they had transferred over in the marriage. Just as they become responsible for other things husbands may have been in charge of during marriage, worrying about crime becomes one more task that divorced women now have on their very full plate. What this means for divorced women respondents is that they can either (1) take back responsibility for safety behaviors themselves or (2) find a way to transfer this responsibility (often unknowingly) to someone else. It makes sense that divorced adult children may transfer fear work back to their parents.

Midwestern research participants Anna and Haley give us a sense of how parents were involved in the safety management process after becoming divorced. For example, when I talk to Anna about how her divorce affected her fear and perception of crime, she tells me that people in her life made her feel she *should* worry more about crime once she was divorced.

> When I'm leaving work that's kind of scary, that is probably like one of the bigger ones. I don't really walk anywhere by myself, and I don't go out anymore [now that she is divorced], so I'm not really alone a lot. Living alone, I've been a little bit afraid of someone getting into my apartment, but I have a dog and a neighbor. I can hear everything between our walls, so that makes me feel pretty safe.

She goes on to explain: "I would say that my mom and my grandma and my step-dad and my aunt, people who are older, think that I should be afraid, think that I should be more careful and think that there is a bigger risk than there really is of something happening."

Anna provides an example of post-divorce fear work transference by explaining that now that she "lives by herself," she is more afraid of crime. Her fear after getting divorced is now greater and has caused her to change her routine activities. Further, her family members, mainly women family members, tells her she should be afraid of crime more now that she is divorced. While she says that they see a more considerable risk than warranted, Anna is also worried about crime and gets advice from her parents and family members as an adult.

Haley, another recently divorced respondent, talks about the role her mom played in her views on crime and fear of crime since becoming divorced:

> My mom worries about me. I remember when I first got my apartment by myself [after divorce], my mom worried a lot that I was going out a lot and coming home late by myself. And I worried a little bit too.... I don't think that had anything to do with my husband, I think that had to do with living by myself for the first time. And I worried about it just because I knew if someone takes me when I'm walking from my car or my house, nobody is ever going to know until late tomorrow when they try to call and call and call and I'm not home. So then there is sort of a flicker of thought. I know my mom thought about that kind of stuff, but you know I would just, maybe if it was one in the morning, I would just call my mom and

say, "hey, I'm pulling into my driveway now, I'll call you after I get inside and walk the dog."

Haley tells me that she never lived alone before becoming divorced. She tells me that instead of taking on new safety measures herself to calm her fears, her mother became the primary safety manager she relied on for safety advice. Haley's safety values as an adult divorced woman were in line with her mother's safety values.

Research studies and anecdotal evidence like we see from Anna and Haley showcase that mothers play a pivotal role in forming safety values both during childhood and in adulthood.[27]

What about Fathers?

How fathers influence fear of crime in their children is not studied very often. We know from the literature that dads (and moms) fear more for daughters than sons.[28] However, how this influences the lessons provided to daughters is not as well known or understood. You may remember different safety lessons from your mother versus your father if you think back to your childhood. If you grew up in a two-parent household, you might remember your father as the one who took care of potentially dangerous situations. Fathers often fall into the "protector role" because of societal expectations.[29]

There are some examples of what women remember learning from their fathers concerning safety. For example, when asked about victimization experiences growing up, Lauren, a Southern woman, recalls a time from her childhood when someone tried to break into her family home. "There are a couple of times we thought people were trying to break into our house. My next-door neighbor was peering into our house with a flashlight, and my sister called the police. My dad went outside in his boxers with a shotgun."

Like Lauren, many women see fathers as responsible for taking care of their safety growing up. Women who view their dads as heroes may recall this viewpoint as a positive part of the father/daughter relationship. However, gendered safety lessons like the ones in Lauren's story ultimately put women on a path to see men as the sole protectors of the family. As women become adults and start to have partners of their own, they rely on their male partners to become the person who takes care of safety at home. Fathers do the same things for their daughters, thus repeating the socialization process. Most women rarely think about how husbands/partners play the same role for their daughters as they saw growing up with their own fathers. In other words, women who watch their dads protect them may unknowingly transfer fear work onto romantic partners later in life.[30] Men become the people who manage safety and potential victimization for their family unit, ultimately passing on gendered safety messages to girls, who become women and propel the cycle of gendered safety values in their own families.[31]

Respondents have also told me they learned how to stay safe from fathers' action-based lessons. For example, whereas you may recall your mother *telling* you to be safe, your father might have *shown* you how to be safe. So, your dad might have taught you how to defend yourself from a potential attack or given you pepper spray and taught you how to use it. In other words, while dads are less influential than moms in the intensity and frequency of safety lessons, the type of lesson we learn from our fathers is significant.

Jennifer, a Southern participant, provides a very spirited memory about what she learned from her dad. She says:

> My dad also taught me that since I was his first daughter, he just taught me, don't take crap from nobody. . . . I used to carry mace with me. My dad, soon as I turned 16, he gave me mace, my mom mace, and my sister mace. When I was five, a little boy was picking on me, and my dad taught me how to fight, and so I kicked the boy 20 times in the nuts. I mean, my dad taught me how to fight at an early age, and I don't carry the mace around with me anymore because it's a pain.

There are a few things that Jennifer's story helps us see. First, we should notice that Jennifer's dad provided gendered lessons. For example, he provided mace to all the women in the house, and this mace distribution with girls tended to be given out when they began having more freedom outside of the house. Second, these actions, for the most part, were in response to stranger danger. Even so, it was undoubtedly the case that the odds of fighting someone in your household or that you knew closely would increase with the protective strategies Lauren learned from her dad. However, the defensive strategies taught to girls and women are almost always based on a fear of strangers, so the focus is on defending yourself against a man outside of the home.

Third, while much more subtle, women also learn a victim-centered crime prevention strategy through these safety lessons. Once girls turn an age that makes them more independent, they are taught they must protect themselves. We can assume from this safety lesson that girls are expected to prevent their own victimization. In other words, by emphasizing protective behaviors taken on by individual women and de-emphasizing lessons with boys and men about not being offenders, we may unknowingly be spreading the myth that victims can prevent their victimization, especially when at the hands of a stranger.

At the very least, adult children recognize that mothers and fathers play different roles in safety socialization.[32] Sometimes the difference is the perceived intensity of advice and worry that comes from mothers.

Jenna, who discussed her mother above, provides an excellent example of the difference between mothers and fathers in safety socialization. When asked about where Jenna learned about crime growing up, Jenna explains that she learned mainly from her parents but describes differences in the lessons she learned from her mother and father.

> Yes, growing up and hearing parents just say "be careful, you could get hurt, don't talk to people you aren't supposed to." . . . Not so much my father, but my mother was very overprotective and was very concerned that something would happen to me and was constantly telling me the worst-case scenario. If she left for the weekend it would be "Okay, well just don't open the door because you could get raped." So I knew the worst case, so I mean in that way, yeah, I heard about crime, maybe not in a real rational way, but not really so much from my father, other than "I always want you to be safe and I love you." It was more "just be very careful."

In the case of Jenna, she recalls her mother as more worried and fearful than her father. She views her mother's worry as irrational, and she also learns particular messages: worry about strangers and worry about rape. Jenna views her father's lessons as more rational and more centered in a place of love.

Thus, we learn a lot about safety values and lessons and their gendered nature from recalling what we learned in our childhoods from our parents.

While all parents serve as socialization agents, when looking at mothers and fathers separately, we can see some clear differences in the delivery of safety messages. Moms and dads teach fear differently. Moms tend to *tell* their daughters what to fear, while dads tend to *show* daughters what to fear.[33] Moms tell daughters what they *should* do: they *should* take precautions, be careful, and worry about crime happening in public places at the hands of strangers. Moms reinforce fear definitions for their daughters and ultimately put the fear learning process into motion. Daughters, then, take on these lessons as they grow up, execute the safety lessons in their daily adult lives (e.g., they stay away from public spaces), and, as we will see later, transmit safety lessons to their children. The cyclical process between mothers and daughters is crucial for fear of crime socialization.

On the other hand, dads don't necessarily tell their daughters what to fear, but they show them what to fear through their actions. Dads take care of scary situations for their younger daughters as part of their protector role within the family unit. Dads teach daughters that women are not typically the ones who manage safety concerns, and dads' concerns are often viewed as more rational then the concerns of moms. When dads do teach daughters how to protect themselves, the messages they teach are gendered and focus on crime myths.

While most studies have found that mothers are more critical socialization agents than fathers in teaching safety values and lessons, I would argue discounting fathers' impact on their adult children creates missed opportunities in previous literature.

In sum, parents are a primary source of education when it comes to safety precautions, as with most things, and often contribute to what we think we know about safety, crime prevention, and how much we fear crime. Other important factors include the type of parenting style and the gender of the parent. We also know that girls are taught to be protected and boys are trained to protect. As one can imagine, gender-specific lessons may also impact thoughts, feelings, and behaviors as we grow up. Finally, it is not hard to imagine that when we are all grown up, we tend to close the learning loop by teaching our children these similar messages.

Safety Socialization in Families of Color

Parental socialization is also a racialized phenomenon. In this book, we are going to talk a lot about white families, since fear of crime myths apply to white women, fear of crime socialization ultimately follows suit. For that reason, most of the literature on the fear of crime focuses exclusively on white participants. A large portion of what we know about popular conceptions of crime, then, is limited, because we still have much more to learn about how families outside of the groups that have received the most research learn different lessons. It is important to recognize upfront that there are social and cultural distinctions in how different groups understand crime and practice safety. We can all agree there are issues with applying ideas about one racial group to another racial group, and therefore I'll try to be careful about generalizations. It is worth mentioning here, as we begin to talk about the gendered and racialized learning process, that the social learning process looks very different for families of color.

Researchers in the field of sociology, for example, have talked to Black parents (Black mothers in particular) about raising their children in the current social world. As Hollins University sociologist Jennifer Turner notes, "through racial socialization, which often occurs via conversations with their children, Black parents educate their children about 'the realities of being Black in America.'"[34] Black parents teach their children how to behave in society (as white parents do), but they also have the additional burden of teaching their children how to navigate growing up in a racialized and racist society safely.[35] Many Black mothers must teach their Black sons that they may be viewed as criminals only because of the color of their skin. Since many Americans still perceive all Black people as poor, independent of their income level, Black mothers must also teach their children how to navigate economic bias as well.[36] Most white mothers and families do not have to think about their duties of socialization in quite the same way with quite the same stakes. The awareness that myths about criminality will affect how others perceive Black men leads many Black men to learn and practice behaviors that assuage the fears of people around them.[37]

Nowhere is this more the case than when we think about the importance of teaching children about the criminal justice system. Many Black mothers teach their children, specifically sons, about the likelihood of experiencing discrimination and racism by police agencies.[38] Studies have found that Black families teach children lessons about the police early and often due to the potentially violent nature of police interactions. For example, Sharon Malone Gonzalez, a sociologist at the University of Texas at Austin interviewed Black mothers from a variety of class backgrounds to better understand the process of the "police talk."[39] She describes police talks between mothers and their children emphasizing the "make-it-home framework." She goes on to explain that this framework is not just about coming home each day but "about black youth learning strategies to stay alive when they encounter the police. The police talk is an attempt by black mothers to teach their children to avoid police violence by becoming aware of their distinct vulnerability to police and how to handle hostile interactions."[40] The police talk socialization process between mothers and their children is particularly salient in Black families.

Another example brought home by Malone Gonzalez is that the police talk often has the unintended consequence of causing fear. However, Black parents and their children, unlike white parents and their children, fear lethal violence from the legal system. If we can think about what a fear of lethal violence at the hands of someone in an authority position might signify in the lives of young children, we can see how fear of police instead of fear of crime becomes a commonplace belief system for Black children in

America today.[41] It is clear, then, why the process of learning to practice safety and fear violence is yet another way growing up Black is a very different experience than growing up white.

As chapter 2 segues to chapter 3, pivoting from the ways people learn to fear crime into the behaviors they undertake in light of those fears, the centrality to the literature of what white women particularly learn and how our society organizes its practices around those fears remains. But just as we recognize that these lessons are not universal and different populations learn to fear different types and sources of victimization, it is also important to recognize those different lessons lead to different learned behaviors to ward off danger through intimidation or avoidance. One specific example of the ways Black men's experiences and responses to potential victimization may be different from the white experience is embedded in the "code of the street." As Yale University sociologist Elijah Anderson discussed in his book *Code of the Street*, part of the survival of Black men in vulnerable contexts stems from their ability to protect themselves from others, given their lack of faith in the protection of the justice system.[42] This "code" serves as an alternative set of informal rules of comportment, interaction, and behavior that are learned culturally and practiced as a defensive strategy.

The consequences of the code is discussed recently by University of California, Irvine, sociologist Kristin Turney, who points to one such consequence: the stressful effects of police stops on adolescents of color and on their mothers.[43] Simply being exposed to police is a stressor that uniquely influences adolescents of color. Given the likelihood that African American males will have a police encounter due to police presence in their communities, such stress can seriously impact their mental health. Researchers John Rich and Courtney Grey also consider the impact of the code of the street for Black men in an *American Journal of Public Health* article.[44] Utilizing the code of the street to understand what this stress is like for Black men in America, Rich and Grey state, "the victims of violence in the present study echoed these views about the police. These victims reported that they do not rely on the police if they feel threatened or fear being confronted by their assailants. Rather, they maintain the belief that if they face a threat, they must 'handle it' themselves."[45] Handling crime and violence without being able to rely on those who are in place for protection (police agencies) can cause anxiety and stress.

Many of the myths discussed throughout this book often leave people of color, especially Black men and women, invisible. While these individuals (and other groups of people of color) have experienced the criminal justice system in very different ways from white people, the lack of research on this topic has meant we do not know how people of color fit into traditional crime myths. We can see how these myths have demonized and criminalized people of color while simultaneously convincing white families that they are vulnerable to victimization. Furthermore, the strategy by Black men to face a threat head-on and handle it is the complete opposite of what we have discussed concerning white women, who will do everything in their power to avoid threats (real and perceived) and seek out traditional authority figures. Such an example shows the importance of racial patterns of fear and strategies for crime prevention.

In sum, the myths continue to preserve racism today, and in the hopes of combatting racism, researchers tracing these effects have concentrated on how white populations understand and perpetuate these myths for that reason. However, this explanation for the limitations of the current state of the field does not excuse the lack of research on non-white families, which is needed to determine exactly what the differences are and the ways different groups form their beliefs about crime and safety.

Learning from Authority Figures at School

Violent crime at school is rare. According to the School Supplement for the National Crime Victimization Survey, in 2017, about 2 percent of children said they had been victims of a violent crime at school over the past six months. If we take out theft, children's chances of violent crime at school drop to 1 percent. The 2018 Indicators of School Crime and Safety report found that from 1992–2018, victimization rates of students aged 12–18 while at school and away from school declined.[46] In that same year, a study conducted by Northeastern University researchers James Fox and Emma Friedel found that four times the number of children were killed in schools in the early 1990s compared to today.[47] In 2021, the National Crime Victimization Survey found approximately 3 percent of children said they had been victims of a violent crime at school over the past six months. Finally, the report found in the 2020–2021 school year, there were 43 deaths of children while at school.[48] So, the possibility of violent victimization occurring at school is infrequent and even rarer when thinking about homicide. Criminologist Matthew Robinson points out that "children are safer at school than in other places" and further that "according to the U.S. Department of Education, there are generally at least 50 times as many murders of youth away from school than at school."[49]

This does not mean that mass school shootings never happen at school or that school shootings are not horrific and tragic. The most recent example of a mass school shooting occurred at Robb Elementary School in Uvalde, Texas, on May 24, 2022, where 21 people, including 19 elementary students, were killed by a lone gunman. The Uvalde shooting incident has spurred discussions nationwide about gun ownership, gun laws, school shooter profiles, and law enforcement responses to school violence. While the lost lives in this incident and others are completely unacceptable, it is also important to note that mass school shootings, like the one that occurred in Uvalde, make up a small fraction of crimes at school.

Bullying behaviors and assault at school (or among school children off school property) are reported more frequently by students. The School Crime Survey through the Bureau of Justice Statistics found that 22 percent of 12–18 year old students said they were bullied in 2019. Bullying, which typically occurs between known people or acquaintances, can cause students various adverse outcomes, including anxiety, depression, lack of desire to be at school, and low self-esteem.[50] A 2019 report found that 6 percent of students avoided classes or school activities because they were afraid someone might harm or attack them.[51]

While school crime is rare, a recent Gallup poll results suggest one in three Americans are fearful for their child's safety while their child is at school.[52] Although school violence, especially school homicide, is sporadic, the public is still fearful that this type of crime might happen. If crime rates are not correlated to higher perceptions of crime while at school, we have to assume that public opinion or policy are shaping such beliefs.

School, then, plays a role in "framing" socially constructed images of crime.[53] Researchers look at how frames contribute to what we think we know about social problems like drugs, poverty, and crime. Further, the frame is an important sociological tool used to make sense of the conversations surrounding an issue.[54] Schools and the media help us form mental images of what something means. Over time, these concepts become normalized, thus institutionalizing the meaning of such objects in the larger society.[55] For example, when I say "school violence," what image pops up in your mind? Is it a school shooter? Is it someone hitting someone? Is it a bully throwing a kid into a locker? While you rarely consider how what you learn affects the image you create with the words "school violence," there is a long history of how these images were constructed, framed, and ultimately normalized in society.[56]

Educational Programming Safety Campaigns

What do you remember about safety programming from schools growing up? How do you think your age influences this? To fully grasp the impact of crime prevention programming safety campaigns, we need to examine how educational programming about crime in schools came to be.

There is a long history of educational safety programming in the school setting. School crime prevention efforts began with the National School Safety Center (NSSC), developed by Ronald Reagan in 1984.[57] The mission of the NSSC was to "promote a continued exchange of information related to school crime and violence prevention through a wide array of resources to assist school boards, educators, law enforcement, and the public in maintaining schools as safe, secure, and tranquil places of learning."[58] Thus, we can see how the focus on safety in school would increase the dissemination of safety prevention information given to children since the eighties. In 1994, such programming was further institutionalized when legislators allotted millions of federal dollars for school safety. As a result, schools began to pour that money into security measures and educational programming.[59]

The frame federal agencies use around school safety has continued to provide school officials and the general public with ideas about what school safety and school violence should look like. For example, each year, a joint report is released from the Department of Education and Justice (this report has most recently been written by the Department of Education and Homeland Security). This report is also endorsed by the president of the United States and is a resource for local, state, and federal school officials. We can see how the framing of school violence changed during a ten-year time period, from 1998 to 2018. The October 1998 report came on the heels of three high-profile school shootings: in Pearl, MS, where two students were killed and seven injured; in Paducah, KY, where three students were killed and five others wounded; and finally in Jonesboro, AR, where 4 students and 1 teacher were killed and 11 other students were injured.[60]

Even in this uncharted horrific and fear-producing context, the executive summary of the 1998 annual report begins by saying, "Most schools are safe. A child is more likely to be a victim of a violent crime in the community than at school. In particular, homicides in school are sporadic events. However, violence does occur in schools, endangering students and teachers and compromising the learning environment. We must not tolerate any school violence." The report goes on to state, "Despite recent tragedies that received national attention, schools should not be singled out as especially dangerous places."[61] Thus, in the 1998 report, though crime rates were higher than they are now and three massive national tragedies had just happened, the U.S. Department of Education and Justice still provides reasonable messages about the rarity of school violence. The 1998 report mirrors criminological interpretations of school shootings and crime in a school context: kids are safer in school than elsewhere. Crime rates are low for children.[62]

However, by 2018, although crime rates were lower than in 1998, the tone and message of the report was alarmed and fearful. For example, the 2018 report begins with a section called "Decades of Problems," stating, "On February 14, 2018, a former student walked into Marjory Stoneman Douglas High School in Parkland, FL, and began firing. He murdered 17 people and wounded many more."[63] While there is no doubt that such a school shooting is extraordinarily horrible and terrifying for the families, community, and the nation as a whole, the panicked and fearful tone of this report seems out of line with crime rates for the time.

Further, there were fewer school shootings in 2018 than in 1998. As a case in point, in the 2018 report, school shootings from 1979 to 2018 were highlighted. Of these 32 school shooting incidences, 10 incidences occurred in the 1980s, 5 in the 1990s, 6 in the 2000s, and 11 between 2010 and 2018.[64] Thus, while the shootings that have occurred are tragic and horrific, from a social construction perspective, the overall prevalence and frequency were still very low in 2018. School shootings have been framed as common and on the rise. The viewpoint is shared by Americans. A recent study asked how confident Americans were in schools to protect students from school shootings; only 27 percent of respondents said that they had a lot of confidence that children were safe from school shootings.[65] These findings indicate that while school shootings are rare, the fear of school shooting is not. Thus, both policy and public opinion shape perceptions of school shootings.

Such a focus on school shootings and elevated crime rates also comes through clearly in the advice given to school officials on ways to keep their schools safe (and ultimately to train teachers and students within their organizations). For example, a quick browse through the U.S. Department of Homeland Security (DHS) website sheds light on how we as a nation see crime at school.[66] Under the "campus resilience program" resource library, there is a "school and workplace violence" link. DHS states, "acts of school and workplace violence, including both active shooter incidents and violent protests, threaten life safety and security, undermine public confidence, and emotionally devastate affected communities. Therefore, IHEs [Institutions of Higher Education] should use these resources to build campus resilience by adequately preparing for and responding to violent incidents." This website is the primary place that school districts and larger institutional units go to determine how to define school violence and how to "prevent, protect, and mitigate" such violence.

The "school and workplace violence" page addresses school shootings but does not include more common forms of school violence. Physical or cyberbullying, for example, does not appear nor does physical assaults between students, two more common forms of school crime. Further, there is no discussion about sexual harassment or relationship violence. This website, then, further exacerbates stranger danger myths and a belief in the prevalence of random violence.

The advice given by the DHS website to local and state school officials goes further than suggestions and recommendations, because it is mandated through legislation in most states. In 2014, 33 states ordered schools to have a "comprehensive school safety or emergency plan." The Council on State Government, a non-profit national nonpartisan organization, provides us with some information about the trends in required school safety plans, saying they need to include the following:[67]

- Requirements for various safety drills, including fire drills, tornado drills, and active shooter drills
- Procedures for distribution of school safety plans and/or confidentiality of such plans
- The role for community and family involvement in the creation of plans
- Involvement of state departments of education and specific school safety entities in the development and implementation of the plans
- General school building and infrastructure requirements for school safety
- Grants and other funding opportunities available to support school safety planning.

What should be noticed here is that all of the school safety plans mandated through legislative action only concern school shootings and stranger danger. The construction of school safety through legislative action showcases another vital part of how safety messages are sustained and persist in society. "Claims makers" give life to a social problem. Claims makers are individuals with power and wealth who can help shape public opinion and, ultimately, law.[68] When claims makers provide information to the general public, eventually, the information they provide normalizes societal topics—for example, the idea that school violence equals school shootings.

Most of the participants in my studies grew up in the 1970s, 1980s, or 1990s and are part of Generation X (those born between 1965–1980). School educational programming during Gen Xers' childhoods likely included McGruff the Crime Dog (to keep kids safe) or DARE (to keep kids off of drugs) but did not include safety drills or school shooting guidance. Gen Xers know a world before school shootings and thus received pre-school-shooting messaging when they were young. Thus, childhood school safety messages focused on kidnappers, dangerous strangers, and drugs. For example, study participants Maya and Sara provided some excellent context about the role of schools in learning to fear crime. Maya, a Swedish participant, says: "Yeah, and in school, they said to us that if an older man was walking around the school, we shouldn't talk to them, and we weren't supposed to take anything if they offered us anything." Over in the United States, Sarah, a woman from the South, recalls a similar memory. She says: "Yes, I remember teachers, parents always said to be on the lookout for people, to give a good description of someone if you need to."

Maya and Sarah's memories are similar in that they remember learning from teachers or other school officials that they should be on the lookout for strangers, especially strangers who may try to lure you over to give you something. This myth stems from the idea that kidnappers approach children by offering them an animal to pet or giving them something they want (like candy) in order to get them in a car. In other words, stranger danger and fear of kidnapping are the two primary messages that Maya and Sarah (along with many other women I've talked with over the years) remember learning from schools. What should be apparent is that neither participant remembered learning about school shootings. How school safety messages change over time is significant and will become critical as we begin to talk about how these children from the 1970s, eighties, and nineties teach fear to their children and how fear for children changes with the framing of school shootings as the only school crime.

Enhanced Security Measures—Safety Drills

The invention and implementation of safety drills by schools today also teaches fear to children. Safety plans and security behaviors of the school environment ultimately influence the children of today as well as their parents' perceptions of safety.

According to University of Texas at Dallas criminologists Michael Huskey and Nadine Connell, there are three ways that schools can conduct safety drills. The first is a lockdown drill, where students are told to go into a locked room and remain quiet. Another is the active shooter simulation drill. Schools that implement this type of drill hire actors who pretend to be school shooters and use air guns to simulate the sound of bullets; some even use fake blood. This type of drill aims to simulate an active shooter attack in as realistic a way as possible. Finally, options-based models are a spin-off of the "run, hide, fight" model: students are taught to run; if they can't run, to hide; and if they can't hide, to fight. Options-based models empower staff to make decisions during an evolving school shooting event. Versions of all three of these drill types are used throughout the United States today.

The psychological ramifications of such drills, especially the active shooter simulation drill, have been shown to do psychological harm, produce anxiety, and make children more worried about going to school.[69] Other studies have shown that safety drills have had less of an impact on students' well-being. This seems contingent on the student's age and less severe drills (like lockdown drills).

In another example of enhanced security measures, a study by researchers Christopher Schreck and Mitchell Miller found that adolescents who attended schools with a variety of security measures were more afraid of crime, even when controlling for factors we might expect would increase fear of crime among students, such as gangs, high drug use rates, or disorder within a school.[70] Further, fear of crime among adolescents was not predicated on the *number* of security measures the school took but on the *type* of security measures used. These results were especially true in public schools. The security measures included metal detectors, guards, hall monitors, locked doors, visitor sign-ins, hall pass requirements, drug education, and locker checks. As the researchers conclude, "the results show that some forms of security do have a statistical relationship with fear of crime: They correspond with higher levels of student fear."

In sum, Gen X children who learned about stranger danger, kidnapping, and drug use grew up to similarly worry about kidnapping, stranger danger, and, to a lesser extent, drug use. However, as discussed, children today are almost exclusively being taught that "safety" means preventing school shootings. This impacts fear of crime for these children, but it also affects the messages parents pass on to children. Gen X children grew up to pass on two kinds of safety lessons to their children: those from their childhood (regarding stranger danger, kidnapping) and those lessons their children are taught at school these days (school shootings). As we shall see, these various generational school safety lessons play into the ways parents teach fear to their children.

Learning from Strangers—the Media

In addition to learning from parents and schools, a third place we learn gendered crime myths is through the media. For example, in a 1991 *Oprah Winfrey Show* episode called "How to Protect Yourself Against an Attacker," Oprah starts by telling viewers, "A woman who uses some form of self-protection is twice as likely to escape," and "fighting back is a choice, a choice that only you can make. If you do choose to fight back, proper training is a must."[71] We can quickly see how this statement ties into the victim-centered crime prevention myth. In other words, women need to learn to act to make sure they do not become victims. Speaking with an expert, Oprah asks: "What is one of the most common mistakes that women make?" Expert: "They let them [strangers] get too close." Oprah, then, asks the experts and the audience a series of questions. She includes three questions. One question she asks the experts is about this scenario—"you've had to work late. You have a long walk to your car. The street is deserted. You feel that someone is following you, what should you do?" Another question is about burglaries: "You are home alone for the weekend, at least you thought you were alone when suddenly you realize there is a burglar in the house and you are in your bedroom." Finally, Oprah has an audience member ask a question to the crime experts. The audience members asks, "my question for you is, what about a woman who is wearing a dress and high-heels and walking down the street? It doesn't seem to me it would be as easy to carry out some of the techniques?" She goes on to explain that "I was attacked and I was in a dress, and I was wearing sneakers because I was walking home from work and I did fight back, and he is now serving time." In answering the question, the detective on the panel says, "good for you!" Another expert answers the questions by saying, "What I'm saying is that women have as much training as possible, and what we train is use your verbal skills, do everything you can, but if all else fails, fight for your life."[72]

Let's deconstruct this *Oprah* episode with an eye toward socially constructed crime myths. First, we can easily see that the entire episode only teaches women how to prevent attacks carried out by strange men. The idea of a stranger attacking a woman as she walks down a street late at night is the archetype of the stranger danger myth.[73] Even when Oprah presents attack scenarios within the home, a more common crime location for women, the attacker is still a stranger (though in real life it is more often someone the victim knows). Finally, women are told they need to fight or die trying.

Second, and perhaps most importantly, Oprah's episode showcases a myth we discussed in chapter 1—that is, the victim-centered crime prevention myth. Specifically talking about the crime of rape, we learn from criminology experts (Oprah's term) that it is our responsibility as women to fight off an attacker. Inherent in these assumptions is that fighting off an attacker will prevent rape. Thus, the reason men rape women is based on the belief that women don't fight hard enough rather than other factors related to the offender or society.

One might argue that *The Oprah Winfrey Show* in 1991 couldn't influence how women during that time thought about crime or the behaviors they took to prevent crime. However, one thing to remember is that most people are not crime victims, and their experience with a crime is often based on socialization sources outside of personal experience.[74] Thus, the media plays a more critical role than we might realize. Further, the 1991–1992 season of *The Oprah Winfrey Show* had 12.6 million viewers. Oprah is an icon in part because of her ability to tap into public opinion. Her show about sexual assault prevention tied in to larger ideas about victims and victim prevention. You just may remember this *Oprah* episode yourself, as I do. We may not necessarily remember where we learned these crime prevention techniques, but we certainly carry out some of these ideas and techniques in our daily lives.

One of the participants I interviewed in the Midwest, Emily, shows how such media stories might influence views on crime. When I ask her what crimes she fears the most, she says "sex crimes." When I ask her to explain why, she highlights very similar prevention strategies to those presented in shows like *Oprah* during this time. She says:

> I think that it would be a sex crime. That would make me probably the most uncomfortable, you know, that's the thing that freaks me out the most. Oh, parking lots. Just to back up a little bit. When I went to graduate school, I was walking out to a parking lot, cause I would stay in my studio until really, really late at night and I don't know why I would always walk with my big key out. I felt like I had absolutely no defense skills whatsoever, but I always felt better if I had my big key out. I don't have any self-defense skills whatsoever, and then, I think this is also from TV shows, the whole, like, slashing of the Achilles heel. Oh my god! In a parking lot I still get a little wave of [shivers] and I get in the car real quick. So, parking lots, that has more to do with sex crime issues than walking at night, that's more random theft. I don't know, like overpowering. I just feel like parking lots are more predator areas than just picking a house. That's totally probably TV, learned as well.

Emily's story is similar to the stories of other women I've interviewed over the years who tell me they are fearful in specific public spaces where strange men may abduct them. The behaviors women tell me they take to protect themselves are strikingly similar but most likely ineffective against an attack. Putting keys between knuckles, carrying mace, and learning self-defense are behaviors that sound very similar to what Oprah's episode highlights, a variety of defensive strategies against strangers. However, taking these precautions will likely not prevent sexual assault or being abducted in a parking lot.

I've explained how popular television shows impact views on safety lessons, but what do other researchers have to say about the role of the media?

Researchers who study media and crime tend to focus on two possible areas. First, they consider something called "media effects."[75] The question here is whether or not the amount of media you consume impacts your worldviews.[76] For example, do people who watch more violent media become more violent? The answer to this question most often is "no." Even if one person watches 100 episodes of a crime show and another person watches 2, it does not necessarily mean that the person with more media consumption will be more likely to act violently because of this media consumption.

A second and more nuanced focus is to examine how the media constructs topics and look at how the media might influence topics as one of many influencers (like parents, schools, and friends, for example). So, as we've seen in this chapter, people likely learn about what a crime victim, offender, and criminal justice professional "look like," "act like," and "do" through a variety of socialization sources, including the media. Therefore, when examining the construction of crime through the media, we can see how some patterns might influence our perceptions of crime but media itself is not a stand-alone socialization agent.

Researchers who study this arena have noted the critical power of the media in formulating public opinions about crime and justice.[77] Researchers have found several patterns. First, crime is presented as stranger-induced, violent, taking place at night, occurring in space that is considered "public," and with a male offender and sometimes a Black male offender.[78]

The connection between media and perceptions of crime is also apparent when talking to people about their views and perceptions of crime. Olivia, a Southern woman, provides an example of how media influenced her own misperceptions about fear of crime for women.

> Yea, *Cops*, *Law and Order*, that's why when I say that homicide and murder are the first things I think of and drugs are the second thing; that is because you see these things [on television]. If there is a major crime its usually that or the other. And so, most of my ideas of crime come from TV. *Cops*, I think, is the most realistic version of crime because it is actually things that have happened. Where some of the movies I watch are just overplayed for how bad it really is.

Olivia very specifically targets where she has learned about crime, that is, from the media. The media do not provide solid guidance on things to fear, like homicide, but as political scientist Bernard Cohen notes, the media do not tell people what to think, they tell people what to think about.[79]

The media has taught Olivia that she should more generally worry about crime because people like her may be crime victims. She learned to focus on stranger danger prevention techniques and the viewpoint that the world is scary. As discussed earlier, the "just world" hypothesis deeply affects how society views crime victims.[80] The more crime television you watch, the more likely you will see the world as a mean and scary place. Thus, while research on the influence of the media on fear of crime has had mixed results, my qualitative in-depth interview data indicates that crime shows influence participants' views of crimes and act as a relevant socialization agent for women.[81]

We can think about how media influences our safety values by way of crime myths. First, the media can significantly impact how we feel about victims.[82] Victims are painted as women, often white women, and are more likely to be blamed for their victimization when they don't adhere to the perfect victim status.[83] An example might be a woman who was out late at night at a bar and was abducted in a parking lot and then killed. In this case, the show might present criminal justice professionals engaging in victim-blame behaviors, such as asking: How much was the victim drinking? Who was she with that evening? Why did she leave the bar alone?

On the other hand, crime is presented as random and as something that cannot be prevented. Thus, media crime victims are often portrayed simultaneously as someone who should have done something in a different way to avoid victimization and as someone who could not have predicted criminal victimization happening to them.[84] The impact of this puzzle is often an increased fear of crime for women who consume crime-related media.[85]

The side of the victim-blame conundrum where victims try to prevent their own victimization is showcased by Jennifer, a study participant from the Midwest. Jennifer talks about what she takes away from fictional crime dramas, saying:

> I watch a lot of crime shows, and I used to test myself on that by watching a lot of these shows, can you identify that victim? You know, can you identify that car? What can you remember from the driver's license? Just little things. Learn how to start protecting yourself. If nothing else, you may remember that license plate number that is in front of you because maybe that person can help you. Maybe if you tell the police there was a car in front of me and maybe he saw the guy that ran past you. Maybe he, you know, could help me; you never know.

While Jennifer isn't engaging in overt victim blame in her answer here, the focus on trying to figure out a way to avoid victimization at all costs does play into the victim-centered crime prevention myth.

Catherine and Lauren provide examples of the other side of the victim-blame messaging: there is nothing you can do to prevent crime. When she is asked what she learned about crime from television, Catherine says: "I mean, what's normal and what's not normal, you know. You hear a lot about things that have happened. That there are a lot of different ways to solve it [crime], and there are a lot of different ways that people come up with a crime."

Lauren also conveys the random helpless part of crime prevention for women, stating: "Even though I'm independent and I think I can stand up for myself that when it comes down to it if some 400-pound man is on top of me, there is no way in the world I would be able to save myself without somebody else being there."

Like Jennifer, women learn from the media that they need to take a variety of limiting and restricting behaviors in public spaces to prevent a stranger-induced attack. Still, like Catherine and Lauren, women also learn that crime is random, violent, and cannot be controlled. It makes sense, then, that women are so afraid of crime.

Do Messages Differ by Media Type?

Researchers have focused on specific media types to see if they differentially influenced perceptions of crime and safety. The news, fictional, and reality crime shows have all been examined by such researchers.

News Stories

Many Americans rely on the news as a primary source of information about crime and justice issues. Studies have examined what we learn from the media regarding offenders, where news stories focus on the most severe, violent, and random crimes; these crimes are rare but seem familiar because of the heavy focus on them in the news.[86] The news portrays offenders as strangers and as Black men and portrays crimes as random.[87] Most news stories focus on recently arrested or recently imprisoned offenders. Rarely, if ever, do news media outlets follow the lengthy (sometimes years-long) process of the criminal justice system to explain the outcome of an original arrest case.[88] The news media is even less likely to provide practical information to viewers or listeners about crime victims.[89] When a violent random crime takes place, news outlets report on that story right when it happens. However, the criminal justice system takes a long time to catch, process, and punish an offender. In real time, this typically means that you, the American viewer, learn about a horrific crime from the news and hear the speculation about what happened. But you never really find out what happened in the long run—who shot the person in a drive-by shooting, what the relationship was to that person, what the skin color of the shooter was, nor much about the victim.

For these reasons, the entertainment element of news stories is widely studied by researchers. "If it bleeds, it leads" is a motto presented by researchers, indicating that the news will cover only violent and horrific crimes.[90] The reality of the news as entertainment is at odds with our perceptions of what the news is and does, especially for older generations, who tend to see news agencies as providing non-biased information rather than entertainment.

As Robinson points out, crimes are only covered by the news if deemed as "newsworthy."[91] He presents five criteria for newsworthiness, including "(1) the nature of the crime, (2) the demographic factors of the victim/offender, (3) the uniqueness of the event, (4) event salience, and (5) various characteristics of media agency." Such newsworthy criteria ultimately lead to one of every seven stories in the news featuring crime, and for every two property crimes featured, eight news stories feature a violent crime. As we know by now, these numbers are out of line with reality. Robinson also notes that the lack of context presented in these stories is problematic. He mentions by not adding cultural context, news viewers are misinformed, and crime is overly simplified. For example, viewers see crime as more widespread than it actually is and that only Black people commit it.[92] Further, news stories make unrelated connections between past and current crimes, and news agencies tend to practice something called "looping," where the same news story is shown multiple times.[93]

The people I've spoken with also show the power of the news on what they remember about crime growing up. For example, Lena, a Swedish participant, says:

> I do remember as a child that I had this fear of being kidnapped. I guess there was a story that was in—we didn't watch much news on TV, so it must have been in the newspapers, that there was some kind of story about somebody. It was some child that was kidnapped and found, and I can't even remember whether alive or dead, sometime in the seventies, probably, the end of the 1970s.

Of all the memories Lena has through her life that she can pull from to remember about learning about crime growing up, this one news story is her first recollection. The pieces of knowledge she recalls and takes away from this story (especially as a child) are that a child was kidnapped and found by authorities. Lena does not even recall if the child was alive, further reinforcing fearful images of children abducted by strangers.

Fictional Crime Dramas and Reality Crime Shows
A lot of criminologists have studied the influence of fictional crime dramas. This influence is significant because, similar to *Oprah*, the reach of fictional crime dramas is immense.[94] Thus, while the stories presented are imaginary, people who watch them start to identify characteristics and patterns of the characters with real-life crime and victimization experiences. *Law and Order*, for example, is the longest-running fictional crime drama on TV. *Law and Order* was on air for 20 years, made 457 episodes, won multiple awards, and produced two spin-offs. The *Law and Order* series has made its legacy and its brand by showing fictional cases that have been "ripped from the headlines." It is argued that the *Law and Order* franchise is so successful because it has found a formula that works. This formula involves an evil offender, a violent crime, and a go-getter officer. It is easy to see how such a formula would provide viewers stereotypical images of criminals and victims that might change how they see crime.[95]

Another popular fictional drama that has also changed public opinion about crime and justice is *CSI*. *CSI* has enjoyed considerable popularity over time. When the show first aired in 2000, it brought in 20.8 million viewers. Even in 2015, as it finished its fifteenth season, the show still had 11.2 million viewers. *CSI* added scientific evidence to the more traditional crime drama (which focused more on crime solving through police officers and lawyers). The idea that crime could be solved by scientific evidence became part of popular culture and became part of crime perceptions by most Americans. A consequence of *CSI*'s popularity has been, "as viewers consume images of *CSI* and forensic programming in news reporting, they may well begin to assume a personal knowledge base formed by the relationship between popular programming and the news."[96] Another consequence of the *CSI* effect has been its influence over court evidence among jury trials. Such evidence can raise expectations that fingerprinting, DNA testing, or blood splatter patterns can help catch criminals. In reality, most states and local communities do not have anyone qualified to study or even in charge of forensic evidence. Many states have only one crime lab, where all data is deposited and analyzed by one crime lab specialist.

Further, the *CSI* effect implies something that must be debunked: that all criminals are caught and brought to justice. Many people who commit crimes are not ever caught. While this is less true for violent crime than property crime, it still shows another crime myth: we always catch criminals.[97]

Some of my work with my colleagues Gayle Rhineberger and Lauren Vasquez examined fictional crime dramas.[98] Analyzing data from a sample of popular crime shows between 2002 and 2009 (*Law and Order: Special Victims Unit*, *CSI*, *Criminal Minds*, and *Without a Trace*), we found some interesting things about the perception of crime and victimization through crime shows. First, we found that strangers were overrepresented as offenders, homicide victims, and white female victims. We also found that victims who had any relationship to the attacker were portrayed more negatively than those who did not know the attacker (adding an element of victim blame). Finally, when comparing the various shows and portrayals of victims, we were surprised to find that *Law and Order: Special Victims Unit*, a show devoted explicitly to victims, was just as likely to blame crime victims as the other three shows. The conclusions of this project easily show how media ties into all three gendered crime myths. That is, fictional crime dramas enhance viewers' belief in stranger danger, the white woman crime victim myth, and the victim-centered crime prevention myth.

Thus, when looking at research about the news, fictional crime dramas, and forensic-based crime dramas, we see some patterns that may contribute to how we learn about the fear of crime. These outlets portray crime as random and violent and as something that is always solved.[99] Viewers also feel that crime is solved more quickly than it is and that forensic evidence is available for all crimes.[100] Real police work differs from the police work we see on television. Police officers arrive at the crime scene on television shows right away and quickly check for fingerprints using a computerized system. These fictional officers then find, arrest, and get a confession out of the offender. The fictional police work process typically happens in 24 hours! Fictitious crime cases are entertaining to watch, but crime is rarely solved using similar procedures or timeframes in the real world.

When examining what the media tells us about crime, we see that criminals, victims, and even crime itself are all painted with broad, inaccurate generalizations. For example, crime is presented as more violent than we see in reality, more likely to happen at night and in a public space, and more often stranger-induced. Victims are also portrayed inaccurately, as white women. The portrayal of victims means that white women have likely seen themselves on television as crime victims much more often than is warranted. As discussed earlier, some research has even found that women of color believe white women are more likely to be the victims of crimes than themselves, even though statistically speaking, this is not accurate.[101]

In closing, this chapter has shown that crime myths must be learned in order for people to believe in and buy into them. The three primary places we learn about crime myths as children (and sometimes as adults) are from parents, at school, and through various forms of media. Parents, schools, and media teach and reinforce notions of stranger danger, that white women are the most likely victims, and that potential victims have the capability to prevent victimization. Next, we turn to a discussion of how women act on these learned messages each day.

3

Living Out Crime Myths

> *I think it's just being aware of my surroundings.... If I have to get out of someplace, where are my exits? If I'm on a subway or if I happen to get in an elevator with somebody, my escape route always comes to mind. When I went to cities, I'd put my purse on with the strap across my chest and just kind of pay attention to the neighborhoods I was in, the area, and who was around me. I think it was just being more aware, visually aware of what was going on, always aware of my surroundings.*
>
> —SALLY, A SOUTHERN PARTICIPANT

How do the safety myths we've learned become part of our daily practices? Like Sally, you may also take preventative measures to lessen the chances of crime happening to you. Take a minute to think about the behaviors you engage in take on or avoid each day because you are worried about crime and safety. As we've discussed, most of our fear of crime is based on myths. Myths, like those surrounding stranger danger, are "carried out" by women each day. In other words, women "live out" the crime myths they've been taught, taking many action-based and avoidance-based precautionary measures.

Perhaps you cannot immediately think of things that you do each day that are crime prevention–focused. Here is an example of another set of prevention measures that may be easier for you to see and recall. I am writing this book during the COVID-19 pandemic. I am struck by how fear of COVID-19 parallels our fear of strangers. In both cases, we take preventive measures daily and perhaps multiple times throughout the day to prevent something from happening (contracting COVID-19/becoming a crime victim). One key difference between crime prevention precautions and COVID-19 pandemic-related precautions is that COVID-19 behaviors are more noticeable and clear-cut than the set of behaviors society expects you to take to prevent crime. For example, if asked about the preventive measures you take to keep you and your family safe from COVID-19, you'd likely be able to rattle off several action-based measures immediately. Preventative measures may include wearing a mask, using hand sanitizer, or staying six feet away from the person in front of you. Most recently, you may have been vaccinated. You know to do this because we've received guidance from official sources like the Centers for Disease Control and Prevention, and we see signs when we enter places ("mask required") and markings on the floor telling us to stay six feet apart. We've seen increased hand sanitizer stations, and we've even experienced government-regulated curfews and lockdown periods. We've also been encouraged to avoid holiday gatherings and large, crowded indoor spaces, such as those you might find at a concert, theme park, or movie theater.

Preventive measures you take because of your fear of strangers are not quite as obvious; there are no dots on the ground telling you where strangers lurk or signs on dwellings telling you to avoid those locations. Given that crime myths target women, it makes sense that crime prevention often falls on the shoulders of women as well. Women, then, must come up with the unwritten, gendered, crime prevention rules and guidelines and make decisions about how to act on their own. As we've seen, preventive measures are another way society puts the responsibility on potential victims but does little to decrease criminal victimization.[1]

Criminologists have a pretty good sense of what precautionary measures people take to prevent crime. They find there are two types of behaviors taken: action-oriented behaviors and avoidance-oriented behaviors.[2] Things like locking the door to your house, turning on a porch light at night, or opening your child's bedroom door after they are asleep are examples of mundane, taken-for-granted behaviors that become part of how we live crime myths daily.[3]

Action-Based Precautionary Behaviors

The action-oriented behaviors studied by criminologists require direct action on your part. Many examples of action-based precautionary measures include taking a self-defense class; owning a weapon for protection; owning a watch dog; adding bars, locks, or extra lighting to your home; and installing a security system. All these behaviors are specifically carried out to alleviate stranger danger. Let's talk about four examples of action-oriented precautionary measures—guns, mace/pepper spray, self-defense courses, and home security systems—and how these play into gendered crime myths.

Guns

Researchers have considered who purchases guns for protection, why they do so, and what impact gun purchases may have on perceptions of safety and fear of crime. We know that opinions about weapon ownership, particularly gun ownership, often develop during your upbringing.[4] For example, if you grew up in a house with hunters, you may be familiar with guns in a way that someone who grew up without hunters in the family may not. We also might imagine that if you grew up in a household with people who work in certain professions, such as police, military, or corrections, you might be more accepting of guns. Finally, researchers have found that people who grow up in certain areas may be more likely to own guns. Two examples would be people who grow up in more rural areas and people who grow up in the Southern part of the United States.[5] We also know that men are more likely to own guns than women, and some research suggests that whites are more likely to own guns than non-whites.[6]

Thus, while a lot of research has focused on who owns guns and for what purpose (hunting, protection), not many studies focus on the second question: what impact might gun purchases have on perceptions of safety and fear of crime? If you own a gun, do you feel safer? Do you feel less fear of crime? Do you believe you can protect yourself from a stranger-induced attack? These are the types of questions that we need to answer before we can understand how we "live" crime myths through action-based precautionary measures.

A research project by Florida State University professor Gary Kleck and colleagues sheds light on this relationship by focusing on guns.[7] Kleck and his colleagues wanted to understand if people were more likely to own a gun for self-protection if they believed they had a higher level of victimization risk or had been victims in the past. They found that people who thought they were at a greater risk of victimization were more likely to purchase a gun for protection. There were a couple of other interesting findings worth noting. First, they found that those who had been previous victims of robbery were more likely to say that they had purchased a gun for protection. Second, they also found that men were more likely than women to say that they owned a gun for protection.

Another recent study by Southern Illinois University Carbondale criminology professors Christopher Mullins and Sou Lee provides clear findings based on gender and the relationship between gun ownership and fear of crime.[8] They found that women were more likely than men to own a gun because of fear of crime. Women who own guns are more likely to come from the South, a rural area, and/or be a working/middle-class white woman. Mullins and Lee also found that women's gun ownership was often tied to men. Women who owned guns grew up in households where their fathers owned firearms, or, as they became adults, they were in romantic relationships with men who owned guns. Therefore, gun exposure by men ultimately influenced gun ownership. The women in this study also said that they were worried about using a gun because they were either afraid of guns or of hurting someone else. Men in the study did not suggest they avoided guns because they were afraid of hurting others. These findings were not part of the responses of the men in the study. The name of this article, "'Like Make Up on a Man': The Gendered Nature of Gun Norms," shows the power of the perceived masculine nature of gun ownership. When we think of guns, our first image is often of a man, not a woman, holding a gun. Further, men that own guns seem more masculine to us. Therefore, it makes sense that women would be less likely to have a gun for protection.

These two studies, then, show us that while gun use is a gendered phenomenon, something society associates with men more than women, the difference between men's and women's reasons for owning a gun is also gendered. For example, women own guns less often and feel less confident in using a firearm for protection. Further, women who own guns do not always experience less fear.[9]

I've found similar things in my studies. For example, Alexandra, a Midwestern respondent, says it best. When asked if she took behaviors to protect herself from crime, she says: "No, not really, because I would still not probably be able to defend myself. I mean, that's like getting a gun. I would never ever ever get a gun because I know the chances are the person would rip it out of my hand and shoot me with it." Like the respondents in Mullins and Lee's study, Alexandra tells us that she is afraid of guns because she doesn't know how effective she would be with a weapon. Thus, owning a firearm for protection is not something this participant seriously considers.

Another example comes from Nancy, a Southern participant who talks to me about a fake gun she owns with her husband. She says:

> We still have it, but part of the reason we bought it was because it looks kind of real. Kind of. Like in the dark, from a distance, it looks like a real gun, so if we ever need it, yeah. Also, my stepdad used to have this, like, porcelain gun, he was in ROTC. They didn't issue them real firearms; they issued them porcelain or something. Ceramic guns that looked real, but they weren't. There was nothing on the inside, and I've always been a little bit interested in those. Like, cause I'm not a big gun person, but I wouldn't mind being, like, "Get out of my house!" But that's just my personal thing. Everybody's got their own opinions about guns and stuff. I'm pretty like anti-gun, but I'm more anti-people coming into my house.

In the case of Nancy, she does not want guns in her house because she thinks they are scary and sees herself as "anti-gun." However, she learned from her stepdad growing up that having something that looks like a real gun without the pressure of using a weapon allows her to put her fears of guns to the side while still getting the benefit of looking like a gun owner. Most research studies examine gun ownership as one crime prevention behavior. However, it is clear from these sources that guns are not women's preferred protective behavior from crime prevention. Women do not own guns very often, and when they do, they are often not as confident with guns and still feel afraid of crime.

Mace/Pepper Spray

Researchers have found carrying mace/pepper spray is a more common precautionary behavior for women, and studies that talk to college students (especially women) have focused on pepper spray as a preventive behavior.[10] For example, one study conducted by Nevada State College researchers Lance Hignite, Shantal Marshall, and Laura Naumann surveyed both men and women college students about behaviors that made them less afraid of crime.[11] They asked students if they carried a weapon to prevent victimization and found that about one-quarter of their participants indicated they had some form of a weapon for protection on campus. When breaking down the 25 percent of the sample who did so, carrying mace/pepper spray was the most common weapon mentioned (55 percent mace/pepper spray, 17 percent knife, 11 percent multiple weapons, and 8 percent guns). In addition, Hignite and colleagues found that among women, those who were white, those who knew about the victimization experiences of others, those who were more afraid of crime, and those with less confidence in campus police were more likely to own mace or pepper spray.

Where do people learn to use mace/pepper spray as a preventative strategy? My research has commonly found that women are given mace/pepper spray by a family member, typically a man. Jaime, a female college professor from the South, explains how she saw this socialization process regarding mace play out with her college students.

> I don't have mace or anything like that. I know a lot of my female students do, and I know a lot of their fathers give them cans of mace to put on their key chains. We were looking at the mace cans in class the other day. I think they were talking about the graphic design [of the can].

In this case, there were enough women in this class who owned mace to compare the designs on the mace cans. Their fathers gave these women mace.

Allison, another Southern participant, mentions mace as a precautionary measure. First, however, she talks about the impracticality of using mace, saying:

> I used to carry like a whistle, and I used to carry mace and things like that, but then it was so bulky, and then I went through the whole situation in my head of if something was actually going to happen and I was randomly attacked, what was the chances that I was actually going to fumble and be able to find my mace and use it effectively on someone else, without hurting myself and then it just became ridiculous in my head, so I threw it away.

In the case of Allison, we see how mace as a precautionary measure often plays out in real life. Women believe they should carry mace, likely because they've been told this by someone of significance in their life (usually a father). Still, once they start carrying it, they realize that it is perhaps not an effective strategy.

Finally, when I ask Mary, a Midwestern participant if she has any advice to give women about fear of crime, she talks about mace, among other preventive measures.

> Such as, like, carrying your keys at all times [and], like, prepare yourself before you get out of the vehicle. I used to carry mace. I know how to use a gun. I know how to protect myself somewhat, if I can remember how to do that. In this situation you know of course I feel like I would be the type of person that would freeze up and be like, "Oh, what do I do?"

In the case of Mary, while she acknowledges that she has owned mace, she does not feel that either mace or the gun she owns would protect her in the case of an attack. Mary fully expects that she will freeze up and not be able to use these things. Also, while she mentions mace, similar to the other two respondents, Mary no longer carries it, which we can assume is because she doubts its effectiveness in preventing crime. Further, while Mary acknowledges a lack of confidence in these preventive strategies, she also talks about mace as part of the advice she'd give to other women to "prepare yourself at all times." So, Mary is telling women to take action-based precautions even though she fully acknowledges that she does not expect them to work. Mary is not an outlier. While women talk about mace as a standard precautionary measure to prevent victimization, they also note they rarely keep it and don't bet on its effectiveness.

Self-Defense Courses

Another commonly mentioned action-oriented behavior taken on by women is the use of self-defense courses.[12] The media and public opinion encourage women to take self-defense courses for protection. While learning these skills might help women prevent an attack, these programs exacerbate stranger danger by emphasizing strategies to protect themselves against strangers. Further, research has shown the primary consumers of these courses are white women, reflecting the belief that white women are the most likely crime victims.[13] These courses also highlight victim-centered prevention by making women think self-defense courses will lower their victimization chances. Thus, self-defense courses are center stage for all three crime myths: the stranger danger myth, the white woman crime victim myth, and the victim-centered prevention myth.

Let's examine an example of the marketing and content of a self-defense course—the Rape Aggression Defense Systems Program (R.A.D.). R.A.D. is considered one of the best programs in the United States and has an extensive reach to the general public. For example, in one state, there are five universities, five police departments (including one large precinct in the state capital), and a couple of other agencies that use the R.A.D. program. In another, slightly bigger, state, there are 35 R.A.D. programs listed with 14 universities as partners.[14]

While the R.A.D. program may have a higher standard of self-defense classes than other programs, this self-defense class still plays into crime myths in significant ways. For example, the program is promoted as follows:

> Rape Aggression Defense, known as R.A.D., is a self-defense program designed specifically for women. The R.A.D. approach to personal safety begins with awareness, prevention, risk reduction, and risk avoidance, and progresses to hands-on physical defense techniques.

We can see how this course description emphasizes stranger danger crime myths by indicating that women who learn self-defense can reduce their risk of victimization. Inherent in this discussion is the message that women will be able to stop a stranger from abducting or hurting them. These courses also tend to target white women as participants. For example, even in states with more historically black colleges and universities (HBCUs), there are very few HBCUs that market this program to their students. Most of the universities that market the R.A.D. Program are predominately white institutions.¹⁵ This suggests that such programs are marketing to white women, at least in the university setting. Again, we must remember that white women are less likely than women of color to be victimized. So, rape prevention marketing strategies are based on crime myths about white women victims. Finally, just from the description, we can see how much self-defense classes put the responsibility of victim prevention on potential victims. Women who take these courses are taught to be "aware," to "prevent," and to use "hands-on" techniques to prevent victimization.¹⁶ Such courses do not highlight that victims, even those who are most prepared through self-defense, may still be victimized or that by knowing self-defense, there will be no impact on the number of rapists and little effect on the number of rape victims. Thus, programs like these reinforce crime myths and may elevate fear of crime.

Taking a self-defense class is also a standard answer and popular choice for crime prevention among the women in my research studies. For example, talking about self-defensive practices, Wendy, a participant from the Midwest, says:

> I'm sure I've been told at some point in my life, "Did you hear what happened to so and so? They were mugged" or you know what always goes around about the shopping malls, like I'm sure you've seen it, where the girl got attacked from the van that was parked next to her and they were in her car or something, and when she got in, he put her in her trunk, and she like busted out her taillight and waved her arms, and that's how she was found or something like that.

In this story, Wendy tells me that she believes that she can be trained to escape from a moving vehicle inside a trunk. We might remember the *Oprah* episode we discussed earlier (or similar shows that discuss safety prevention), which taught women to protect themselves from a stranger. Also important here is the story's outcome; we see a positive ending because the potential victim fought back and got herself out of the dangerous situation.

Karen, a Midwestern participant, focuses on self-defense as a critical prevention strategy. She says:

> I guess I feel that if somebody did try to attack me, then I'm going to fight back like hell because if I'm going down, they are going down with me. It's not that I'm being cocky or anything, but I guess your mentality [is essential]. If you kind of curb your feelings a little bit and are prepared, it makes you feel better and not necessarily as afraid as not being prepared.

Karen's answer focuses a lot on physical strength. Other participants expressed a more mixed assessment of the effectiveness of self-defense classes. Teresa, a Midwestern, married participant, expresses a belief that while women should take self-defense courses, she is not confident the training could prevent victimization. She says:

> I wouldn't say that they protect me, but I will say they make me feel a little more empowered. I wouldn't say they necessarily protect me because if a dude is 450 pounds, 6' 6". I mean, I know I'm kind of tall, but I think he could easily do whatever if he wanted to.

Donna, another Midwestern participant, also has a mixed assessment on the effectiveness of self-defense but believes the positives outweigh the negatives. Donna, talking about self-defense as well, although more about self-defense classes than self-defense acts, says:

> I always encourage people to take self-defense [classes] when they can, and like I said, it is empowering. It is not about knowing how to fight off an attacker cause you don't know if you're going to be able to fight him off, but that feeling of empowerment is, you know, a huge part of that, it's going to help, at least. I'd tell them, yeah, take safety measures if you feel like that is going to help.

Donna labels self-defense classes as "empowering," giving women the confidence they might need to get themselves out of a dangerous situation. Interestingly, Donna also admits that knowing self-defense may not prevent an attack but feels self-defense gives women a fighting chance. The idea that women in potential victimization situations can control a dangerous situation stems directly from the victim-centered prevention myth: women are victimized because they did not do enough to prevent victimization.

While women often cite self-defense courses as a primary way that they think women could protect themselves from crime, they also are not as likely to believe that such prevention efforts would likely pay off in an attack. Criminologist Alex Campbell notes one crucial benefit of self-defense.[17] While self-defense classes emphasize crime myths, they may also give women confidence about their bodies. Self-defense programs may have a similar benefit to programs like CrossFit, an exercise program that focuses on healthy bodies and building muscle.[18] Thus, while the effectiveness of self-defense courses on crime prevention or fear of crime is not strong, there is support for other benefits.

One last point about self-defense is that it is a prevention strategy that targets multiple identities—since it is often something that white women (rather than just white people or all women) take on. So, then, it makes sense that prevention measures related to self-defense play into the white woman crime victim myth.

Sociologist Kristine De Welde provides the most comprehensive examination of white women's prevention efforts through self-defense classes. De Welde spent three and a half years attending and working with white women participants of a self-defense safety course.[19] She conducted 320 hours of observation and 30 in-depth interviews with participants. She found that there were three primary reasons participants took the course. They took the course because they were about to go off to college, because they had been crime victims, or because they were afraid of crime. De Welde says, "the particular focus on 'the attack' is suggestive of a broader angst about white women's general vulnerability in public spaces. This is consistent with discourses suggesting that women are simply not safe outside of their homes and are especially unsafe without a male protector. . . . These fears also suggest that women's dread of being victimized [on the street] limits their lives. Fear then functions as a social control."[20] Thus, self-defense courses are marketed to counter fears of attack but actually play into fears that constrain women's activities.

Home Security Systems

Women think about protective precautionary measures not only in public spaces but also in private spaces. At first glance, this should make criminologists feel a bit better since women are most likely to be victimized by a known man, often one they are romantically involved with. Thus, taking preventive strategies in the home seems like a step in the right direction. Unfortunately, women do not typically worry about these known men or romantic partners. Instead, women consider stranger danger when they think about preventive measures to protect their private dwelling. Women are worried about strangers entering their homes and see home security as a way to prevent such victimization from happening.

Home security systems are a precautionary strategy taken by both men and women to prevent their homes from being burglarized. Home security systems are big business, and millions of people have a security system for their home.[21] Several studies have examined what having a security system does to your fear of crime. In one example, a survey conducted by researcher Carlos Vilalta examined how home security systems might influence fear of crime in large metropolitan areas like Mexico City.[22] Surveying 1,549 households, Vilalta found that those who lived in neighborhoods perceived as unsafe were more likely to own a home security system than those who did not perceive their community as dangerous. When he broke down the characteristics of individuals who own security systems, he found that women, minimum-wage earners, and young people were more afraid of crime than their counterparts (men, higher-wage earners, and old people). Further, he found that having a home security system had no impact on fear of crime. In other words, this behavioral prevention strategy did not make people feel less afraid of crime.

One must ask why people would purchase security systems if they do not make them feel less afraid. Perhaps people see security systems as an option they should pursue based on societal pressure, but once they purchase a security system, it does not have the effect they hoped for. In other words, having a security system may be a common response to crime myths, but because the system doesn't curb fear, it becomes a preventative action without much of an outcome.

One study by sociologist Allen Liska and his colleagues uses National Crime Survey data, where 6,500 people across 26 major cities were surveyed.[23] They found a circular loop between fear of crime and preventive measures. So, someone is afraid of crime, which causes them to take precautionary measures, which causes them to be more fearful of crime. For example, imagine buying a security system for your house because you are worried about break-ins. Each time you set the alarm or touch the buttons, you are reminded of the potential that crime may occur and, thus, feel more afraid. As discussed earlier, studies have found that precautionary measures, even avoidance behaviors, do not necessarily decrease fear of crime and may actually increase fear of crime.[24]

Another point to mention about home security systems is that they are often income based. Women who can afford to own homes and who live in areas where home security systems are common are more likely to have an economic privilege that allows them to buy these systems. Unfortunately, there hasn't been much research on how income influences behavioral precautions in preventing fear of crime. Still, it seems likely that such income-based decisions would be an essential part of selecting action-based precautionary measures like home security systems.

If security systems do not reduce fear of crime, we must ask where the desire to purchase one comes from. ADT, a large home security company that made approximately $5.3 billion in 2020, is a leader in the home security business.[25] This company is well known in part because of its large base of commercials and advertising. Most of you have seen one of these commercials, although you may not have connected ADT commercials to crime myths, stranger danger, or fear of crime. However, if you think about it, these ADT commercials have been constructed to do this very thing—to make us more afraid of crime and to believe that the only way to reduce our chances of victimization is by having a security system.

For example, one recent ad campaign focused on getting a security system before something terrible happens.[26] This popular commercial begins by showing a married couple sitting on a couch in their lovely home. The wife, a white, attractive, middle-aged woman, starts by saying, "I got ADT because I walked in on a burglary once." As she tells her story, the viewer sees a flashback of the woman and her white elementary-school–aged daughter walking into the house. They see a white man standing in their living room. He has demolished the living room, and glass is broken, lamps are knocked over, drawers are open and rifled. He runs out when they enter the house. The mother picks up a broken picture frame with a picture of a boy, which the viewer assumes is her son—the scene changes to the daughter's bedroom at night. We see the mother going into the bedroom to hug and comfort the daughter, who cannot sleep because she is so worried about someone breaking into their house again. We hear the mother's voice as we watch the scene unfold. She says, "The physical damage was pretty bad; the emotional toll was even worse. My daughter had nightmares. What that robber took from us was our peace of mind. With ADT, we got it back." Thus, the mom tells viewers that security systems will prevent victimization and, if you have been burglarized, ADT security systems will alleviate your fear and worry. The ADT ad exemplifies how the stranger danger crime myth plays out in real life and how effective this commercial might be for white, economically privileged women who have been taught to fear strangers.

In conclusion, action-oriented prevention measures target the prevention of stranger-induced criminal victimization. The most typical action-oriented behaviors taken on by women include using mace (especially young women), taking a self-defense course (especially white women), and owning a home security system (especially those with more income). Under rare circumstances, women see guns as a viable precautionary measure.

Avoidance-Oriented Crime Prevention Strategies

While women take on action-based behaviors, they are most likely to take on avoidance as a primary way to live out gendered crime myths. These include behaviors like avoiding places at night, avoiding going places alone, and avoiding areas altogether. We know this because studies comparing action- and avoidance-based behaviors among women have found that women take on avoidance-type behaviors way more often than action-based behaviors.[27] For example, my work with my colleagues David May and Sarah Goodrum used survey data collected from 2,091 residents of Kentucky.[28] It investigated women's use of precautionary behaviors in comparison with men's use of precautionary behaviors. First, we found significant gender differences; that is, women are more likely to take avoidance precautions than men. Second, women are more likely to say that fear of crime had prevented them from doing things they would like to do in the past 12 months.

Thus, while action-oriented crime prevention efforts are sometimes taken on, women, in particular, are most likely to engage in avoidance-oriented crime prevention behaviors. For example, suppose women can avoid confronting a potential attacker instead of engaging them (through fighting or using pepper spray or a gun). In that case, women will pick avoidance nine times out of ten. Avoidance-based behaviors include things like changing routines and times of travel because of fear of crime, avoiding places during certain times of day (usually nighttime), avoiding going certain places altogether, and avoiding going places alone.[29] Such behaviors are so much a part of being a woman that you likely do not even know when you choose to take on avoidance behaviors.

Avoiding Places

Researcher Hannah Scott found that women are more likely than men to take many avoidance-based measures, including avoiding walking alone at night, not taking public transportation, not leaving the house when alone, and avoiding parking garages when alone, among other things.[30] She found the greatest impact on women's behavior was harassment by strange men: being followed, receiving unwanted attention, or receiving obscene phone calls. Harassment behaviors predicted fear of crime even more so than being a crime victim. This finding is pretty intense and shows the power of gendered crime myths. Scott concludes from this study that fear of stranger danger is more relevant to determining behaviors than other reasons, such as direct experience with crime. Scott also highlights the significance of this finding, saying, "It is ironic that this study demonstrates, for the most part, that women fear the danger posed by strange men even though statistics show that women are more likely to be victimized by individuals they know. They are most afraid of the surprise sexual attack by the unknown assailant, despite the fact that statistics and public service media campaigns are making women aware of dangers of dating and marital situations. It is argued here that there is something more at stake with the unknown assailant: predictability. Level of intimacy between the victim and the offender, with few exceptions, offers a buffer to thoughts of victimization. . . . In essence the author is suggesting that knowing someone allows for a false sense of security in that one may feel that they can predict more accurately, and thereby possibly control, the behavior of someone if they have met in the past."[31]

A study by Queen's University sociologist Carl Keane also examined the significance of women's avoidance behaviors.[32] Using data from the Violence Against Women Survey (which surveyed 12,300 women over 18 years of age who lived in Canada), Keane sought to understand women's use of avoidance behaviors. Women who participated in this survey were asked how often they avoided walking in their neighborhood or using parking garages, and then they were asked if they would do those activities more often if they felt safer from crime. Keane found that 67 percent of participants said they would walk in neighborhoods or use parking garages more often if they felt safer. This may seem like a "no brainer"; of course women who feel safer in public spaces would be more likely to use such areas. However, we must remember that women who are avoiding these spaces are doing so independent of actual victimization chances.

Further, it is very unrealistic to expect that such public spaces will ever feel safer for women. How likely is it that parking garages will be updated in a way that gives women peace of mind? Again, this is not a feasible reality. Keane concludes that "what appears to be happening, then, is that some women, because of fear, feel unable (or at least unwilling) to take full advantage of their immediate environments. Hence, many women may be currently restricting their daily activities to avoid the settings described here, and likely many other settings, because of worries about their safety."[33]

The participants of my studies have overwhelmingly verified such research findings on avoidance behaviors. Moreover, most women point to avoidance behaviors as the most common strategy to manage their fear of crime.

Sophia, a Midwestern woman, explains how avoidance behaviors are part of her daily life. For example, when asked if she avoided going places at night, here is what she has to say:

> I mean, I wouldn't go. There are things I just wouldn't do, I mean what they are, I'm not really sure, but you know, like, if I had to go somewhere and I had to park, like, three blocks away, and it was dark, and I was alone I wouldn't go there. You know, I'm not going to go walking around somewhere where I'm going to have to walk anywhere alone besides in and out of a building after dark. So, that's about it really.

So Sophia completely modifies her life by avoiding all activities at night. Even when she cannot avoid being somewhere in the dark, she takes precautions ahead of time by making sure that she parks as close as possible to minimize her time in the dark. The most striking part of this conversation is in the very last sentence, when Sophia says, "so, that's about it really." It seems for Sophia, completely modifying routine activities around darkness is not a big deal. The nonchalant nature of this statement shows us just how truly rooted in tradition these behaviors are for women. Women take precautions without agonizing about it and do so because these are just things that women do.

In addition to women talking about all the various places and events they avoid, especially at night, it is interesting to note that women also talk about avoidance as a key advice strategy to give to other women. It is one thing to take precautions yourself and another to advise others about the precautions they should take to keep themselves safe. For example, when asked what advice she would give other women about how to stay safe, Tina, a Midwestern participant, explains:

> Basically, what I've been saying, just, first of all, we try to avoid situations where it is really, really dangerous. If you can't, then, you find street lights, find people that are going into the building, coming out at the same time, just small steps, because most attackers are probably not going to come up if there is a group.

For Tina, she feels it is essential to tell other women to avoid perceived dangerous situations at all costs. If they cannot do so, they should make sure they take precautions to the best of their ability. Tina sees these as "small steps," even though avoiding situations in public spaces is not as easy as Tina makes it seem. The expectation that women should see these avoidance strategies as common and not that big of a deal gives us another example of why gendered behaviors persist for women. We avoid people and places in public because we think this will keep us safe from criminal victimization. However, as we've already established, these things are not based on the reality of our victimization chances.

Studies also point out the gendered nature of avoidance behaviors. For example, based on focus group data with men and women, University of Oregon sociologist Jocelyn Hollander concludes that "these patterns of perceived vulnerability and dangerousness are not simply cognitive constructs; they have concrete consequences for the everyday lives of women and men. . . . Women report constantly monitoring their environment for signs of danger, hesitating to venture outside at night alone or even in the company of other women, asking men for protection, modifying their clothes and other aspects of their appearance, and restricting their activities to reduce their perceived risk of violence, thus limiting their use of public space."[34] So, avoidance is both detrimental to reducing fear of crime and a gendered phenomenon.

Changing Routine Activities

Almost all people engage in routines each day. These routine activities are typically done in the same way and even in the same order each day. A morning routine might include going to the gym, getting ready for work, getting your kids ready for school, dropping kids off at school, and heading off to work. We cannot modify some activities, such as more fixed activities like work times or children's drop-off times. While we cannot change fixed activities or the timing of such activities because of fear of victimization, we can modify or change how we arrive at the fixed activity. So perhaps we walk down the same sidewalk each day to get to our car at the end of a workday. One day, we see a man we do not know walking down the same sidewalk, causing us to feel afraid. So we might change our routine activity by walking to the other side of the road or taking a different path to get to our car in the future. In this case, we've modified our route but not the routine activity.

When it comes to leisure activities or things we do for fun, we have a lot more leeway in which activities we do and don't do. A lot of research has shown that women change their routine leisure activities if they are worried about crime. So, for example, at night perhaps you choose to go to the gym instead of running down the road. Maybe you run with a buddy instead of alone, or you change up your running route every day. As another example, perhaps you choose not to go to a party in a part of town that makes you uncomfortable or worried about crime. Or maybe you don't go to the grocery store at night because you are concerned about crime. These are just a few of the ways women might change their routine activities.

This sentiment was expressed by a Midwestern woman I interviewed. Angela, a runner, said:

> If I'm running by myself . . . it's mainly men [I worry about]. I don't think I ever worry about a woman, but it's a man. I'm not saying I won't go run or something, but I find myself getting a little nervous if we are on a sidewalk [and he is] coming near. I find myself thinking for a moment, you know, what if that happened? Typically, if you just say "hello," most people say "hello" back, and that's fine. But there might be a moment that I'm like, "Okay, is anybody around?" Something could happen, you know.

Angela tells us something fundamental, that is, she is not only willing to change her routine activities if approached by a man, but she also is constantly struggling internally with the possibility that an assault could happen.

Sociology researcher Gustavo Mesch also studied how women changed their leisure activities because of fear of crime.[35] Through surveys with approximately 500 respondents from Israel, Mesch examined how one's fear of crime might impact evening leisure activities. He found that women, married people, and those with less education were less likely to go out at night to public places because of fear of crime.

Another study conducted by Rutgers University criminologist Andres Rengifo and University of Missouri criminologist Amanda Bolton expanded these points.[36] These researchers examined not only avoidance behavior itself but the space where people engaged in such behavior. They were primarily interested in exploring the different behaviors people engaged in depending on whether activities were voluntary (like leisure activities) or non-voluntary (like grocery shopping or work). Interestingly they found that perceived risk and fear of crime were higher among those who were in voluntary spaces (i.e., leisure spaces) as opposed to those in non-voluntary areas (i.e., workplace, home). So, people were more likely to modify their actions in spaces they chose (i.e., voluntary spaces). In one example, fear of crime and perceived risk in a disorderly neighborhood did not influence actions in non-voluntary areas (i.e., home, workplace). These findings highlight that when we feel we choose our space (i.e., voluntary spaces), we are more likely to adapt our behaviors. On the other hand, when we are required to be in an environment (we have no control over the decision), we do not change behaviors or our perception of risk. So, in what ways do you modify your behaviors based on the type of space you are entering into? Do you notice a difference in the areas where it is voluntary versus non-voluntary?

While some research focuses on behaviors, other studies focus more on the space itself. For example, a study by criminologists Bonnie Fisher and Jack Nasar focused on fearful landscapes—places with the potential to increase someone's fear of crime. They found that people were more likely to avoid public areas where potential stranger attackers could hide. So, areas with a lot of bushes and greenery and places with the lowest prospect of escape (e.g., a location with a wall or a large bush) caused participants to feel more fear of crime. In other words, if people saw a place with good visibility, they felt less fear. Thus, people were most likely to avoid places where they did not think they could escape and where they also could not see if an attacker was lying in wait.

Geographer Alec Brownlow also examined how fear landscapes differentially affect men and women.[37] In this study, Brownlow conducted focus groups with students participating in a class that took place in a local park. The students were very familiar with the park. They were shown pictures of specific areas and asked about their perceptions of safety in those areas. He found that men were three times more likely than women to say that they felt relatively safe when alone in the park. Moreover, women and men handled perceived unsafe areas differently. Women were more likely to say that when approaching perceived dangerous parts of the park, they would avoid those areas altogether. On the other hand, men were most likely to talk about confronting a potential attacker in these perceived dangerous areas. As part of the ways they accomplished masculinity, men suppressed fear of crime and did not view avoiding locations as a crime prevention strategy. Brownlow suggests that women and men perceive environments differently, and perceptions of dangerous environments are very gendered.

People I've interviewed change routine activities absentmindedly. For example, a Midwestern woman, Carrie, talked about her behavior changes, which she notes are "small," and she does not see them as a big deal. She says:

> I don't know that you necessarily should be afraid or always be constantly watching your back or worrying that something is going to happen, but I think there are small precautions you can take as a woman, such as not going places alone by yourself at night and locking your doors and things like that. I do not think being a woman makes you need to be afraid, but as a woman, you probably need to be a little more cautious.

Unpacking Carrie's story, think of how restrictive it is to never go by yourself at night to public places. These restrictions are a substantial commitment to crime myths and stranger danger in particular. Further, it is a good example of modifications of voluntary versus non-voluntary behaviors, since Carrie tells other women to avoid or modify their behaviors in voluntary spaces. Finally, it shows us that Carrie is willing to altogether avoid public spaces in the evening hours if she is alone.

Sociologist Esther Madriz found similar things in her focus group study regarding modifying routine activities among New York City women. For example, she says, "in discussing their different strategies, some women at first said that they did not do too much to protect themselves, because I am not really afraid, while in the next sentence, they shared the different manners in which they respond to the fear in their lives."[38] She found that women shared several restrictive, self-isolating behaviors. She found that they avoided certain places in New York City, even areas that were not really crime-prone. Instead, these women commented that they avoided "unfamiliar" places. The women of Madriz's study also avoided going out at night. As Madriz notes, women's control of leisure is not merely a matter of personal enjoyment and gratification; it is "an integral part of social relations."[39] She argues that women miss out on social solidarity, so not only are they keeping people they think might hurt them at arm's length, but they are also keeping those who are not harmful at arms-length and, therefore, limiting the amount of social interaction they may have with other people. Avoidance of space, especially when avoiding voluntary activity, then increases women's fear of crime.

Avoidance Privilege

What about those who cannot avoid places or who cannot change their daily routine activities, even if they want to? Working women, especially those who work hourly jobs, more than one job, or shift work, may not have the option to avoid public spaces completely, even at night. These women, who are more likely to be women of color, do not always have the avoidance option. We can think about women taking public transportation at night, going to potentially dangerous locations, or even women who must walk from their workplace to their vehicle late at night or when alone. While these women may feel the same fear that all women feel, they don't have the same options that other women do. In other words, believe it or not, avoidance because of fear of crime is a privilege. It is an economic privilege; only those who can afford to avoid may do so. From statistics, we also know that as a social group, Black people tend to have lower household incomes than white people do and Latinx people in comparison to non-Latinx groups. So, avoidance privilege attached to economic disadvantage is also linked to racial privilege.[40] It is a racial privilege, one that benefits white women.[41] Avoidance privilege is one part of how the white woman crime victim myth plays out. Women of color, especially economically marginalized women of color, recognize higher victimization chances than white women. Still, they do not have the privilege to act on their worries.

While we know that many messages are thrown at white, middle-class women about managing their fear of crime (including avoidance strategies), less is known about the impact of these messages on African Americans and other women of color who are economically marginalized. To gain some insight on this topic, a study by criminologist Jennifer Cobinna and her colleagues is helpful.[42] They looked at the precautions that urban African American women living in disadvantaged communities took because of fear of crime. Using in-depth interviews with 33 African American women, the authors found that strange men in public spaces produced fear. However, they found that participants did not adopt protective strategies but did adopt avoidance strategies, such as changing daily routines or avoiding locations when possible. This study shows these women also buy into the messages about safety for women, but, perhaps because they have fewer financial means to do so, they are less able to use protective strategies and even more likely to use avoidance strategies when feasible.

In sum, we have learned a lot about how women live out crime myths. For example, women are more likely to take avoidance-based than action-based behaviors. Women with privilege are even more likely to do so than those who cannot avoid such activities and events. But what about women who are scared of crime but do not use action-based or avoidance-based behaviors? What do these women do instead?

Adaptation

While most of the research has found that women are likely to engage in either action-based or avoidance-based behaviors, women's strategies are not always so black and white. There is a gray area also; that is, women might find ways to adapt to the pressure to engage in either avoidance or action-based preventive measures in a way that both adheres to prescribed gender-appropriate safety options while simultaneously giving women some wiggle room in how they put these options into action.[43]

Why would women need to adapt how they live out crime myths beyond taking action-based or avoidance-based precautionary measures? For starters, not all women can avoid going out in public spaces (avoidance-based behaviors) because they need to do things and go places. While most women fear strangers and believe that they personally have some chance for victimization, the idea that women can shut themselves into their homes and never leave is not realistic or viable. Instead, women may need to go to their workplace, an event, the grocery store, or to pick up children at various activities. The traditional avoidance-based strategies may not work in a wholesale fashion, and likely most women have realized that "living in fear" is not a strategy that they can adopt in all circumstances. On the other hand, women may be aware of action-based techniques (like carrying a weapon, taking a self-defense class, or owning a security system), but they may not take these actions for several reasons. As we saw, it could be because women don't feel comfortable taking specific measures, whether it be owning a weapon, carrying pepper spray, or signing up for a self-defense class.

Another reason women may feel they need to adapt may be because they do not think any strategy (avoidance or action-based) will be effective.[44] For example, some women may feel that physically, no matter how much they train in self-defense, they just couldn't take on an attacker effectively. Finally, many women may not choose to take action-based behaviors because of the cost associated with these behaviors. This is especially the case with home security but can also apply to programs that teach self-defense or weapons that cost a lot. So, for various reasons, women may not be able or may choose not to take action-based behaviors. In other words, many women who still believe and buy into gendered crime myths (e.g., the stranger danger, white women, and victim-centered crime myths) may also find other ways to live out crime myths. Simply because women cannot avoid or act does not mean they just stop living crime myths; they must either figure out ways to adapt or make the conscious choice to resist living out crime myths. Two examples of adaptation are using self-talk and taking a (preferably male) companion into perceived dangerous situations.

Self-Talk: The Inner Voice

A subject of psychological research and self-help books, the "inner voice," or what is sometimes called "self-talk," is an essential adaptation technique when avoidance or action-based behaviors are not possible or available to women. According to *Psychology Today*, "Many people are conscious of an inner voice that provides a running monologue on their lives throughout the day. This inner voice, or self-talk, combining conscious thoughts and unconscious beliefs and biases, provides a way for the brain to interpret and process daily experiences."[45]

We can all think of times and ways we engage in self-talk, and as psychologists tell us, these conversations can be both positive and negative. People talk to themselves for various reasons, such as motivation, self-reflection, and self-regulation. We also know that self-talk can help us work through painful emotional experiences, provide perspective on challenging situations, and/or help us learn to regulate our emotions.[46] One such feeling where self-talk may be used is to conquer fear. Fear of crime may be regulated and better understood through self-talk.

The importance of the self-talk adaptation technique also solidifies a core safety belief women have learned throughout their lives: the idea that fear is irrational. I've found that people see admitting to fear of crime as a weakness or as taboo. Fear as weakness has been the case for both the men and women I've interviewed. Both men and women are likely to tell me that they are not afraid, but that, yes, they do worry or are careful when it comes to crime. It seems that no one wants to be viewed as fearful but being labeled as "cautious" is considered acceptable. For example, one young woman I interviewed in the Midwest put it best. I asked Charlotte if she was afraid of crime, and she said: "I'm not saying I'm not careful, but I'm not real scared or paranoid that something is going to happen to me; where other people, they're more cautious." This theme of "I'm not going to live in fear" is prevalent in my research findings for both men and women. One significant difference between men and women is that when prompted about behaviors for safety, women will talk for a half-hour about all the actions and preventive measures they take to keep themselves safe. On the other hand, men only take a few precautions, which are usually taken to keep someone else safe (usually women in their lives).

The participants I've spoken with over the years give clear examples of how self-talk as an adaptation strategy works for women. For example, Julie, a Midwestern participant, explained how self-talk works for her. She said:

> I kept thinking some crazy person was going to jump out of the bushes and attack me, and then I kept thinking, why would someone be waiting in the bushes on the off chance that a woman was to come walking down the street, that's stupid. That's really stupid, but I thought about it quite a lot . . . lot of times, I just tell myself it's ridiculous. I mean, a lot of it is sort of that self-talk where you sort of say this probably isn't going to happen. It is probably irrational, so I'm not going to participate in those kinds of feelings because I'm not. Something is telling me to be afraid as opposed to I've never actually experienced any physical crime, I haven't known anyone in terms of a family member, and like the person that was killed in my apartment building, that was by family, that was not a stranger. Most of the crimes are done by family members, they're not strangers, so there's a lot of things that I try to say to myself. This isn't rational, I'm not thinking clearly, and I gotta stop doing this, and I keep saying it until it works.

When Julie is not able to vary her behaviors (either through avoidance or action), she adapts by using self-talk. She tells herself that she is not rational in feeling fear and tells herself to change her behavior. Many women say similar things about feeling "silly," "irrational," or "ridiculous" in a moment of fear, and they use internal self-talk to help them get through the situation.

This disconnect between not acknowledging the fear of crime but engaging in numerous safety precautions happens for two reasons. The first reason is that women seriously do not realize the number of behaviors they take each day for their fear of crime. Like brushing teeth or hair, women may take such behaviors completely absentmindedly. A second reason is that women recognize the gendered societal expectations and norms regarding safety and behave within the limits of these expectations. Similar to most socialization processes, there is a combination of tradition (we just have always done things this way), absentmindedly engaging in/avoiding behaviors (I put my keys in between my fingers when I walk to my car at night), or wanting to make sure that such behaviors are viewed as appropriate behavior (I avoid going shopping late at night). I have found the combination of these reasons best explains women's disconnect between fear of crime and behaviors.

Regardless of why women believe that fear may be irrational and the numerous behaviors they take to reduce fear of crime, it is clear that self-talk is a crucial way that women adapt to societal pressure to act on crime myths.

Male Romantic Partners as Escorts

While many women would rather avoid what they perceive as a dangerous location since it's perceived as dangerous for any number of reasons—location or time of day—this is not always feasible. There are times when women must go into places that are perceived to be filled with possible dangerous strangers. An adaptation strategy to this problem involves using others as a precaution—that is, having a companion to act as an escort, one who can minimize perceived safety threats.[47] This comes in two forms: male romantic partners and female friends.

In this clever adaptation strategy, women rely on others, particularly men, to get them where they need to go. Romantic partners who are men are a viable precautionary measure.[48] Women recognize that they are being told they should avoid dangerous places. They also acknowledge that they have stuff to do and cannot stay in their houses all the time. So, one strategy is to go with their husband/partner to a perceived dangerous space. They rely on men to escort them or accompany them to places they would avoid alone (basically anywhere at night in public places). They count on men to figure out what household safety precautions will be put into place.[49]

Women I've interviewed have also shared stories with me about using men as a precautionary measure. For example, when interviewing wives in both the Midwest and the South, husbands' presence was used as a common precautionary measure. Diana presents one example of how this works with husbands. She says:

> Probably I've felt a little safer just having a man here, and he kind of makes more decisions than I would've thought about. I mean, he is more "Make sure you lock the doors," and sometimes it bugs me, but all in all, that makes it safer and just makes me safer to have him here. If somebody comes to the door, I can just look at him and say, "what do I do?" or I'm like, "There's somebody at the door," you know what I mean? And if he is here, he's gonna get it, not me, but if I'm here by myself, I feel trapped like, "Oh gosh, What do I do? Do I go the door, do I not go to the door?" So it makes me feel safer just that he is there. You know, if we go to the movies, I'm not walking out with a girl; I'm walking out with a guy. My husband's not a big

guy, just something about having a guy there, and I don't know, I'm not as worried.

Here, Diana tells us that she feels safer with men accompanying her places. She also tells us that if she wants to go someplace, Diana doesn't avoid that place (the movies in this case) or engage in more action-based precautionary measures; instead, she takes her spouse along with her.

Another respondent, Cheryl, is also concerned about a stranger breaking into her home and explains how having her husband in that space makes her feel safer. She says:

> Because then I know that if somebody came through my windows and saw a man, they'd think twice about coming in or doing something. I mean, that doesn't stop a lot of people, but you know they may think twice about doing that. It just makes you feel safer because I'll know that if someone does try to come in and it's just one person, and he's attacking me, I know he'll go, you know, trying to do something to stop the guy or whatever.

So, for Cheryl, we see that she feels much safer in her home when her husband is there. When she runs through scary scenarios, one that particularly troubles her is a man climbing in her window. She adapts to this perceived possibility by remembering that her husband is there in case something happens. She believes his presence would be enough to deter criminals, and she feels better.

In both cases, romantic partners who are men become shields that keep women from having to use other forms of preventive measures—either avoidance or action-based measures. Such precautions are but one part of a more extensive process for women. That is, as I've noted in my research, women who are in long-term serious relationships with men start to do something quite interesting. They engage in a process I call "fear work transference."[50] Women, well, at least married women in my studies, come to associate precautionary behaviors and safety with their significant other, and they "transfer" the "work" that comes with managing security to these partners. Women then check safety off the mental list of things they need to worry about each day; it becomes part of the division of labor within their households. While wives may pick up kids for doctor's appointments, husbands are the ones who check the locks on doors and accompany their wives to nighttime outings. This adaptation technique (relying on the strength and size of men) may make women seem like they are using or manipulating partners into protecting them or emphasizing traditional gender norms. Still, by understanding that fear work transference is an adaptation to living out gendered crime myths, it makes more sense. Women do not have the option, especially in today's modern world, to avoid or act on stranger danger all the time. Thus, because of their upbringing and social learning cues, they recognize that they can turn safety decision-making over to the men in their lives.

Interestingly, most women I've interviewed over the years are not what I'd call entrenched in traditional gender roles. They talk to me about their careers, about having equal partnerships with their spouses, about teaching their girls to be strong and independent. It has always been fascinating that in this one element of life—safety and fear management—women expect traditional gender norms to be part of their relationships.

The Buddy System

Another adaptation to living out crime myths in everyday life is for women to take along female friends as escorts in perceived dangerous situations. This process is more commonly known as the "buddy system." We learn as children that when we go into a public space where strangers might be, we should always have a buddy to take with us when we leave the larger group. The buddy system is used as early as preschool with children who go on field trips or outings. Children at this age are taught to hold the hand of their buddy and go together to get lunchboxes, to walk to or from school, and even to walk to the bathroom. While both boys and girls use the buddy system as young children, this system fades into the background for boys, while it stays relevant for girls as they grow up. For example, girls often go to the bathroom together or dance in groups in high school and are cautioned to avoid going places alone.

Canadian researchers Sydney Cherniawsky and Melanie Morrison note "victimization-focused prevention strategies (e.g., instructions to avoid poorly lit areas, use the buddy system, or never leave your drink unattended) are particularly under-researched."[51] While how the buddy system is used as a precautionary measure may be under-researched among college women, women's advice is not. As women enter college, the buddy system advice continues. College women are often told to make sure they always have another friend with them in social environments. Women often go to parties, social events, school events, and even to places they eat with other women. This is especially the case at night. During their orientation, many freshmen are told to make sure they always take a buddy with them when going into perceived dangerous spaces.

For example, the National Association for Student Affairs Administrators in Higher Education provides some guidance to university administrators about campus safety, including the familiar use of the buddy system.[52]

They tell university administrators to "consider adding these personal-safety guidelines, provided by the National Crime Prevention council to your campus' student safety resources":

- Inform security, peers, or a family member if you're going to work or study late and when you expect to be back. Leave the building with a peer or security escort.
- Leave a record of your appointments with a peer; let someone know where you're going and when you expect to return when leaving for off-campus activities.
- Be careful in stairwells and elevators. Avoid using dark or isolated stairwells. Stand next to the control panel while riding in an elevator with a stranger. If you're attacked, punch all the floor buttons so the door will open on each floor. Yell for assistance every time it opens.
- Trust your intuition. If someone in an elevator appears threatening or suspicious, get out and alert security.
- Use a buddy system. Tell a peer when you're going to the restroom or running an errand.[53]

These common safety messages often allude to taking a female friend along as an escort. While these messages are not gendered, they seem to play on the stranger danger fears we know women (but not men) have been sold and focus on preventing crimes women fear the most (e.g., abduction or sexual assault). Thus, such messages create underlying signs and messages for women to follow regarding behavioral modifications they should take or participate in. In fact, given this advice, it would be the rare male college student who sees these strategies as something they need to pay attention to or act on.

This message has also come through in interviews I've done over the years. For example, when I ask Arianna, a Midwestern participant, what precautions she takes to stay safe, she mentions relying on a woman friend as a safety strategy. She says, "I go to the drive-through at the bank; I don't go out alone. If I'm going out of town, I make sure my best friend and I are together, and one of us can stay sober at all times."

Victoria, a Southern participant, also discusses taking her husband or her girlfriend with her as a precautionary measure. She says, "I am normally with people walking, like whether it's with my husband, or a friend, you know, you arrive together, and you leave together. Or you walk out together; even if you came in separate cars, you walk out together."

Other participants have similarly talked about the buddy system as a safety strategy when advising other women. For example, when I ask Jaime what advice she might have for women who are very afraid and what would she tell them to do, she says:

> [I'd tell them to] go places in groups, I would definitely give that advice. I would definitely say go places in groups.... I think that is something I would suggest. If you could get together with a bunch of women, could you find a way to do things together, to shop together?

Cathy, another participant, had similar advice to give other women about how to stay safe. She said, "Always go with a friend and trust your instincts."

These women, then, have experience taking women friends with them into perceived dangerous situations. They rely on this strategy enough that it is evidence that they find it practical, and thus give other women similar advice to take along a buddy when worried about safety.

Thus, women are adapting to traditional and expected avoidance strategies, whether using a spouse or a female friend to go to perceived dangerous situations (usually public spaces at night).

Adapting through Resistance

Resistance is a rare strategy taken on by women managing safety expectations and crime myths. Most women have had traditionally gendered safety precautions drilled into their heads from a very young age. As we discussed, such precautions are reinforced throughout adulthood as well. So then, women who take on the resistance strategy would have to (1) recognize the gendered expectation and (2) make a conscious effort to reject the norm.

Study participant Jaime provides an example of how resistance to safety precautions play out in her life. She says:

> Working out, I think. I think I feel a lot better about it because I lift now. I used to be really concerned about my body image, so I would, like, you know, not eat to get thin, and now I sort of don't do those things. And this way of getting fit is much more empowering, and I feel much better to take care of myself, not that I would need to. You know, just better about my body, stronger maybe, I feel physically stronger. I practice running, for example, which is something I wouldn't have done before. That makes you feel better [about crime]. You know, I can run if I have to run.

As Jaime discusses here, feeling better and having a confident body image makes her feel less pressure to meet the expectations for women and safety.

Therefore, her primary motivation for working out is to have a better body image. Doing so allows her to take care of herself and not need others to protect her from perceived dangerous situations.

Another place I've seen some resistance in my work is when talking to women who feel comfortable with guns. An example shows how this works for this small group of women.

Allison, a Southern woman, talks about how guns made her feel more confident about being able to protect herself. While gun ownership doesn't make her feel totally safe, it does bring her some comfort. She says: "I know how to use a gun. I know how to protect myself somewhat, if I can remember that. I have a gun under my bed, and it is very lawful right now. I have the papers." Unlike some other women who found gun ownership to be something that makes them uncomfortable or something they would not use themselves, Allison feels good enough about using a gun that she keeps one under her bed.

When Alyssa, a Southern participant, is asked if she owns a gun, she tells me she does not but she also goes on to tell the story of how owning a gun made her friend feel like she could go out at night without her husband (or without him knowing). She says:

> We drove from one area of the beach to another town, and it was at night, and she said, "Well, my husband would just die if he knew that we were doing this, so I'm not gonna tell him." And I was like, "really, that would bother him?" because I don't think my husband would care at all, and she was like, "oh yeah, he doesn't like me to be out at night by myself," and she said, "and I keep a loaded gun with me." And I was like, "you're kidding."

Alyssa is both surprised and somewhat awestruck by her friend's decision to go someplace with a loaded gun but also sees this is a precautionary measure that works for her friend.

Thus, while most research shows that women avoid or take preventive actions daily because of crime, there are small ways that women adapt to or resist these norms.[54] For example, they adapt through self-talk and taking others along as a precautionary measure. In rare circumstances, they make a commitment to fight by becoming physically fit or showing confidence with guns, which keeps them from feeling as worried about crime.

Dutch researcher Gwen Van Eijk examined this very idea.[55] She argued that we should look at "ambivalence and deviations in responding to questions about fear."[56] In this study, she interviewed heterosexual couples about how they handled safety in their relationship. While she found many examples of women participants who consciously or subconsciously engaged in preventive measures based on their perceptions of "appropriate feminine expectations" (the more traditional action- and avoidance-based precautionary measures), she also found moments of adaptation and resistance. For example, the women participants in her study talked about balancing safety with freedom. Thus, we can see how juggling safety and freedom might be an adaptation strategy. Talking about respondents, she notes, "as these interviews illustrate, women may indeed recognize that their risks are higher, but at the same time they resist the idea that they need protection let alone restrict their behavior, neither by avoiding places nor by keeping their partner informed about their whereabouts."[57]

Eijk notes, as I do, that how women "do" gender and "do" fear must be seen on a continuum.[58] At one end, we have women who 100 percent buy into gender norms and act accordingly. In these cases, women will avoid places or engage in more action-based behaviors without question and will see doing so as part of what it means to be a woman and as part of their identity. This makes up most of the women I've talked with, and Eijk also found a similar group of women makes up the base of those she interviewed. On the other end of the continuum, there are those women, whom Eijk labels as "independent women," who resist the gender norms about safety, behaviors, or stranger danger entirely. These women report feeling stronger when they are alone, and they do not think they need the protection of others. In both Eijk's and my studies, we have only found a handful of women participants who completely resist or reject the gendered norms and behaviors surrounding living out crime myths. The remainder of women reside in the middle of the behavioral precautionary measure continuum, buying into and engaging in safety behaviors and focusing more on freedom only at times.

Consequences

So, knowing now how women "live out" crime myths, through avoidance primarily, along with some action-based behaviors and adaptation strategies, we need to ask: what are the consequences for women of living myths in this way? There are two really serious consequences of how women live out crime myths: perpetuation of victim blame and social control of women.

Women fear stranger-induced crime because of the societal pressures on women to protect themselves from potential victimization.[59] The victim-centered crime prevention myth relies heavily on victim blame and ideas surrounding the perfect victim.

As we have already discussed, when we learn that victimization can only be prevented by potential victims (rather than by likely offenders or society at large), it makes sense that our behaviors and daily routines will be affected. In other words, part of the reason you likely do not go out alone at night is because of your safety values, for example, the idea that women who are attacked when they are out at night probably should have been a little more careful. Victim prevention, then, keeps women living the same crime myths they were taught. All daily behaviors are made to take control of potential victimization at the hands of strangers—whether that outcome is realistic or not.[60]

It is interesting to think about the ridiculousness of this concept—can you imagine a world where all men are taught that they could become rapists at any possible moment? And therefore, they should take a bunch of precautions to avoid that possibility from becoming a reality? Yet, this is how it is for women in society, who learn from a young age that it is ultimately *their responsibility* not to get sexually assaulted, and if they do, it is perceived by others as their own fault. Furthermore, most women feel fear of crime at some point in their lives because of the power of these gendered myths. Thus, taking these gendered precautionary measures adds fuel to the already burning victim-centered crime prevention myth.

University of London criminology professor Elizabeth Stanko noted, "as a consequence of fear, women police themselves by restricting their activities in public because of the anxiety about potential violence and by using, in public and in private, more safety precautions than do men."[61] Stanko was one of the first researchers to argue that fear of crime served as a social control mechanism in women's lives. This may not sound intuitive to the reader here. How could it be that an individual, internal, and often uncommunicated emotion—fear toward possible criminal victimization—is a way that we control women in society? We can see several pieces of evidence of how fear of crime may contribute to the social control of women.

Using some of the lessons from this book, we can establish that women are less likely than men (generally speaking) to be victims of crime.[62] Second, and in contradiction to crime statistics, women are taught the powerful and deep-rooted crime myth that women, especially white women, are more likely to be crime victims than men.[63] Third, women are also taught an important lesson about accountability. When women "do gender" outside of gendered norms, they will be held accountable by others. Given the gendered nature of crime myths, women who do not act as society expects them to may be held responsible for their own victimization.[64] For these reasons, women live out crime myths just like they were taught to do—by avoiding public spaces and strangers and by believing that they are responsible for their own victimization. Women make most decisions about safety based on notions of stranger danger and rely on gendered stereotypes about gender-appropriate behavior.[65]

Gender scholars would argue that how we do gender is very much based on the social control of women.⁶⁶ I would take this a step further and say that how women live out crime myths is yet another form of the social control of women.

Women are socially controlled through every day, taken-for-granted precautionary measures. Society keeps women outside of public spaces, forcing them to rely on others for protection and live in a state of fear. Let's imagine for a second that it is opposite day, and everything women do regarding fear of crime is flipped on its head. Women are not constantly worried about strange men. They do not feel the need to avoid spaces and are comfortable being alone. What would this world look like for women? One quick answer is: free. Freedom is the opposite of control.

Women, then, take on a considerable burden through daily preventive measures. Women take on avoidance behaviors and also action-based behaviors. They also use adaptation strategies when necessary and resist the pressure to conform to gendered fear of crime practices on rare occasions.

In the next chapter, we talk about what happens to those women who become moms. What role does parenthood play in perpetuating gendered crime myths? Once women add children into the mix, how does this change women's daily gendered behaviors? What do moms teach their children about safety, behaviors, and fear of crime?

4

Raising Gen Z Children with Gen X Safety Values

Gendered crime myths are learned through childhood and acted out during adulthood. To make gendered crime myths a permanent feature of how we teach fear of crime, we must next pass them on to others. At no time is the passing of gendered crime myths onto others more apparent than when parents have children of their own. In this chapter, we ask ourselves, what safety values do we instill in children, and how do these values crystalize into how we teach fear to others?

When adults become parents, the cycle of teaching fear in traditional and gendered ways continues so that parents, either unintentionally or intentionally, "teach fear" to children in the same ways that they learned. Parents draw from a well of personal experience and socialization to determine how to talk to children about crime and teach them age-appropriate safety lessons.[1] There are strong forces at work leading parents to believe that dangers to children are tremendous and that parents can prevent such victimization from happening to their children. As we shall see, such lessons and values about safety are easily recollected and merge with current trends and new risks. Rather than seeing the world through rose-colored glasses, parents see the world through risk-colored glasses. Such a fearful lens is exhausting and requires parents to constantly monitor and eliminate potential threats.

Parents instill values in their children based on gendered crime myths such as the fear of strangers, public spaces, and kidnapping. Society expects parents to teach perceived appropriate safety values to their children. Thus, societal expectations of safety values is something that most parents do not realize they engage in or buy into; they do it as part of their parenting duties. Those parents who do not follow proper parenting protocol may be held accountable to others.

Many would say that keeping children safe is one of the most important goals of parents. While this desire, need, and societal requirement is indeed essential for the well-being of children, the things we fear and teach children to fear are not always realistic. We need to understand parental fear for children because research shows parents fear significantly for their children, and such parental fears creep into their children's fears.

University of Amsterdam psychologists Evan Altar, Milica Nikolic, and Susan Bogels call the process the "inter-generational transmission of worries."[2] While their research does not focus on crime-related worries, it shows how children translate parental worry or fear of crime into their own emotions and anxieties. Their study found that parents passed on both nonverbal and verbal communication of stress and fear to children.

University of Texas at Austin researchers Mark Warr and Christopher Ellison surveyed 1,600 people in Texas about their fear of crime, and their findings are informative.[3] First, they found that whereas 60 percent of the respondents reported fear for themselves, 70 percent said they had a fear for others in their household. Of the 70 percent of respondents who reported fear of crime for someone else, 83 percent were afraid for their male children, and 86 percent were worried for their female children. This study also found that parents feared for younger children independent of the sex of the child. Fear for children also varied by race and ethnicity. For example, Black parents were more likely than white parents to fear for sons (as opposed to daughters), whereas white parents were more likely to fear for daughters than sons. Latinx parents were also more likely than white parents to fear for sons. Parents of color, then, have a more realistic fear of crime for their children than white parents. Since men of color are more likely than white men and women and women of color to be victims of crime, there is less of a mismatch between victimization rates and fear of victimization rates. White parents, especially parents of white daughters, who are sold images of white children as victims, overestimate the chance of victimization to their children. Warr and Ellison showed that parents, especially white parents with girls and parents with younger children, particularly fear for their children.[4]

A study by University of Western Australia researcher Jacinta Francis and her colleagues focused not on racial differences in parents' fear of crime for children but on how economic marginalization influences parents' fear of crime for children.[5] Their focus group results found that while all parents had a higher perceived fear of strangers than warranted, their degree of fear was socio-economically based. Although parents with a mid- to high socio-economic status (SES) believed the *risk* of crime happening to their children was low (an accurate assessment), their *fear* of crime was still moderate to high. The parents from the lower quartile of SES believed the *risk* of crime happening to their children was medium to high (an accurate assessment), as was their *fear* of crime. Those parents in the lower quartile of SES have similar fear and risk levels for children. In contrast, mid- and high SES quartiles have an elevated fear compared to their lower perceived risk. Thus, parents, especially those whose income is in the middle to upper SES levels, often misjudge how much fear they should have for their children in comparison to actual risk of victimization.

Parents' fear for children, then, varies by race, gender, and economic standing of parents.[6] Still, it is also essential to remember that all parents fear more for their children becoming victims than is warranted by crime statistics. Francis and colleagues report the significance of this, stating, "While the term 'safety' captures concepts such as road safety, personal injury, bullying, and harm from strangers, parents are more fearful of strangers harming their children (i.e., stranger danger) than any other sources of harm. Furthermore, parents continue to fear strangers despite knowing the probability of a stranger abducting or abusing their child is low. Indeed, children are less likely to be harmed by strangers than by family or acquaintances."[7] As we've discussed previously, children are most at risk from criminal victimization in their own homes and with known people (like parents). Still, safety lessons concerning the victimization of children at home remain a taboo topic. We find it difficult to talk about child abuse and mistreatment within the home.[8] Thus, the stranger danger myth is a potent myth deeply buried in the core of parents' belief systems and within parenting itself.

Newcastle University human geographer Rachel Pain puts this another way; she calls this phenomenon "paranoid parenting."[9] By constructing childhood as risky, we see children as vulnerable, innocent, and in need of constant surveillance and regulation. Such a construction puts parents in a position to regularly worry about their children and feel that they must protect them in situations they think are dangerous. Mary Ann Stokes, a researcher, explains the paranoid parenting process, noting,

> If stranger danger is to be considered a social problem, in either the realistic or constructivist sense, it has the most significant impact on parents.... It appears to be somewhat of a "vicious circle," with parents influencing the media and that, in turn, shocking more significant numbers of parents. It eventually snowballs to the point where it is unthinkable that children should be unsupervised at any time, increasing the pressure to "chaperone" and "helicopter" the child's life.[10]

Most parents do not want to be labeled a "paranoid parent" but also see some of these characteristics in themselves. I've found in my research that parents feel a strong desire to calculate risks when determining children's activities. Anna, a Swedish participant, shows how paranoid parenting works, saying:

> I should be worried about traffic because that's really a big [problem] in the city as well, the people with the bikes, they drive like crazy, but I, of course, you have those fantasies about someone kidnapping them. I know that risk is so tiny, I mean, he would walk through the city center where there are a lot of people everywhere. His school is just in the center and that risk is—that's not what I should worry about, even though I have, of course; you have this fantasy brain.

Anna provides an excellent example of how paranoia can take over a mother's thoughts. She recognizes that she should be more worried about bicycle safety, but her imagination runs wild, and she has a hard time not imagining someone kidnapping her child. Anna is less concerned about her child getting kidnapped when other people are present, playing on a fear of being alone in public spaces. Thus, Anna spends a lot of time in her head worrying about things that are unlikely to happen, which she recognizes, but she still has a hard time not worrying about her child getting kidnapped. The risk-colored glasses are hard to take off.

Swinburne University of Technology researcher Karen Malone also discusses this phenomenon and how it applies to fear of crime for children.[11] Discussing Generation Z (those born between the mid-1990s and the mid-2010s), she says, "with the outside world presented as a dark, dangerous and high-risk place, childhood for many Generation Z children is increasingly becoming an indoor activity. . . . Children are being chauffeured around their neighbourhood, often for very short distances, because of the increased fear of traffic and 'stranger' danger. This is despite evidence that Australian suburbs are much safer for children than they were three decades ago."[12] As we shall discuss shortly, Gen Z children are experiencing quite a different childhood from their Gen X parents.

Paranoid parenting also contributes to the "bubble-wrap generation."[13] In other words, parents today are so afraid that something might happen to their children that they would bubble-wrap their children if they could, taking out all risk of injury or harm. Parents of Gen Z children are also more likely to "helicopter" their children.[14] Helicoptering children involves constantly knowing what is happening with children in every situation at all times. With both bubble-wrapping and helicopter parenting, parents attempt to fix or solve problems for their children. In the case of safety from crime, parents are under a lot of pressure to keep children safe.

Instilling Safety Values

A study by University of Iowa psychologists Elizabeth O'Neal and Jodie Plumert considered how mothers instilled safety values in their daughters.[15] While this study did not focus on crime but safety hazards, we can still glean some insight. Each daughter and their mother were shown photographs of potentially dangerous situations and asked to use these photos to provide a safety rating. Some examples included a photograph of a child burning an arm on a hot stove, a child using a knife to cut an apple, a child climbing on a ladder, and a child riding a skateboard into a road. Once mothers and daughters made their safety rating for each photograph, they were then asked to provide a rationale for their ratings. Researchers then talked to the mothers and daughters and compared the ratings/rationales. They found that mothers discussed the *outcome* rather than the *features* of the dangerous activity shown in the photograph. For example, mothers taught children to worry about burning an arm on a hot stove rather than talking about the stove being hot. The authors argue mothers tend to focus on outcomes more than features to make children understand causal connections. In other words, we teach children not by explaining what the object of concern is (a stove) or its features (it is hot) but by explaining the outcome of what can happen to children if they aren't careful around the object of concern (they will burn their arms). Mothers instilled safety values through this process.

We teach safety lessons about crime in much the same way. We teach children by explaining to them what can happen (becoming a crime victim/getting hurt), rather than focusing on the object of concern (a public space) or its features (it's a place where strangers may reside). For example, if a mother is worried about a child running off from her in a park, she might say, "stay with me, so you don't get hurt." By focusing on the outcome, the bad thing that might happen to kids if they wander off, we teach children from a young age to know they should fear without understanding why they should be afraid. By focusing on the outcome instead of the feature, we also teach children that their behaviors can change an event. Following the rules (staying with their mother) determines the outcome (the child will not be hurt). In most cases, the truth of the matter is that victims, especially children, cannot prevent their victimization no matter what they do. By not explaining the features, we ultimately are not giving children the tools they need to understand safety and crime. The lessons learned about stranger danger become crystalized safety values as children grow up.

There are two ways parents instill safety values in their children. First, parents teach their children the same safety values they were taught by their parents growing up. In the case of Gen X parents, they rely on safety messages learned in the 1980s. The second kind of safety values parents teach their children are about modern-day crimes. In this case, parents adapt to the current culture, which has changed quite a bit since they were children. Today's children, primarily Generation Z children, live in a very different world than their parents did. For example, Gen X, for the most part, did not have to navigate internet safety, cyberbullying, and school shootings during their childhoods. Safety lessons from the past and the present provide parents with the tools they use to teach children safety values.

Using Safety Lessons from the Past

Parents' first reaction when deciding how to teach safety lessons to children is to use what they were taught as children.[16] Many parents may be surprised to hear themselves saying the same things to their children that they heard from their own mothers and fathers. To a small child, we may say, "don't ever take candy from a stranger." To an adolescent who begins to stay home alone after school, we may say, "always lock the door and don't ever let anyone into the house that you do not know (no matter what they say)." Parents views on safety haven't changed much from when they were children. Children are no more likely to be abducted by a stranger today than they were in the eighties or nineties, for example.

The parents I've interviewed in my research studies provide many clear examples of safety lessons taken from childhood. We can see how Barbara, a Swedish mother, uses past lessons about strangers to parent her children. When answering my question about if she fears for her children, she says:

> Yeah, but I'm not extremely worried. I mean, it is not like it [worrying about safety] takes a lot of my energy, but I see to it that they call. They often walk alone to school, and then I see to it that they call me when they are at school. When they have a ride, in a sense, that is also weird because if something would have happened to them, how could I prevent that? Do you see what I mean? It makes sense that you want to hear that they have arrived there.

I then ask Barbara, "so, they call you when they leave home?" She says:

> Yeah, they leave the home and then they call me when they arrive at school. And then [they call me] when they get home as well. I mean, my son does, at least. My daughter, I fetch my daughter, and she is

not allowed to go on her own. She is up in the morning with neighbors, and then [in the afternoon] she is with my son. My son, he can go home alone but then I want to know when he is on his way home so he calls me before going home.

Barbara then talks about several traditional safety values likely learned in her childhood. First, she teaches her children that they need to call when they arrive at every destination when they are away from their parents. In Sweden, where Barbara lives, traveling to school and back home alone is more common than in the United States. In Sweden, safety from crime is less of a concern.[17] However, it is interesting to note that Barbara still wants the children to call her when they get to each location. We aren't sure what Barbara tells the children regarding why they must call her, but we see that she asks them to call each time and as soon as they arrive at the location. Barbara also teaches gendered safety values. While her son is older and has more responsibility, her daughter is tightly supervised, sometimes by her brother. The gendered safety lesson is that boys protect girls from potentially dangerous situations. Barbara's past safety values are also evident here since Barbara only worries about the children calling her when they go in and out of public spaces.

Barbara is not an outlier of the mothers I've talked to over the years. Her parenting style is not what we might put in the "paranoid parenting" category. Still, while Barbara tells us that she isn't apprehensive about safety, she spends a reasonable amount of time ensuring her children check in and avoid potentially dangerous situations.

Maya, another Swedish participant, also provides an example of how safety values learned during childhood inform how she teaches her children about safety in the present. Like other Gen X parents who learned about stranger danger as children, Maya reports that locking doors is a priority lesson. When I ask Maya if she ever discussed safety precautions with her children, she says:

[I've told them] they have to lock the door. Yeah, it's important to lock the door [to prevent a burglary] so we have all our things here when we come home. But it is also like a norm [for people to lock doors]. They see it everywhere, all of their neighbors, their friends, everyone is locking their doors. So it is nothing to be worried about.

By teaching children that locking doors is standard operating procedures, we continue to teach children traditional stranger danger safety lessons. This lesson teaches children to fear what is outside the locked door rather than what is inside it. Locking a door seems like an innocuous and mundane behavior. However, when a child locks a door, the action can cause them to think about the potential of crime and increase their fear of crime, especially of strangers outside of the home.

Kidnapping

Gen X parents also lean on another fear from their childhoods, the fear of getting kidnapped. When Gen Xers were children, as discussed earlier, they learned to fear kidnapping.[18] Once Gen Xers started raising Gen Z children, we see the old fear surrounding kidnappings resurface.

For example, Hannah, a Southern mother, talks about the fear of crime for her daughter. She says:

> Especially with my daughter. I don't want to be out by myself with my daughter because when you talk about my daughter, I always think about keeping her safe with me. Her getting kidnapped is something that goes through my mind now more than ever. A child or a child being victimized is extremely different as opposed to someone who does not have children.

When I asked her what precautionary measures she took for her daughter, she said:

> I'm trying to think, I mean I know I do. I mean, with her, keeping her very close would definitely be one [precaution]. I mean, not letting her run off at a store or something like that. Not taking her places that I think would be an unsafe place. If there were such places, I just would not take her there.

Hannah, then, is worried about her daughter being kidnapped by a stranger. Her primary prevention strategy is to over-supervise her daughter, keeping her "close" at all times. Even though it comes from a good place, we can see how her fear might be the early sprouts of "bubble-wrapping" her child. When she and her daughter are in a public space, she keeps her daughter very close. The action serves as a non-verbal cue to her daughter: being away from her mother in a public place like parks is dangerous. As Hannah's daughter gets older, she might lack confidence in being alone in public spaces and feel she must depend on other people for her safety.

As we see from Hannah, old kidnapping fears resurface when one becomes a parent. It does not help that parenting fears are reinforced through high-profile kidnapping media stories and educational campaigns that focus on child abduction.[19] One such example comes from fingerprinting programs. These programs provide fingerprinting services to parents. If a child goes missing, law enforcement then has more information to find the missing child. The National Child Identification Program (NCIP), one of the largest of these programs, provides Child ID kits to parents, including an inkless fingerprint card, a DNA collection site, and an inkless applicator.[20] NCIP has national reach through multi-million-dollar corporate sponsors like the American Football Coaches Association, Ford Motor Company, American Airlines, and Kroger. While fingerprinting a child is not harmful, in the case of fear and safety messages, fingerprinting programs emphasize child abductions by strangers. As we've discussed, kids are more likely to be kidnapped by a known offender. The NCIP does provide accurate information on their website by showing statistics about the likelihood of children being taken by non-family members (a small percentage).

However, the facts on the webpage are overshadowed by the general marketing material, which highlights stranger danger. For example, under the prevention portion of their website, they give the following advice to parents:[21]

PARENTS SHOULD:
- Avoid clothing and toys with your child's name on them. A child is less likely to fear someone who knows his/her name.
- Check all potential baby-sitters and older friends of your child. Never leave your child alone in a public place, stroller, or car, even for a minute.
- Always accompany young children to the bathroom in public places.
- Always accompany your child on door-to-door activities.
- Create an environment where a child feels safe to talk to you. Let him/her know that you are interested and sensitive to their fears.
- Teach children that the police are their friends and that they can rely on them if they are in trouble.
- Keep an up-to-date color photograph of your child, a medical and dental history, and have your child fingerprinted.
- Stay involved in your child's life by communicating daily to prevent your child from running away.[22]

Of these crime prevention strategies, six of the eight pieces of advice address strangers kidnapping children. The two remaining pieces of advice address children running away from home and an open line of communication with your child. Thus, when most people hear about Child ID kits, their first thought is most likely stranger-induced kidnapping.

There is a perfect storm when parents rely on safety lessons from the past and the present about strangers kidnapping their children, one that increases parents' fear for their children. Most Gen Xer parents can recall the pictures of young girls taken by kidnappers during their childhood. Such images are ingrained in parents' brains and ultimately translate into the safety lessons they then teach their children. Such fears tend to be gendered and apply differentially to girls.

For example, Paige, a Midwestern mother, discusses her fear for her daughter and why she is worried about her. When I ask her if she worries about crime for her child and, if so, why, she says:

> PAIGE: Completely and all the time. There are just way too many crimes today happening with children. Abductions and everything involved with children. It is just hard to let her go outside and play without worrying about her.
> NICOLE: What are you worried will happen?
> PAIGE: Her getting taken. That would happen first, foremost, is her being taken because she is a pretty little girl.

Researchers who have focused on non-crime-related injuries provide insight into how we instill different safety values in boys and girls. As Paige notes, parents often teach girls different messages from boys. It is easy to see how mothers who view crime as a primary concern for girls would differentially react and have conversations with daughters versus sons.

Psychologists Barbara Morrongiello and Tess Dawber studied how mothers responded to injury-risk behaviors on the playground and how responses were similar and different for boys and girls.[23] Specifically, they answered the question, "Do mothers differ in what they identify as injury-risk behaviors, the speed of their intervention, or the nature of their intervention in response to sons' as compared to daughters' risk taking?"[24] Their study found that mothers were more likely to encourage and tolerate their sons' risk-taking activities on playgrounds than their daughters'. When looking at how mothers interacted with daughters concerning injury-risk behaviors, mothers also referenced the injury-outcome process, providing a much fuller explanation to daughters about the consequences of getting injured than they did with sons. Morrongiello and Dawber conclude that gender-specific feedback resulted "in girls, more so than boys, internalizing an appreciation for injury processes, including developing a tremendous appreciation of their vulnerability for injury and the potential severity of injury."[25]

Gender-specific safety lessons about crime are given to children as well.[26] As discussed earlier, studies have shown that parents fear more for their daughters than for their sons.[27] A study by Northeastern University criminologist Kevin Drakulich highlights some significant findings in how fear is transmitted to children by first highlighting the concerns of parents.[28] He found that mothers reported more concern for their children than fathers and that both mothers and fathers were more concerned for daughters than for sons. Girls and women are most likely to be feared for by others. Daughters are a focus of concern, and this concern likely changes how parents supervise, discipline, and allow daughters to participate in structured and unstructured activities.

Social scientists who study gender (but not fear) would not be surprised by these findings since we tend to see similar patterns in other areas of social life.[29] There are several reasons mothers' influence over children might be more prevalent in shaping safety values. First, research shows that parents treat sons and daughters differently in various areas, including supervision.[30] Some scholars have argued gender socialization is learned most often from the same-sex parent, especially in two-parent households. So, gendered social learning is passed from mothers to daughters and from fathers to sons.[31] Other research has found that mothers tend to oversee parenting for both same- and opposite-sex children because of the gendered division of labor and tend to be more responsible for modeling behaviors to both daughters and sons.[32] There are many structural reasons, then, why mothers have more influence over children's safety behaviors.

A study conducted by Ball State University psychologist Katie Lawson and her colleagues would also support the claim that mothers are more "in charge" of safety values for children.[33] They state, "On average, mothers spend more time with their children than fathers and mothers and fathers engage in and encourage different kinds of activities: Fathers tend to encourage more risk-taking, exploration, active leisure, and taking the initiative, whereas mothers tend to engage in more role-playing, object-mediated play, and childcare."[34] Mothers, then, teach their children to be risk-averse, whereas fathers teach children risk-taking behaviors.

It is not a stretch to imagine that mothers' concerns about their daughters' safety would influence daughters' safety values. We can see how mothers' attitudes about gender and overall parental modeling are essential in forming young adults' attitudes about various topics, including crime prevention.[35] In other words, in families with traditional gender attitudes and values, their children are likely to grow up with similar gender attitudes and values. Even in families with less traditionally gendered family values, teaching girls to fear crime and boys to not is a common parenting practice.

In sum, gendered safety values learned by children rely heavily on the safety lessons (i.e., fear of strangers, suspicion of kidnapping) learned during parents', particularly mothers', upbringings. Mothers pass on safety lessons to their daughters, thus continuing the cycle of teaching fear of crime.

Remembering the Past Nostalgically

Parents teach safety lessons to children through a nostalgic lens. As scholar Rachel Pain explains, "The cultural processes are widely felt to have sharpened in the 'risk society' (Beck 1992), owing to the central place of children and childhood within it: 'today we live in a climate of heightened risk awareness coupled with a nostalgia for an imagined past in which children played safely throughout a carefree innocent childhood.'"[36] The fear and paranoia parents feel for their children are exacerbated by how much parents believe the world has changed since they were young.[37] Gen X parents who grew up during the eighties and nineties remember a different world, one where unsupervised outdoor play and greater independence were a part of their childhoods.[38]

For example, Greta, a Swedish mother I interviewed, recalls a story from her childhood that shows the importance of nostalgia in determining how to parent her children:

> I know my mother let me, like at three or four years old, play alone in the sandbox outside. She was feeding my baby sister and didn't know what I was doing. She couldn't look after me because she had to sit inside and feed her. I was totally alone, maybe some other children were there but I do not remember. I do not recall grown-ups [being there], and [when I asked her about this] she said no, there were not always grown-ups. Back then, that was natural, you could just play and she came back 15 minutes later and I was still there. I would never leave my children like that today. I don't know why
>
> We were actually very free when we were children. I biked to school all alone through the woods and on a little biking road. Nobody knew where I was. We walked a lot alone, we were playing away from home in some woods around, a bit away. I had a watch and my mother told me, you come home at two o'clock. I left at ten and I came back at two. They never knew where we were.

Relying on memories from the past, then, which may have gotten hazy over time, parents such as Greta see the world as more risky and dangerous today than it was.

Parents manage nostalgic notions of a safer past by over-supervising children.[39] Over-supervision of children manifests itself in two ways: restricting supervised play and restricting unsupervised play.

Brandy, a Southern participant I interviewed, discusses how restricting supervised play makes her believe her child is safer. She explains:

> We played outside as kids, and we were gone for hours each day. We would be gone eight hours and come home for dinner, and my family wouldn't think anything about it. My children will not do that. They will stay where I can see them at all times. Even if that means I have to sit outside and watch them. I am afraid that someone is going to abduct them or hurt them, you know?

Sandra, another parent from the South also talks about how she restricts supervised play, highlighting the disconnect between her childhood and how she feels she must parent in today's world. She discusses how she manages the worry she feels about her daughter being kidnapped by a stranger. After discussing her fear for her daughter, I ask Sandra how she handles her worry for her daughter. She says:

> I keep her inside, or if she goes outside, I will go with her. I tell her there are boundaries and I only let her stay in the backyard if she wants to play outside. She can't go in the front yard, she can't go past my car, she has to stay in this small area where I can see her.

In Sandra's case, she feels her best defense against crime happening to her daughter is to make sure she can see her inside or out.

The surveillance of children is an important safety strategy for parents like Brandy and Sandra. Studies have shown parents reported the importance of being able to see their children when they were in public spaces. When parents' views of their children were obstructed, parents felt more fear of crime. Areas of concern for parents included public restrooms, areas of dense vegetation, or crowds that blocked their views of their children.[40] The message parents teach children here is to always be visible to parents, but they don't really explain the object of concern or the features of that concern. It is easy to see how nostalgia and over-supervision of children can go hand in hand for parents.

A second way parents over-supervise their children manifests itself through tighter restrictions on unsupervised recreational activities.[41] Jenny, a Swedish participant, explains how things have changed since she was a child and the impact of these changes on parenting. She says:

> When I was growing up both as a child and as a young person, there was so much more freedom than there is today. This is something

that has changed dramatically, I think between my growing up and my kids' growing up. We were always allowed to go on our own everywhere. We were never taken by parents to practices or friends' houses or cinemas or anything like that and that has changed. Kids now, they are being driven everywhere, and part of it is for safety reasons, I think.

Sara, another participant in the Swedish study, also recalls her childhood and how this impacts the way she is raising her children differently during unsupervised play. She says:

I don't let, I won't let them run around in the city on their own. I want to know where they are. That is the big difference between me and my parents. Even though I grew up in a quite poor area, we could be, when I was seven, eight, nine, we could be gone for hours running around. My parents had no idea where we were. But I would never let them [my children] do that now. At least I won't let them do it for many years. I want to know where they are. I want to be able to see them or just arrange with some other parents [to be with them] just that someone is with them.

In both Jenny and Sara's case, they believe that children today need to be restricted in their unsupervised recreational activities. They have found ways to do so through monitoring children's activities and, in some cases, relying on other parents to help them with this goal.

Thus, participants in my studies and in studies conducted by others show a connection between fear of crime and over-supervision of children in supervised play and more monitoring of children's unsupervised activities.[42] Parents recall their childhoods with a bit of nostalgia, believing that they were freer to run around the neighborhood and spend hours unsupervised than kids today. It is difficult to imagine that these restrictions do not influence the nature and frequency of outdoor and indoor recreational activities. It is also difficult to imagine that such limits do not impact fear of crime.

Safety rules, while well-intentioned, may have dire consequences for children's development.[43] First, such safety rules could increase the fear of crime for both parents and their children. For example, a study conducted by Ding and colleagues examined the relationship between restrictions on outdoor play and fear of crime.[44] They specifically examined the connection between parental fear of stranger danger and parental rules for outdoor recreation. They surveyed 287 parents about their fear of crime, perception of crime, demographic characteristics, and their parenting rules. Ding and colleagues asked parents about several rules about outside play, for example, making sure children were close or within sight of the parent/home, not allowing children to go places alone, or making children check in with their parents frequently. Also interesting was that they asked explicitly about fears of stranger-induced crime. The results from this study confirmed what we might expect: there was a strong connection between fear of stranger danger and parental rules for outside play. Parents who had more fear of strangers were less likely to allow their children to play outdoors unsupervised. Further, parents with the youngest children had higher levels of fear of strangers.

Another consequence is that children who avoid outside play are less likely to exercise than those children who have outdoor playtime.[45] The benefits of exercise in children are well known, including physical health outcomes like healthy weight, body mass index, and heart and respiratory functions.[46] There are also benefits to children's mental health; that is, they can better focus, learn, and sleep, and have lower levels of anxiety and depression.[47] Thus, while unintentional, parental restrictions concerning outdoor play may have health effects on children. Another consequence of keeping children indoors more often is that children are less likely to make decisions independently and feel confident and secure in their world. Research has shown that children who are over-supervised may feel just as afraid of crime as those children who are under-supervised.[48] At first glance, this doesn't make much sense. How is it that over-supervising children has the same effect as not supervising children at all? The reason researchers think this happens is because children who do not have the opportunity to make mistakes or become independent beings can lag behind their peers in decision-making processes.[49] Children who are over-supervised do not have the opportunity to fail and grow.[50]

Teaching Fear with an Eye to the Future

While Gen X parents must control for fears they learned growing up, they are now also responsible for managing a new host of "dangers" that they did not have as children. These new fears must also become part of the safety values parents teach to their children. The vastly different world that many Gen X parents grew up in ultimately frames a different set of concerns for their Gen Z children.

There are a few areas we've seen change over time regarding safety lessons. The largest of these new areas revolves around the online world. Most Gen X parents, especially those born in the early end of the Gen X time frame, did not grow up with computers or cell phones. Smartphones or social media were not a part of Gen X parents' childhoods. It is sometimes hard to imagine what life was like before we had these things, so a brief reminder is in order. When Gen X kids wanted to talk to each other, they had to call from their home on a corded phone (no cordless phones yet); there was no option to pick up the phone privately because cell phones were not a thing yet. When Gen X children went out and played with friends, they had a time of day they were supposed to arrive at home (usually dinnertime), and if they were late, their parents called the homes of the other children. If Gen X kids grew up in a two-parent household, decisions about who picked up which kid and at what time had to be decided in the morning before everyone left for the day (and no changes could be made because there was no way to communicate). If parents were late to pick kids up from an activity, the child just had to wait until their parents arrived (since there were no cell phones yet). There was no texting. It is hard to imagine a world without texting now, given how much we text each other, but if Gen X children wanted to talk to their friends after school, they had to call them on the phone. The internet wasn't yet a thing. To find out information about the world, people in the eighties and nineties had to read a newspaper or watch the five o'clock news. Most people during that time frame saw news sources as legitimate and credible ways to learn about the world, crime, and politics. People in the eighties and nineties had to be patient to get information; there was not a way to immediately know everything all the time. If Gen X children wanted to play games, they pulled out Life or Monopoly. Because there were not yet smartphones or the internet, there was no online gaming. Gen X children made friends from school and through activities and did not have friends worldwide, as children can today (unless they met them at camp or wrote letters to a pen pal). Once Gen X children graduated from high school, unless very socially connected in small communities, the details of their adult lives were not public knowledge, as they are now through social media platforms like Facebook. Gen X kids could keep their embarrassing moments private instead of having these memories posted publicly, as kids do today.

Safety values have had to keep up with the technological advancements of today's world and the numerous changes Gen X kids have been through. Parents cannot rely on their childhood experiences in this new arena of parenting. While safety myths may not have changed with recent advancements, the execution of crime myths have morphed into more modern-day territory. Crime myths are still part of teaching safety values to children. Still, because of the lack of personal experience with technology, Gen X parents are forced to rely on information from others to keep children safe from these new threats.

The New-Age Boogieman

The image of the stranger has changed for Gen X parents. As discussed earlier, the boogieman jumping out of the bushes is a familiar image for Gen Xers.[51] Safety messages in the eighties and nineties were more straightforward: avoid locations where potential boogiemen might lurk, such as a park or outside of school.[52] Fear of the white kidnapper van and educational stranger danger campaigns like McGruff the Crime Dog were based on the boogieman idea.

Today's boogieman is more complex. The internet has become a place where anyone can pretend to be whomever they want by disguising their true identity. The internet has made the "bad guy" unknowable, unimaginable, and unpredictable. During Gen Xers' childhoods, a grown man could not pose as a child who wanted to be your friend. Such new threats have forced parents to pivot in the types of lessons they teach their children. They must still teach stranger danger in the traditional sense, but the new boogieman can be any stranger your child meets on the internet.[53] It becomes difficult to control this unknown. There is no way to honestly know someone's identity on the internet, so parents are expected to constantly monitor kids online. As discussed earlier, Gen Z children are sometimes called the "bubble-wrap" generation. It is hard for parents to find bubble-wrap that will prevent online victimization.

Carla, a Midwestern participant, talks about the unknown now presented by the internet. When I ask if she is fearful of crimes happening to children, she says:

> Probably, I mean just because times have changed, like when we were kids, you know you just roamed free and that doesn't happen. I don't even think you play in the front yard by yourself nowadays. So probably [I would be afraid for children], or like you always hear about online people [predators]. I always wonder how people with kids are dealing with this, you know? Your kid is going to be on the computer so like how do you deal with those kinds of situations?

Carla points out some of the elements of the new-age boogieman. First, she acknowledges that today's parents did not have to think about or worry about computer crimes, especially online predators, when growing up. She also says that in today's world, parents are faced with additional challenges because they must navigate a world where their children have access to technology they didn't have growing up.

Another factor making the internet boogieman more complex is that it is entirely possible that children know more about how the internet works than their parents.[54] Gen Z children learn to use computers at a young age and learn about computers at school. Whereas most Gen X parents took a typing class or perhaps learned how to use a computer at a basic level, Gen Z children learn how to type along with foundational elements of computers, including how to deal with internet security and use computer programs of all types. Many schools give out iPads or chromebooks to every student, and the kids take tests, do lessons, and complete homework online. Clearly, this is a different world than Gen X parents grew up in. Parents' lack of knowledge makes it harder for them to control online safety because they don't always know what they are controlling or how to make decisions about safety.[55] It is hard to teach others about things you do not understand yourself.

Ghent University researchers Martin Valcke and colleagues refer to this as "reverse socialization," where children have better skills in an area than their parents do and often teach their parents about the area.[56] Such a reverse socialization process requires parents to educate children differently than they would for other areas of socialization. In online learning, children have more knowledge about the internet than their parents, but parents still have to supervise this space. Parents then must learn to negotiate and mediate such complex issues.

London School of Economics and Political Science researcher Sonia Livingstone and her colleagues more recently considered how parents modified parenting strategies to "maximize opportunity" and "minimize risks" for children in the online environment.[57] Surveying 6,400 children in European countries, they found that there are two primary strategies parents take to level out opportunities and risks, "enabled" mediation and "restrictive" mediation. "Enabled" mediation involves active mediation of internet safety and general internet use, along with technical controls and active parental monitoring of online activities. "Restrictive" mediation involves strategies where parents completely restrict internet activities. They found that parents are more likely to use "enabling" types of mediation with younger children and more "restrictive" mediators for older children.

Livingstone's study also considered the importance of parental risk perception. They define "risk perception" in relation to crime and harm from things like bullying and found some interesting results that may apply to parental safety lessons for online crime. They found that parents with slightly higher risk perceptions were more likely to use enabling mediation rather than restrictive mediation strategies. They argued this is likely because when parents fear a bit for children, they want to be more hands-on and see if their fear is warranted. However, parents with high levels of risk perception had high usage levels of both enabling and restrictive mediation strategies. The authors of this study conclude that "parental risk perception is positively associated with children's greater online opportunities and risks. It is not possible to determine causality here, but it seems likely that parents more sensitive to or concerned about risk may also be aware of their child's online activities of all kinds."[58]

For example, social media is a significant concern of parents.[59] Monitoring children's social media seems to be an added responsibility of parenting today. A recent Pew study found that two-thirds of parents said that parenting is "harder today than 20 years ago." These parents cited social media and smartphones as two primary reasons they thought parenting is now more challenging.[60]

Social media and technology also impact parents' fear of crime.[61] Australian researchers Jacinta Francis and her colleagues considered key factors in how children's media use affected parents' fear of strangers.[62] Mothers in particular said they worried about social media because children might be exposed to sexual predators pretending to be children.

One mother interviewed in the South provides an example of how this works in the real world. Melanie says:

> [My daughter] got this game, and here is where it is and here's how to download it and she downloaded it. I did not know that it had a privacy thing to it, I thought it was just a game you played on your phone but I didn't know it was over the internet with others. So, it [the privacy setting] was set to the public [instead of private]. I caught it pretty early on but still. [Children] don't, at that age that she was then, they don't understand the difference between public and private. They don't really understand the internet. They don't really understand how somebody could take something as innocent as a silly picture of yourself and then turn around and use it on you when you're 13 to bully you, you know what I mean? Like, I was trying to tell her, I was like, whatever you put out there, it is out there and you can just assume that it is out there forever and that it can be shared to anybody in the whole wide world. Do you want that to happen? That is the question you should ask yourself before you write something to somebody else, would I want this shared with the pastor of my church?

Melanie gives us a solid picture of the complexity of parenting children in the internet era. Parents may not always realize all the intricacies of downloading apps or games (privacy settings are a good example). Further, children may not understand that what they put online at 11 years old may affect them when they are older; someone may use their information in ways they did not intend. Thus, parents are required to explain why the internet is dangerous to children who may know more than their parents about the internet. However, the underdeveloped emotional and social skills of children may restrict their ability to see that they should not put themselves out in a world that seems completely open and safe to them.

Combatting the New Boogieman

Since anyone can be a boogieman now, how do we combat the new threat? One way to combat the new boogieman involves the constant supervision of children.[63] As we discussed earlier, Gen X parents control kids' use of public spaces by over-supervising recreational activities.[64] Parents have also tried to get educated on risks associated with the new boogieman.[65]

With all the added potential online threats, parents have turned to technology themselves for help.[66] One strategy has involved purchasing programs or apps that can track kids who have phones. The use of these apps and under what conditions to use them is a hot topic of debate among parents.[67] For example, a *Washington Post* article called "'Don't Leave Campus': Parents Are Now Using Tracking Apps to Watch Their Kids at College" talks about the debate of using tracking apps on adult-aged children.[68] While some parents in the article felt that tracking their adult children with apps was a violation of privacy, most parents thought that the app was a helpful way for them to keep track of their children's whereabouts. One of the primary motivations of parents who use the program with teens and adult-aged children is to help minimize safety concerns. A college-aged daughter interviewed in the article said she did not have a problem with her parents using the tracking program because it was for safety. So there seem to be pros and cons for parents using tracking apps. Regardless of this debate, such apps are popular with consumers.

A *Parents* magazine article called "The 11 Best Apps for Parents to Monitor Their Kids" starts by saying, "these apps for parents can monitor phone use, location, and more to give you some peace of mind when it comes to your child's safety."[69] By framing tracking in terms of safety, the tracking of kids, while not agreed upon by all parents, becomes an option for worried parents to combat the new boogieman.

The Life360 app, a popular app in today's tracking market, focuses on and frames the tracking of kids around safety concerns. Their website says Life360 provides services like location sharing, driving safety, identity protection, safety assistance, and emergency response. They label their services "all-in-one safety for on-the-go families."[70] Life360 tells potential consumers in their marketing tagline that Life360 will make you less of a helicopter or bulldozer mom, so you can just be a "mom" mom. In other words, Life360 is playing on societal expectations that mothers' primary child-rearing concerns should be for safety. They tell moms that to be a good mom, you need to over-supervise children.

These apps play into the stranger danger myth because the apps provides 24-hour surveillance, but tracking apps also tap into a newer construction of the victim-centered prevention myth. That is, mothers are not only expected to figure out ways to keep their teen/adult children safe from unknown scares, but they are also held responsible if they do not constantly supervise their children. In other words, if something happens to a child and their mother wasn't over-supervising (through tracking apps or otherwise), the mother is held more responsible. The new pressure on moms today for 24-hour surveillance of their children adds stress to mothers. The idea sold to mothers through tracking companies is that all mothers, especially "perfect" mothers, are tracking their kids, so why aren't you? In a way, this idea causes mothers to "keep up with the Joneses" by participating in tracking their children.

The popularity and use of tracking apps are still too new to know the future ramifications on fear of crime for parents and their children. However, a study from the 1980s on fear of crime may provide insight into what we might expect tracking apps to do to parents' fear of crime. As discussed earlier, State University of New York at Albany criminologist Allen Liska and his colleagues found a reciprocal relationship between fear of crime and the use of preventive behaviors.[71] In other words, the more you are afraid, the more you take precautionary measures, which causes you to be more afraid. It makes sense that the constant ability to monitor the whereabouts of children/teens may also increase parents' fear of crime for their children. The tracking of children will be an interesting extension of fear of crime research in the future.

In sum, there is a whole new world of boogiemen out there, whether through a home computer, a laptop, or a smartphone, for parents to be afraid of. Unlike other areas of socialization, children have the upper hand in many ways with the online world since they know more about it than their parents and learn to use the internet at a young age.[72] Parents, then, must act in ways that they may never have imagined, like watching their child's every move, to feel they are keeping kids safe and keeping up with other moms/parents who already track their children.[73] Perhaps the lack of predictability in the online world is the most challenging safety issue for parents. It is more difficult to control children on the internet than to keep kids out of a park. Keeping kids away from and out of the online world is not an option. Parents must negotiate the unknown world in ways they never imagined with little direction or experience in how to do so. Ultimately, the fear of the new boogieman in combination with the old boogieman impacts how parents teach the fear of crime to their children and how their children will ultimately grow up to fear crime.

The Devil You Know—Cyberbullying

Parents are most afraid of an unknown person posing as someone else to a child online, but there is also a new threat children face: cyberbullying. If you ask a Gen X parent what a bully is, they will likely describe someone in a school trying to beat up a kid, push a kid into a locker, or steal a kid's lunch money. These bullies are hard to deal with and, for many children, extremely scary, making the school environment unwelcome. Traditional bullying is still a part of today's school environment. However, with the advent of the online world, children today have to contend with online bullies.[74]

For example, Madison, a Southern mom I interviewed, talks about her fear of traditional bullies. When discussing things that she fears for children, she says, "I am afraid of some bully at school hurting them. I mean, it is a meaner world than when I was growing up."

Parents also understand that cyberbullying is something to be concerned about.[75] A Swedish dad I interviewed, Daniel, talks about how difficult it is to teach kids about cyber safety and social media. When I ask him what he talks about with his children, he says:

> Cyber safety—technically, I would talk a lot about that because they are also interested in what are hackers, what are cyberbullies, and stuff like that. But also hate crimes and stuff and how you behave on social media, stuff like that. They spend so much time behind the screen, they should also really be aware of the other stuff that is not good.

Daniel, then, discusses several online fears, including the new-age boogieman and cyberbullying.

There is a lot for parents to unpack about cyberbullying, such as understanding what cyberbullying is, what it involves, what behaviors it includes, and what a cyberbully is trying to accomplish.[76] Stopbullying.gov defines cyberbullying as "bullying that takes place over digital devices like cell phones, computers, and tablets. Cyberbullying can occur through SMS, text, and apps, or online in social media, forums, or gaming where people can view, participate in, or share content. Cyberbullying includes sending, posting, or sharing negative, harmful, false, or mean content about someone else. It can include sharing personal or private information about someone else, causing embarrassment or humiliation. Some cyberbullying crosses the line into unlawful or criminal behavior."[77] In other words, cyberbullying goes way beyond physical alterations. It involves humiliation, privacy violations, and the posting of false information. These scenarios are not things Gen X parents ever had to navigate themselves.

While the frequency of cyberbullying is difficult to pinpoint, according to the National Center for Education Statistics, about 22 percent of students between the ages of 12 and 18 said they had experienced bullying at school.[78] About 16 percent of students in high school reported that they had been bullied online in the past 12 months. Female students, white students, and students who identified as gay, lesbian, or bisexual were more likely to report cyberbullying victimization in comparison to males, non-white students, and heterosexual students.

Cyberbullying can be overwhelming and highly confusing to parents.[79] First, most parents do not know all the places cyberbullies might be lurking; most parents are not as adept at these forms of social media, whether it be Snapchat, group chats, or TikTok, as a cyberbully (or their children). Put another way, cyberbullying is often conducted outside the realm of adults. Parents may not even have the same social media platforms as their children.[80] So, kids today are part of an unstructured environment ripe with the potential for bullying without parental presence. Second, because social media is constantly morphing, cyberbullies have realms of online space that they can pivot to if adults get close to bullying behavior. If a bully can no longer bully on TikTok, then they move to another form of social media. Cyberbullying is a moving target that is difficult to pinpoint and confusing for parents. Finally, the nature of cyberbullying is different than traditional bullying. Cyberbullying allows people to engage in emotional, rather than physical, warfare with their victims.[81] There are relational and social elements to cyberbullying that make it difficult for parents to combat. The reach of cyberbullying is more significant as well, since the online environment is global rather than contained to one hallway or one school. So, with traditional bullying, four people might witness a bully/victim interaction in the hallway at school. With cyberbullying, a person can send an embarrassing picture or harmful rumor about a victim to hundreds of kids with the click of a button.

Because cyberbullying is more common among girls, and white girls report this behavior more than non-white girls, we can see how this plays right into crime myths.[82] Recall the white woman crime victim myth, which targets white women as the most likely crime victims. The idea that white women are more likely to be crime victims than anyone else is a myth. In the case of cyberbullying, white girls do make up a significant proportion of those victimized by cyberbullies. White parents, especially affluent white parents who can afford crime prevention devices and services, may be the target audience for stranger danger and child abduction campaigns.[83] We can speculate that this group of parents may also become the target audience for cyberbullying campaigns. Informational and public service campaigns may focus more on white girls, then, potentially increasing fear of crime among white parents with daughters.

Cyberbullying also plays into the victim-centered crime myth since victims are perceived to bear the responsibility for their victimization. For example, if a picture is taken at a party showing a high school girl drinking, others who see the photo may think the girl deserves to be shamed since she was acting inappropriately. This takes the blame off of the offender who took the photo and posted it without permission. It is clear these new virtual fears play into parents' fear of crime.

The Unknown School Shooter

Another new threat parents must think about is the school shooter. Both school administration and parents reinforce school safety messages about school shootings.[84] School shootings fall under fear of the new-age boogieman because, as University of Texas at Dallas criminologists Michael Huskey and Nadine Connell point out, Gen X parents have a different understanding of school violence than Gen Z children.[85] Huskey and Connell argue that people who went to school before the 2001 Columbine school shooting have a very different perspective on school safety than children do today. Columbine, and its significant media coverage, changed everything Gen Xers knew about school safety. Gen Z children have always lived in a world where school shootings existed. Thus, preparing for such a possibility seems logical to kids who have also been doing safety drills or living with active shooter training all of their lives. Thus, school shooting prevention drills may not impact kids' perceptions of safety in the same way they do for their parents. Huskey and Connell argue that different learning experiences of Gen X and Gen Z have caused a generation gap in safety values surrounding school safety.[86] The generational gap of school safety may mean that Gen X parents grew up without fear of school shootings but now fear school shootings happening to their children very much. Gen Z children learn from school that school shootings are possible, and the narrative taught to children about staying safe includes information about school shootings from a young age. Gen Z kids, then, may find school shooting prevention activities to not be that big of a deal.

While kids today will experience these safety lessons at school whether they want to or not, as we discussed earlier, parents also reinforce the school shooter boogieman. The post-Columbine world is full of media coverage regarding school shootings.[87] For example, in a horrific school shooting in 2012 at Sandy Hook Elementary in Newtown, CT, a lone gunman took the life of 26 people, including 20 kids who were between the ages of six and seven.[88] Nothing causes more terror for parents than watching the pictures of 20 young children who are no longer on this earth because of a school shooter appear on the television screen. This particular school shooting also received extreme attention from the media. As Texas State University criminologist Jaclyn Schildkraut and Miami University criminologist Glenn Muschert explain, "Since the Columbine shooting, other school shootings have occurred, some with higher body counts (e.g., Virginia Tech) and some seemingly taking place as copycat crimes (e.g., the May 20, 1999, shooting in Conyers, GA), but none have garnered a comparable level of media attention until Newtown."[89] They note that the Sandy Hook shooting was the second most-followed news story of the entire year in 2012 (following the presidential election). When comparing newspaper articles about Columbine and Sandy Hook, the authors conclude that the media framed the Columbine and Newton stories very differently. With Columbine, the media were more likely to frame the story around the offenders, who they were, and why they did what they did.[90] With Sandy Hook, the media focused more on the crime victims. As the researchers explain,

> Coverage of Sandy Hook also exhibited a significant departure from Columbine concerning how the story was told. The mass media discourse notably changed with Sandy Hook, following the lead of the earlier shooting at the Aurora, Colorado, movie theater. In both cases, coverage of the shooters was extremely limited and instead focused on the victims. In fact, very little significant information was released in the media about Adam Lanza or the investigation, particularly in the first week of coverage. Instead, the media focused on telling the stories of the heroic educators and the losses of innocent children. These groups especially fall in line with what Sorenson, Manz, and Berk have identified as the "worthy victim." Such victims, who typically garner increased media attention and are considered the most newsworthy, are those who are "White, in the youngest and oldest age groups, women, of high socioeconomic status, killed by strangers."[91]

It is highly likely then that after the Sandy Hook Elementary shooting and the media attention it received, Gen X parents were thinking about school shootings in elementary school perhaps for the first time. The conversations that followed with children would have reflected those worries and fears from parents and school officials. While parents' discussions with kids about Sandy Hook are not the focus of much research, the parents interviewed in a recent study I conducted with Courtney Heath and Maggie Hagerman reflect a larger fear of school shootings. When we talked to parents about their safety concerns, they mentioned school shootings as a genuine concern. Bailey, a Southern mother, talks about school shootings when discussing her fears for her children. She says:

> So I think we were just explaining that sometimes, we don't want them to be afraid when they go to school, but there have been cases where people have gone into schools with guns and shot people, and people have been hurt and killed. I think we tried to just give them the facts and I know I try to explain some of the meaning behind it—the sadness with what must happen, what must lead someone to be able to go in and shoot people. I guess try to draw the compassion for the whole situation to help them have a bigger perspective of it wasn't just some really bad person who went in and killed some people.

Bailey frames school shootings in a way that she hopes will minimize fear while simultaneously teaching safety values about school shootings through facts. The lesson also focuses on compassion, but it is still a lesson framed around school shootings and violence that happens at school.

Another respondent from the South also focused on school shootings, although through a less compassionate lens. Ashley explains:

> I'm going to think about how I want to say this. I have a friend who has a really weird kid and I've been joking since he was three that he is going to be a serial killer when he grows up. Something is not right. It has been a joke but I'm always like be nice to him because when he wears the trench coat to school and pulls out the shotgun, we want him to remember that you were nice and skip you kind of thing. I say it sort of jokingly, but it's kind of my general philosophy. Be nice to people because that is probably your best prevention.

Ashley, then, teaches her children that they should be nice to others so that they don't stand out as potential victims for a potential school shooter. In both cases, Bailey and Ashley have framed talking to children about school safety in terms of being friendly to those who potentially might shoot up a school. The safety guidance given to children about school shooters is that school shootings are a possibility. That school shooters tend to be mentally unstable loner types who target mean people. These ideas most closely align with the media's presentation of the school shooter.[92]

A *Time* magazine article from December 2012 titled "Sandy Hook Shooting: Why Did Lanza Target a School?" explains:

> For all the disbelief and dismay, we actually know pretty well that most such events are committed by individuals with a particular set of characteristics. As my colleagues Mark Coulson, Jane Barnett and I noted in a 2011 article in the *Journal of Police Crisis Negotiations*, school shooters have generally been found to 1) have a history of antisocial-personality traits, 2) suffer from mental illnesses such as depression or psychosis and 3) tend to obsess about how others, whether other individuals or society at large, have wronged them. . . . These individuals seethe with rage and hatred and despondency, until they decide to lash out at individuals or a society they believe has done them great wrong. Mental health, as well as our failure to address it as a society, is at the core of these events.[93]

While not a completely inaccurate picture of school shooters, kids with these traits make up only a tiny fraction of school shooters.[94] Most students who are loners, wear long coats, have mental health issues, or are antisocial will never become school shooters. The truth of the matter is that school shootings are sporadic, and while the small group of people who are school shooters bear some of these characteristics, there are plenty of other students with these same characteristics who do not. The lessons taught to children by parents is that school shootings and school crimes are predictable, that there is a profile of an offender, and that there is no prevention plan except to be nice. These safety lessons may cause fear and will not prevent a school shooting. Whereas schools are given the primary responsibility of teaching safety lessons about school shootings to children, parents often worry about their children and, therefore, reinforce the safety lessons schools teach.[95]

We now have a good sense of what parents teach their children about safety, risk, and how to fear crime. Parents teach fear to children through safety values. Safety values are based on old fears of the traditional boogieman from Gen Xers' childhoods, like the belief in stranger danger and in the high likelihood of childhood abductions. However, Gen X parents have also had to adapt to new-age fears in the modern-day world. Whether it be internet safety, cyberbullying, or school shootings, parents have to incorporate these new crimes into their discussions about safety. Parents also have new forms of over-supervision to consider when teaching safety to children. Tracking children/teenagers' whereabouts is in fashion currently, and parents may feel pressure to engage in such behaviors to keep children safe.

Parents then manage and instill safety values in their children through old-school and new-school ways.

What do children make of all of this? Very few studies have attempted to determine what children think about their parents' lessons regarding safety. Children's interpretations of the safety lessons learned from parents and their thoughts about crime and safety more generally are the focus of the next chapter.

5

What Kids Hear and What Kids Fear

You may recall playing a game called "telephone" as a child. A group of children sit in a circle, and a child thinks of a phrase. The child whispers it to the person next to them until the last person in the circle says the phrase out loud. The phrase is undoubtedly different from what it was at the start of the game and usually does not make sense. In this chapter, we ask ourselves if children come to understand safety values and fear of crime in a similar fashion. When we teach safety values to children, do those messages get passed on like in a game of telephone? We can better answer questions about what children learn from parents and school officials by asking children themselves.

We need to know what kids hear when they are told safety lessons, and we also need to know what kids do with this information. What do kids do with the lessons from their parents and school officials? Do kids buy into, resist, or feel apathetic about safety lessons? Do these safety lessons alleviate the fear of crime, cause more fear of crime, or have no impact on fear of crime at all? Studies have not been able to answer these questions because researchers rarely ask kids about what they learn from their parents concerning safety.[1] Researchers have assumed that children hear what parents say, understand the intention and meaning, and then act on these lessons, which may or may not be the case.[2] Since most researchers study parents who speak on behalf of their children they cannot fully understand children's viewpoints and beliefs about crime.[3] However, to fully understand how society teaches fear of crime from generation to generation, we need to understand the viewpoint of children in their own words.

We can gain insight from more recent child and youth scholars, who argue that kids are more than sponges; they also have some agency in what lessons they incorporate into their thoughts, beliefs, and identities.[4] By interviewing children themselves (and sometimes both parents and children), these researchers can gain a more in-depth understanding of the perceptions and viewpoints of children. More contemporary scholars argue that the only way to understand children is to ask children themselves what they think.[5] This chapter attempts to give voice to children. In their own words, children will share what they hear parents say about safety and how this influences their fear of crime.

What Kids Hear Parents Say

Most researchers have not asked children "what have your parents told you about safety?" I have also not focused exclusively on children and what they hear from parents about safety. However, my study with families in southern Sweden asked kids about safety, and my most recent study, with my colleagues Courtney Heath and Maggie Hagerman, interviewed families about safety in the Southern United States. Both studies provide meaningful guidance for future research on children and fear of crime.

In both the Swedish and Southern U.S. studies, when children were asked what they heard their parents tell them about safety, they most easily recalled conversations about stranger danger. Researchers agree parents are the most critical socialization agent, so what kids hear parents say about safety, crime, and fear is extremely important.

For example, when Lisa, a Swedish child, is asked what her parents teach her about safety, she says:

> Yeah. So, for example, when I bike to and from school alone, my parents have told me that I shouldn't talk to strangers. Like, for example, if someone says, come here, I've got some candy maybe you want some, I'm supposed to not talk to them and just bike past. And the same if someone tells me, hey, I've got a puppy at home, maybe you'd like to come see it and have it, I'm also not supposed to go home with the stranger. In the same way, I'm just supposed to not talk to them and bike on.

Lisa's answer about stranger danger mirrors the concerns around stranger danger presented by parents in chapter 4. The classic "don't take candy or a puppy from strangers" sounds like it is right out of a 1980s after-school special. Lisa's answer shows that she understands from her parents that she is to avoid strangers, that these messages are clear to her, and that she should not be tricked into going with a stranger under any circumstance. It is also important to note that Lisa also says she is worried about crime in public spaces.

However, later in the interview, Lisa shows how stranger danger messages may not translate to her contextual understandings of what she should fear. Lisa explains why she would be afraid in a particular area of town. She says:

> So, for example, I feel very safe in this house [her home], and of course, if the door wasn't locked, anyone could just come in here, but we can lock the door. And also the house is very colorful, and it's not—it's not run down, but it's sort of a nice house, and, for example, if I'm around run-down houses or scary houses, or when there—when it's very dark and run down, I feel more afraid. Like, for example, if the houses are very one-colored, so if they're only black or only white or only gray, I don't like that very much either.

In this example, while Lisa understands she should fear crime in particular neighborhoods, she doesn't exactly know why she should worry about those places. The color of the houses and their condition could represent a dilapidated neighborhood where crimes rates are statistically higher. Thus, she is likely correct that the area she describes is a higher-crime area, but the part of the messages about higher-crime neighborhoods, likely learned from her parents, has gotten lost in translation through the game of telephone. Lisa thinks the neighborhood is dangerous but doesn't necessary understand it is a high crime risk area. Lisa's story shows us that parents need to contextualize safety discussions that make sense to a child and teach the reality of crime more clearly. Parents could make explicit that dilapidated areas have higher risks of being dangerous and explain why this is the case.

Cleo, another Swedish respondent, also talks about what she learned from her parents about crime. She says, "I learned about if strangers take me or something, like that, I scream and fight, and if the strangers is only coming to talk to me, then I just go, and if they follow after me, I run. So run away."

Cleo learned that children should be afraid of strangers in public spaces. Specifically, she knows that she should scream, fight, and run away if she feels worried about a stranger. Again, she translates her parents' messages correctly: she should fear strangers. These messages also favor protecting yourself from strangers in public spaces. However, what Cleo should do about her fear of strangers is a little bit unrealistic. It seems unlikely that parents would tell their nine-year-old daughter to fight off a stranger, likely an adult man. Also, fighting and running away seem like opposite strategies. This misinterpretation of her parents' words of wisdom may be confusing and cause more fear of crime. Although, as Lisa and Cleo attest, parents emphasize safety advice and prevention tactics, the context of safety advice is often lost in translation.

Another lesson kids hear from their parents involves safety surrounding the perimeter of their home. Most kids we've interviewed tell us they feel very safe in their homes. While kids hear parents say they are very safe inside their homes, kids also listen to parents cautioning them about dangerous people trying to get inside their homes. So, kids hear parents talk about things like locking doors, being cautious of visitors, and protecting the home from potential intruders. For example, Caroline, a Southern child, heard her parents talk to her about preventing strangers from entering the house. She says:

> We lock our doors and stuff. Whenever I'm at home, or they're out on a walk that I didn't have to go on, I keep the door locked and don't answer it for anyone unless it is a friend that I know is safe or it is them [her parents] because they didn't bring a key since I was at home.... It's stuff they [parents] tell me. Keep the door locked, don't answer it unless I know who it is at the door, and even if it is an adult and I know who it is, just say that my mom and dad are not home, so come back later or something like that. I had a friend come over to ask to borrow a book, and my mom was ok with that because she knew who it was, and I knew who it was. She knew the parents, and she knew she probably wasn't coming to do any harm.

In Caroline's case, she learns from her parents to always lock the door and be cautious and non-trusting of anyone attempting to enter the house. We can see how Caroline's childhood restrictions might become part of her adult safety values.

Holly, another respondent from the Southern United States, also talks about learning to fear strangers entering the house. When discussing what her parents taught her about safety, she says:

> So my mom is like, if someone [either Holly or one of her siblings] answers the door, make sure [to check] if there is a parent home. If we are in the shower or something, don't answer the door, or if they [parents] are not home, don't answer the door. We don't have windows [in the front door], but if it is someone we know or something,

we get our chairs [to stand on] because we have a little, tiny peephole, like one of those little, tiny things that hotels used to have, so we'd stand on a chair because we are not tall enough and so we need to stand on a chair and look through. If it is someone we know, like *know*, we would answer the door, or if our parents were expecting someone [we can answer that]. But if it's not, we text mom and dad, and we don't answer the door; we pretend like we are not home.

Holly, then, also hears her parents say she should fear someone coming to the door. She learns a myriad of rules about deciphering the safe level of a person at the door and that adults (and not children) determine if someone is safe or not. Such an understanding of safety may cause children to rely on others rather than themselves to decide if someone can be trusted to enter the home. The parents get to determine if the person is a stranger or not. Children, then, seek the "all clear" from parents before they allow people in their homes.

Whether in public spaces or the home, as the children we've spoken with in our interviews demonstrate, children hear parents tell them that they should fear strangers in public areas and that it is important to keep strangers out of the home. However, children rarely learn from parents to worry about people they know or to take precautions against potential crimes happening in private spaces—like inside their homes. Finally, children learn from their parents that they are not as qualified as adults to be decision-makers on what is and is not (or who is and is not) safe.

Translating What Kids Hear from Parents to What Kids Fear

What kids learn about safety from their parents may also impact kids' fear of crime. Researchers have measured kids' fear of crime primarily by asking parents to speculate about what kids are afraid of.[6] Other studies ask parents to self-report what behaviors they take to keep children safe from crime.[7] Finally, some studies ask parents how fearful of crime they are for their children.[8] While these studies are important, they do not ask kids what they are afraid of and why.[9]

When researchers talk to children directly about fear of crime or safety, they often speak to adolescents or young adults.[10] Unfortunately, by focusing only on teenagers, these studies have missed out on the potential knowledge we can learn from younger children.[11]

For these reasons, research in criminology and fear of crime lacks a general understanding of kids' opinions about their fears.[12] We can learn some from a study conducted by Canadian researcher Mariana Brussoni and colleagues.[13] In a study of 105 kids, they did walking tours through the children's neighborhoods and talked to them about meaningful places. While this study was more about children's views on unsupervised outdoor play, some of their findings involved safety concerns related to crime. The 10- to 13-year-olds said their perceptions of the "neighborliness" of people influenced how safe they felt in their neighborhoods. Neighborliness might mean that these children felt a sense of community with the people in their area. On the positive side, having people, primarily known people, in unsupervised spaces brought a sense of security to children. On the flip side, people who didn't fit this mold were perceived as potentially threatening and made children feel less safe in their neighborhood. For example, the respondents felt more fear in areas with many homeless people or places perceived as having drug addicts. Brussoni and colleagues also found that kids felt less safe in their neighborhoods when it was getting dark, and kids also avoided areas where kids known to be bullies hung out. While some of these findings mirror studies on adults' perceptions of neighborhood safety—like feeling less safe when homeless people are on the streets—some of these findings also highlight experiences specific to children. The idea that bullies congregate in certain areas of a neighborhood and should be avoided is not likely something we'd hear if we interviewed adults about their own experiences or the experiences of their children.

The last finding of interest from the Brussoni study was that children who had more confidence in their ability to get out of a dangerous situation felt safer.[14] Kids from this study who talked about having good observation skills or having exit strategies like running fast generally felt safer than kids who didn't have similar strategies. Children, even younger children, have unique thoughts and opinions about safety. Only by talking with children themselves can we truly understand what children fear and what they do not.

Similar to Brussoni and colleagues, I found similar things with the kids from my Swedish and American South studies. For example, Iza, a Swedish child, talks about what she is afraid of. She says: "So I think it's a little scary to be home alone. I don't like that." Alice, another Swedish child, tells me she is afraid of outside spaces in the dark. When I ask why, she says, "[because] you are walking on empty or deserted streets, and there may be dangerous people around." She further clarifies what a dangerous person looks like to her, saying, "A person that maybe has taken drugs or alcohol or a person with a weapon." In both cases, Iza and Alice are worried about strangers. It is also interesting to note that both Iza and Alice reference darkness or nighttime.

Lisa, the Swedish child I referenced earlier, provides a perfect example of how fear at night ties into perceptions of safety within the neighborhood. She says:

> I go outside of school to learn to play an instrument, and so once my Mom and I were biking, and we were biking across a cemetery. Even though—and it sort of feels uncomfortable and scary, like, even though I know that there's no one there, that no one's watching me, I feel like someone is watching me, or, like, something can see me. So that feels very uncomfortable, even though I know there isn't anything there, so I felt very scared, and I kept looking over my shoulders and looking around, even though I knew there was nothing there. And that was scary.

Lisa, then, is afraid of darkness and nighttime in her neighborhood, even with her mother nearby. We aren't sure if Lisa is scared of a stranger pursuing them or if Lisa is scared of ghosts, but in both cases, darkness makes her feel more afraid.

While Lisa is not yet a teen, how teens manage their risk and fear of public places also sheds light on kids' safety perceptions. Another study by scholar Danielle Van der Burgt talked to Swedish teens about managing their perceived risk and fear of public spaces.[15] Unlike studies with parents, who can likely only guess what teens think or do in public areas when they are alone, Van der Burgt gets the information directly from teens. Her study found three ways teenagers dealt with public spaces perceived as risky. First, avoidance strategies were prevalent among teens. So, when teens were worried about places, they would do their best to avoid those areas. This pattern is what we generally see with adults. Similarly, teenagers also avoided places or times of day (like night time) when they were most worried about crime happening to them.

The second way teens dealt with risky spaces was by using risk-confronting strategies. Risk-confronting tactics were similar to adults' use of protective strategies when feeling afraid of crime. For example, teenagers might take items with them to help them feel safer (e.g., a weapon or some other thing they could use for protection). Van der Burgt's study also highlighted teen-focused risk-confrontation strategies that we do not typically see discussed in studies with adults. First, teenagers used social skills as a risk-confronting strategy. Teenagers assessed social situations while they were in them and, if necessary, thought about ways out of those situations that would prevent escalation. Teenagers also used their social network to tip them off about places to avoid. Friends were often the source of whether or not an area was safe. Teens rely on these social networks to keep themselves safe. Van der Burgt also noted that teens rely on spatial skills as part of their risk-confrontation strategies.[16] In this instance, teenagers monitored the spaces they occupied. By being aware of the surroundings in a public area, teens could still occupy the space and hang out with friends but felt their risk was diminished.

In addition to avoidance and risk-confrontation strategies used by teenagers, Van der Burgt added a third category called "empowerment and boldness" strategies.[17] Stemming from the concept presented by University of Helsinki researcher Hille Koskela of the "bold walk," Van Der Burgt similarly argues a few teens resist societal norms that expect kids to avoid public spaces altogether.[18] As Van Der Burgt explains, "an active use of unfamiliar public space seems to provide children and young people with a sense of agency and promote feelings of confidence and boldness."[19] However, similar to what I've seen in my research with adults, Van Der Burgt notes this last strategy is rare. Of those who used the strategy, she found "boldness" could come in the form of going places and doing things that others might find fearful. The "I'm not letting fear run my life" mantra applies here.

One interesting boldness strategy found among teens is what Van der Burgt calls the "auditory bubble." She explains, "the sound of music in headphones provided some teenagers with a feeling of safety and calm when moving through public space. It kept them from thinking fearful thoughts and letting all the sounds in the surroundings frighten them." Teens' use of headphones makes sense when thinking about how comfortable kids are with technology and with incorporating it into their lives. However, while adults are typically not asked about headphones as a strategy for safety, I would bet that adults do not use this strategy. In other words, researchers would not get this information from asking parents what their kids do or from talking to adults and trying to apply these findings to teenagers. Thus, we only have a true sense of what teens fear and their strategies for minimizing the fear by talking to kids and teens.

Our research study with kids interviewed in the Southern United States also provide examples of the ways kids manage fear through avoidance, risk, or boldness.

Henry provides an example of how fear of crime is tied to safety prevention strategies. He says:

> If I'm in a public place alone, I don't really like doing that unless it is on [Name] Street where there are not too many people, and it is all spread out. In Walmart, everybody's on one aisle, and I don't really like that. I like being with my parents and my siblings [in this situation].

In Henry's scenario, he sees his family members as a safety strategy, similar to how women sometimes use men or girlfriends as escorts to help alleviate worry about crime. Since places with many people or tight spaces (like an aisle in Walmart) cause him to worry, he makes sure he is with family members who help him stay safe.

As should be clear from the findings provided by these studies, we can see how fear of crime is unique for kids and teenagers. Kids and teenagers may look out for bullies who congregate in groups within the neighborhood or use the "auditory bubble" and spatial avoidance as preventive strategies. These strategies are unique to kids.

In sum, we, the grown-ups of society, often think kids do not listen to what is being said by their parents, and perhaps we do not think of kids as having much agency. However, the studies presented here show that kids have a unique view of what they should fear and how to manage it. Kids' fears of strangers, darkness, and public spaces are directly translated from their parents' safety values and lessons. However, kids also have a different worldview than their parents. Children's differential worldviews are based on age but are also part of growing up in a different generation from their parents. Therefore, parents can more realistically and efficiently help their children navigate safety concerns by understanding kids' safety concerns.

Kids at School

Schools are another place where kids hear about safety and crime prevention.[20] My Swedish study and the U.S. Southern study with Heath and Hagerman have found that kids feel safe at school most of the time. These findings are consistent with large-scale surveys, which have found kids generally feel safe at school.[21] For example, according to the National Center for Education Statistics, in 2018, only 5 percent of school-aged children between the ages of 12 and 18 said they were worried about crime happening to them while at school.[22]

What does a fearful kid look like, and what are they most afraid of? When we look at the characteristics of scared kids in school, one study conducted by Mississippi State University researcher David May and West Virginia University researcher Gregory Dunaway surveyed a sample of Mississippi adolescents.[23] They found that perceptions of safety at school influenced youths' fear of crime. The more a kid perceived their school as unsafe, the more afraid of crime they were. May and Dunaway also found important gender and race differences.[24] School-aged girls were more afraid of crime than school-aged boys. However, whereas African American school-aged boys were more scared than white school-aged boys, the race of school-aged girls did not impact fear of crime.

Another study that provides some information on the characteristics of a fearful student was conducted by criminology researchers Christopher

Schreck and Mitchell Miller.[25] Using data from a nationally representative sample of students (the National Household Education Survey), they found that kids who attended schools with more preventative security measures were more afraid of crime. Also, kids who attended schools where official records pointed to gangs, weapons, or drug dealers had a higher fear of crime.

Thus, we can use these studies to understand the profile of a fearful student. Whereas most kids feel safe at school, kids in schools with more security measures or those from perceived vulnerable populations (girls, racial minorities) fear crime at a higher level.[26] However, we are unsure how this translates to other students, mainly because kids (especially young children) are not usually asked about what lessons they hear regarding safety at school and how these lessons influence kids' fear of crime.

According to kid participants in the studies I've been a part of, there are two primary safety messages kids learn at school: school shooting prevention and bullying prevention.

School Shooting Prevention

American children were more likely to talk about school shooting prevention than Swedish children because historically, American children have been more inundated with images of school shooters. In our Southern U.S. study, when kids were asked what they learned from school about safety, they told us that school officials focused almost exclusively on school shooting prevention. This should come as no surprise given our discussion in chapter 2 about schools and safety messaging surrounding school shootings. Noah, a child in the U.S. South, provides an example of what is learned at school through safety drills. As previously discussed, safety drills, emergency drills where kids prepare for the possibility of a school shooter, have become a standard part of educational programming at school.[27] Noah discussed what he heard from schools about safety, lessons that emphasized safety drills. He said:

> At school, we do stuff like fire drills and tornado drills. We do school shooting drills now, shooter drills, we call it, I guess. I guess that's pretty much all we do. And we do talk about safety from bullies, not really safety, but don't bully, we talk about that. But that's pretty much all safety-wise.

For Noah, he equates a safety drill with emergency weather procedures. "Shooter drills" are commonplace in schools for Gen Z kids.[28] While Noah also mentions learning about bullies at school, the focus is on bullies, not the prevention of bullying. Thus, for Noah, the primary messaging he is receiving at school is focused on school shootings.

Noah also talks about the impact of safety drills on his fear of crime levels. When he is asked if he feels safe at school, he says:

> Yeah, I feel safe at my school. I don't really [worry about] any threat, really. The only thing I would be scared of, probably, is a school shooting but it is pretty unlikely. Well, now it is more likely [than it used to be]. I'm not worried about it. I used to be. When I was younger, I had fear problems, and I used to be scared. Whenever a lockdown drill would happen, I would be scared. But not so much anymore.

So, for Noah, we can't know for sure that he fears school shootings because of ongoing safety drills. It could be that he fears school shootings because of the media or because of something his parents taught him. However, it does make logical sense that safety drills may cause Noah to be more afraid of school shootings. Also, given the rare and unpredictable nature of school shootings, we have to ask ourselves if the benefits of safety drills in schools outweigh the potential psychological damage children face from being forced to go through an exercise to prevent a rare school shooting.[29] For kids like Noah, fear of crime may be an unintended consequence of such school safety drills.

While Noah is greatly affected by safety drills, other kids we talk to are not as affected. For example, when we ask Amelia if she ever worries about safety at school, she tells us she does not. We then ask if she ever attended school safety talks. She says:

> AMELIA: Well, sometimes they do these weird internet safety videos, but it's very rare. Like, don't tell people your information, and that's basically it.
> INTERVIEWER: Do you feel safe at school?
> AMELIA: Yes.
> INTERVIEWER: Has there ever been a time when you maybe didn't feel safe at school?
> AMELIA: Nope.
> INTERVIEWER: Do you ever talk about stuff like school shootings or anything like that?
> AMELIA: When it just happens, maybe, or if it [a school shooting] was in the newspaper. We would just really talk about what happened.

While Amelia is a kid of few words, the words she says are essential here. As Amelia notes, while she is privy to the same safety lessons as all Gen Zers surrounding school safety, she also seems less affected by what she hears at school. The safety messages at school (the weird safety videos) don't provide her more comfort or alleviate any concerns, but they also do not seem to increase fear of crime, either. She also notes that they talk about school shootings but she doesn't seem that concerned about what she learns or hears.

There is not a lot of evidence that safety drills make children feel safer in schools. If the anecdotal responses of the participants here are any indication, procedures surrounding school shootings either make kids more afraid or have no impact on fear of crime at all.[30] We have such little research on kids' viewpoints on conversations with schools regarding safety. We can only speculate on the connection between what kids hear at school and what kids fear at school, and it seems a good place for future research studies to take a closer look.

Another pattern from the kids we've talked to involves the fluctuation of fear of crime among kids. In other words, fear of crime does not remain a static constant level for kids but changes depending on the situation. We saw this when we heard that Noah used to be afraid of school shootings but is not so much any longer. Joseph also provides an example; when he is asked if he ever worries about school shootings, he says:

> Yeah. I sometimes worry about that. When I first heard about the one in Florida, that kind of worried me because it's not good to do that at school because there are lots of kids who are too young, and I get scared sometimes when I hear about it and go to my school and like what if they're here? What if they're going to shoot up our school? And I'm just worried overall whenever I hear about it.

It seems clear that Joseph is very worried about school shootings, and we would expect this fear to be constant or pervasive throughout the school day or school year. However, when Joseph is asked if he talks to his parents or other people about his concerns, he replies, "Not really because I forget about it. Like throughout the day because I'm having fun and learning things, and I just forget about it, and I just don't think about it."

Joseph, then, showcases a critical point. Even though children sometimes fear school shootings happening at their schools, they also don't worry about school shootings happening all day or every day. It could be that children's fear of crime is more fluid than their parents' fears, especially in the school environment. However, we need to spend more time talking to kids to make sense of the contextual nature of fear of school shootings.

Bullying Prevention

Bullying at school is another point brought up by kids when we talk to them about safety concerns at school. For example, P.J., a Swedish middle schooler, talks about bullies. He says, "if it is bullying, I usually seek protection from my friends. Well, we don't often have bullying in my class, but all don't like [the name of boy], and one of the boys moved to a different school because of this boy."

P.J. indicates that he is worried about bullying, although he does not clearly state that is the case. However, he does tell us that he relies on his social network of friends at school to help him avoid bullies. This strategy is similar to the Van der Burgt study discussed above that found teens often use social networks as a crime prevention strategy.

McKenzie, a Southern participant, also talks about bullying when asked about safety concerns. She recalls talking to her mother about her fears about bullying at school. She says, "I mean, I usually talk about bullying if that is going on to anybody that I know or even if it is involving me sometimes."

McKenzie talks to her mother about bullying and the ways to work through bullying prevention. McKenzie implies that she has been bullied, although she doesn't clearly state that is the case. We are not told by McKenzie how her mother reacts or if she engages in help-seeking on her behalf.

Henry, another Southern respondent, also talks about relying on his parents to deal with bullying at school. He speaks of a bad experience he had when his hair was very long when he was younger. He says:

> In fifth grade, I had long hair. So I was bullied about it, and so it wasn't fun. People would tease me, and they would flip my hair when they would go by, so I told my parents, and they took care of it.... I was walking, and they [bullies] would—they did not like me having long hair, so they called me names and stuff, and I told my mom, so I got my hair cut.

In Henry's case, he was singled out for his hair—he describes these bullying experiences. The outcome of these experiences was to cut his hair, and while Henry does not explicitly discuss fear of crime, it makes intuitive sense that fear of future bullying experiences might stem from this experience.

There are a few commonalities to point out here. First, P.J., McKenzie, and Henry all talk about bullying as a safety concern. They could mention other crimes, but they bring up bullying. However, while they bring it up, they do not explicitly tell us that they feel unsafe or afraid of crime. Second, children's discussions of bullying at school are vague. The vague nature of conversations about bullying is a lesson to those who work with young people. It may be that talking about bullying is hard for kids, and they may not relate to or answer questions about being a victim to a bully. As is done in other victimization areas, focusing on bullying victimization indicators (e.g., someone with bruises, someone who is being made fun of on social media, someone who stops coming to school) may make more sense than more generally talking about bullying in school assemblies or through school educational campaigns

Another point is that kids we've talked to do not mention learning about bullying or bullying prevention from schools. This should be surprising given what we discussed in chapter 2. Schools are putting in great effort and dollars to curb bullying at school. However, it may be that the messages kids are taking away from these efforts are not what schools intend for them to hear. The kids we've talked to tell us that they feel more comfortable talking about bullying to their parents or close friends than school officials. Unlike school shooting prevention, kids do not see bullying prevention as a topic discussed by schools or as a legitimate focus of school programming. As mentioned in chapter 2, this is important because school officials believe they are teaching kids about bullying prevention. Still, these messages may be getting lost in translation (through the game of telephone) or might be overshadowed by conversations about school shooting prevention.

Other Things Learned from Kids

In addition to learning about strangers from parents and about school shooting prevention and bullying prevention from schools, three more findings will hopefully be a jumping-off point for researchers and administrators alike regarding children's fear of crime. First, rather than only asking kids about scary things, the Swedish and the U.S. Southern studies asked kids the opposite—that is, what makes kids feel safe. As we shall see, this slight change may be a more fruitful way to understand kids' experiences with safety and fear of crime. Second, the kids in the research studies I've been a part of talked about disguising their feelings of fear and why they did so.[31] The ability of kids to downplay or mask their fear is an essential indicator of children's agency and gives parents/schools insight into kids' fear of crime. Finally, we will discuss how kids teach other kids safety and fear of crime. This discussion will take us full circle to the beginning of this book, where we started by understanding how parents learned safety messages as children and passed these messages on to their own children. We'll close the safety learning loop by looking at how safety messages and fear of crime are taught to kids by other kids.

What Makes Kids Feel Safer?

Adults are usually asked about what makes them worry or makes them feel afraid. When kids are asked these questions, which is rare, the questions similarly revolve around fear and worry. However, because kids are different from adults in various ways, asking kids about feeling safe rather than afraid may garner better implications for policy. If we know what makes kids feel safe in the home, outside of it, and within schools, we may be able to build child-centered safety programs.

The first finding is something that kids talk about in both studies, and it will likely be a pleasant surprise to many people reading this book. Kids, even pre-teenagers, tell us that their families and their parents make them feel safe. For example, McKenzie, a Southern respondent, tells us, "I feel pretty safe because of my mom [laughing]. She would do anything to save me." Louisa, a Swedish respondent, tells me that her father makes her feel safe, and Anton, another Swedish respondent, says to me that his mom and dad make him feel safe. Most of the kids in these studies talk about their families/parents making them feel safer.

The kids from these studies also talk to us about the importance of place or their community in making them feel safe. One thing they mention is that growing up in a small town makes them feel safer. For example, when talking about why they are less worried about school shootings than they might be otherwise, Amelia says: "I don't know. I just think that would happen more in the bigger cities." Another kid from the United States, Josiah, also talks about feeling safe because he lives in a smaller community. He says:

> But I still feel safe at my school. Like, just lock the door, and then they have to like get in, and then we have a lot of sharp things in there we can fight back with. We're in a small town, too. So, it's pretty unlikely that any mentally insane someone will come in.

Finally, Henry specifically explains the importance of place:

> Well, we don't have any big cities, and there's not a ton of people that aren't from [name of state]. Everybody is really nice there because it is kind of a small town and everybody knows each other, so it's really fun. Some of the parents went to school together, like my base-

ball coach knows my daddy and my football coach, so it's cool. It's really cool.

So, growing up in a small town creates a sense of community for the kids in our studies. While we don't have other studies to compare the Swedish and U.S. studies to, we can rely on researchers who study the importance of place and of having a sense of community.[32] Canadian researchers at McMaster University Peter Kitchen and colleagues define a "sense of community belonging as a social attachment among individuals, which involves 'social engagement' and 'participation in communities.'"[33] They use Statistics Canada, an extensive representative data set, to assess how others' sense of community belonging might tie into the health of Canadian residents. It turns out that people who have a greater understanding of belonging in their community have less depression and stress.

Further, the relationship between a sense of community and health depended on the size of the place. For example, respondents who lived in smaller communities reported a stronger sense of community. Unfortunately, the study did not examine how safety concerns might impact a sense of belonging among Canadian residents. Still, we can imagine how having a sense of belonging might be a protective factor for kids.

The takeaways here are that kids might feel safer because there is a sense of community belonging in their smaller communities.[34] Because they feel this sense of community, they may feel less fear or worry about safety. We also know that people who live in smaller communities are more likely to have social networks and relationships with others within the community. We might apply this information by putting fewer kids in each classroom, allowing the children and their parents to form more secure social networks.

The kids in the Swedish and Southern U.S. studies also discuss teachers as an element that makes them feel safer. For example, Joseph from the United States talks about how teachers make kids feel safe. He says, "yeah. I feel like there is trust [at] school. The teachers are nice, and I feel like they can trust me, and I can trust them."

So for Joseph, having a sense of trust in the school and with teachers, in particular, is essential for him to feel safe. Holly also talks about teachers alleviating safety concerns for her. She says:

> Because I always want to stay safe but not really because I know our teachers will take care of us, and if anything happens, I know our teachers will handle it, but I don't really—like I do worry about these things and stuff I try to always do things to keep me safe.

Another kid from the United States talks about teachers as well. When Oliver is asked if he worries about crime, he says: "No, because I think the teachers could break it up. There are a couple of teachers that have broken up a fight this year, and they've done fine." So, for Oliver, teachers at school provide a sense of security.

The mere presence of teachers can alleviate kids' fears and make them feel more at ease while at school. These findings mirror the study by U.S. Department of Education researchers Deborah Lessne and Christine Yanez, who found that kids felt safer in environments where they believed teachers at their school would help or care for them.[35] Students may believe that teachers would take care of a potentially dangerous situation or reduce the chances of victimization, which can alleviate worry.

In addition to discussing certain places (small towns) and people (teachers) that make them feel safe, kids also discuss how various things within a school make them feel safer. Preventative measures have been the source of much research about adults. For example, we've talked about the preventive and precautionary measures taken by women for self-protection and also by parents who want to protect their children.[36] However, we are not sure how preventative techniques impact kids' views of a safer community. As discussed above, Schreck and Miller found that security measures in schools did not permanently alleviate fear of crime.[37] As I also mentioned above, the studies I've been a part of have found that school safety drills do not make kids feel safer. However, two things in the Swedish and Southern U.S. studies made the kids we've talked to feel safer and are worth mentioning.[38] First, kids talk about the importance of ID badges at school. For example, one respondent says:

> I feel a lot safer at [name of school] because we have our IDs now, and they care a lot more about passes since a lot of the kids look grownup. Like eighth-graders, they look like a lot—kind of like adults. So they make the sixth graders walk with teachers for anything, but unless it's like to go to the front office or something, they give you passes. And we have to wear our IDs. If they don't see that you have an ID on, they're like, where's your ID? And if you don't have your ID, they'll either send you back to your teacher or say, where's your hall pass?

In this case, the ID badge serves as a way for kids to know that others in the hallway (others they may not know) belong in the school. They can be assured that those people are not intruders.

Another participant talks about the importance of locks and the possibility of barricading from potential offenders if needed. Hope says:

And I don't think A Building would be, either. Cause we have multiple buildings, and well, B Building is the first building that if you drive up, you would see it. So, it would be B and C. And I feel like the back building, E, and go upstairs would be the safest really because you'd have to go through all of the buildings to get there. And there are multiple ways to get in, but there are also multiple ways that you cannot get in. They always keep the gate locked, for instance. Let's say for electives, if the electives are not going on, they lock the gates. You can only go through a [specific] gate if you are a teacher and the teacher allows you to because there's gates leading out and stuff like that. So, I feel like we'd be very safe at our school, and if that does happen, we would be scared because we wouldn't know what is happening. They wouldn't tell us for own safety.

As is apparent from these two kids, such protective measures make them feel safer. This is interesting because most of the research with adults talks about these precautionary measures as causing more fear or having a feedback loop.[39] When we don't talk to kids themselves, we miss out on the opportunity to learn what kids do when they are worried about safety and how this influences their fear of crime. Future research should focus on this area since it may tell us a lot about making children feel safer at school.

Disguising Fear and Teaching Others

Another interesting finding of these studies involves kids' ability to disguise their feelings of fear. I've found adult women also sometimes hide their feelings of anxiety to keep their kids from feeling afraid. Moms do not want their kids to worry, for example, so they downplay their concerns to their children. However, I am unaware of other studies that consider how kids disguise feelings of fear and under what circumstances. Among the Swedish and Southern U.S. studies, kids mask the fear of crime for several reasons. First, while not the focus of this book, many children have childhood fears that have nothing to do with crime or safety. Kids may fear various things like snakes, bugs, thunderstorms, monsters under the bed or in the closet, or scary movies. Second, as we've discussed in this chapter, kids also fear certain things because they are worried about crime. In both cases (childhood fears and fear about crime), kids may decide to disguise fear if they don't think their fear is valid.

This was apparent in our interviews when we asked kids how they disguised feelings of fear to others and with whom they shared their fear. Lisa, a Swedish respondent, provides an excellent example of how fear and imagination work together. She says:

So, most of the time, my mom knows what I think is scary, but otherwise, when there's something really—when there's something scary, I usually tell her. But sometimes, when I think it might sound too ridiculous, or there may be too many explanations, then I don't tell my mother because I'm thinking it would be silly.

Lisa doesn't talk about her fears sometimes because she thinks her parents would find her fears silly or trivial.

Payton, a Southern child also speaks about how she feels afraid and comes up with scenarios to get out of her house if a stranger enters, but she doesn't feel comfortable telling her parents about these plans because she thinks they might not take her very seriously. She explains:

> I remember recently last week; I was with my friend. I had my friend over. I showed her what I was going to do if I ever heard a robber come to my house. And I have this closet. . . . It is one of those where these two doors open up, and they fold in half. My room is at the top floor [and the closet is] slanted, which I think is cool. I put my feet up there. Since it's curved, the door where the hangers are, like the metal pole. It can't go all the way back because then there's only about from here to here with this much space. There's a good bit of room, about this much room in the back of a slanted [closet]. My plan is if there's ever a robber—I never talked about this with my parents. I always think of weird scenarios in my head if things like that ever happen. I would get out of my bed. And if I had time, I would grab a little, tiny, pocket knife that I keep in a purse. Well, I don't really know. If I had time pending. I'll part my clothes in the hangers. I would climb over. Because there's a little drawer also to keep my shorts and stuff. It can also be a hiding place. I'd also have to grab my phone. When they go away, I could call somebody or something or warn my parents before they got upstairs. This has never happened, but I practiced it with my friend.

Payton's story gives us a birds-eye view into her world and showcases how children make sense of safety during their childhoods. Payton has thought through plans for protecting herself from a robber, creating a safety drill with her friend who pretends to be a robber. She also thinks about things through a child's eyes by telling us all about her closet and her fear of being alone and that she believes she has a plan that would prevent a crime. Finally, and perhaps most importantly, she does not share these plans or her fears with her parents, indicating that she believes her parents might think her safety plans are not worth fearing or wasting energy on. While she doesn't name these feelings, the fact that she has developed such a detailed plan yet not shared it with her parents suggests this might be the case.

Whether fear of strangers entering the home, fear of bullies at school, or childhood fears like a fear of ghosts, kids' ability to move between these arenas is more advanced than we may be giving children credit. They can name their anxiety and can articulate why they are afraid of these specific things. Further, they can hide their fear of crime from others if they feel it is best to do so.

Another critical point to consider is why kids might feel they need to disguise their fears about crime from their parents. While there may be a lot of possible explanations, there are four that stand out to me. One possibility is that kids disguise their fear of crime from parents because they do not want their parents to worry that they are worried. Put another way, kids in this category may believe their fears would be an unnecessary burden on their parents and so they pretend they are not afraid.

As we see from Lisa, a second possibility is that kids disguise their fear of crime because they don't want their parents to think they are silly or childish. Kids might want their parents to see them as more grown-up and think being afraid of things is weak. This possibility would fall in line with what researchers know about gender differences. Boys who show emotion are often portrayed as soft or not manly. As British researcher Jo Goodey found in her study, boys are taught that crying and other emotions are unacceptable for men.[40] As part of masculinity and "doing masculinity," boys do not show emotion.[41] Even for girls (like Lisa above), it may be the case that they do not want to be viewed as childish by their parents.

A third possibility is that kids do not have confidence in their parents' safety messages. For example, a child may disguise fear of crime because they have a parent who is overly worried and takes too many precautions on their behalf. On the other hand, it could be that the child views their parents' safety values as paranoid and does not want to tell parents about fear to avoid additional restrictions or supervision of their daily activities.

Finally, and perhaps most simply put, kids may disguise their feelings of fear to avoid additional conversations with their parents about safety. Some kids, especially pre-teens, may want to avoid the extra time talking to parents. Because of the lack of research with children about where they learn safety messages and the impact of safety messages on fear of crime and psychological well-being, we cannot generalize to all children. Still, the information from these kids is telling.

Kids Teaching Other Kids

The name of this book is *Teaching Fear*. In this last section, we close the social learning loop by seeing how kids teach other kids what they know, believe, and fear regarding crime. We've debunked the idea that kids have no thoughts or opinions about safety and crime. We have opened the door to talk about how kids teach other kids about safety. There are two ways that researchers can consider how kids teach fear to other kids. The first is by listening to stories that come up organically about teaching safety lessons to other kids. While not "teaching fear" per se, kids may unknowingly be teaching fear to others. For example, Iza, a Swedish participant, talks about how this process works for her when talking to a friend. She says:

> So, I talked to my friend about this. A lot of people think she's my little sister, but she's not. But we talked about this because, in third grade, she is also gonna get to go home alone from school, but her parents haven't talked to her about how to stay safe, so I've talked to her a bit about that.

It is also interesting to note that Iza sees herself as a "big sister" to her friend and perhaps feels an added caretaking responsibility for her friend's safety.

Caroline, a Southern child in the United States, also mentions conversations about safety with a little sister. She says, "I trust my little sister, she is responsible, and she knows what to do. She already knows [what to do], but [I tell her] you just keep the door locked, don't answer unless it is a friend or Mommy or Daddy, or me." Caroline tells us she has faith in her sister to take care of herself, but just in case, she follows up with some advice points to keep doors locked and only answer for someone the sister knows.

Finally, Alice, a Swedish respondent, teaches other kids about bullying by serving as a peer mentor at her school. She explains it like this:

> So I'm a peer mediator, and so during the breaks, we have a certain designated time where we help people solve their conflicts. At first, we are taught specific phrases to use by our teachers. Then next time there are training sessions, these students teach other students, and so on and so forth, so eventually, we have maybe about 50 peer mediators that are out and available at different times.

Schools have implemented the peer mentor program model by giving agency and power to kids to help combat bullying behaviors. Alice teaches bullying prevention techniques to other kids, thus teaching safety values regarding this specific crime.

These examples with Iza, Caroline, and Alice showcase the ability of children to teach other children safety values and beliefs. In these cases, the safety values reinforce what the children have been taught. Such traditional safety lessons may increase the fear of strangers among kids, especially when home alone.[42] Alice's story, though, gives us a different outlook. Alice gives us a kid-centered crime prevention program where peer mediators intervene when bullying occurs. In the case of peer mediator prevention programs for bullying in schools, we see a more recent and perhaps less traditional safety message emerge.[43] The safety message here is to be a good bystander (when you see something, say something to peer mediators), a message that emphasizes power and agency among children and also focuses on a crime with a potentially known victim/offender.[44] Alice, a peer mentor, teaches kids how to mediate conflicts and decrease bullying behaviors. It is difficult to say how these less traditional safety messages will translate to adult behavior among Alice and her fellow peer mentors. Still, these types of programs provide hope that teaching fear and safety messages can be done differently.

Another way we can learn about kids teaching fear is to ask them directly if they do so. For example, I have always asked all participants I've interviewed: what safety advice would you give others about how to stay safe from crime? I have found answers to this question fruitful to understand fear of crime and safety practices. Questions about advice to others also help us understand kids' safety beliefs and practices. The answers to this question provide insight into how kids would teach fear and safety to other kids if they needed to or were given the opportunity. For example, one way children teach other children about safety seems to rely on respect for authority and trust in adults. Holly, a Southern U.S. child, provides the best example. She says:

> Listen to your teachers or your parents. Because if we had to do that [give advice to other kids] . . . I would tell them to be safe, listen to your teachers, and only listen to your teacher. Don't listen to anybody else because you don't know what they want. You always know that your teacher will keep you safe or your mom and dad will keep you safe, don't listen to anybody else.

So, for Holly, trusting authority figures is an essential piece of advice. Another Southern U.S. respondent, Noah, also stresses the importance of listening to parents. He says:

> I guess just know who you're talking to. If it's a stranger, don't approach them unless you need to kind of thing. And if they do

approach you, just be polite and always be ready if you need to run. I guess it depends on the age range of the kid. If it's an eight-year-old, just tell them to stay with their parents kind of thing, I guess. Just listen to their parents.

Noah's advice is about stranger danger and focuses on the importance of teaching others to listen to parents and authority figures to determine what to do to stay safe.

These safety messages perpetuate children's reliance on authority to understand what and who is safe and what and who is appropriate to fear.

Finally, Henry provides an example of focusing on listening to authority figures and trusting them to keep kids safe. He says:

> Just to watch out for people you don't really trust or strangers trying to talk to you and not really acting too friendly and just be safe when you're out in public places or if you don't feel safe at school, just tell somebody. Maybe that could be—somebody could make you feel safer.

For Henry, there is again a focus on stranger danger and public spaces. We don't know who the "somebody" Henry refers to is: a teacher, administrator, or peer mediator (if there is one available). Still, it seems likely that it is someone in an authority position. So, fearing strangers in public spaces and asking for teachers' help if you have issues at school are ways that Henry would teach other kids to worry about crime.

As should be clear, when we talk to kids themselves, we see that they teach fear in particular ways. There is still a focus on stranger danger and public spaces. There is also advice given on trusting authority figures and even respected peer mediators at school. Being a good bystander (helping someone who is potentially in a dangerous situation) seems to be a message that kids today are getting more than grown-ups did as children. Perhaps this safety message will slightly alter how these kids grow up to teach others.

To sum up, talking to children, especially regarding what they think about safety, their concerns, why they have these concerns, and what they do about them, is a sporadic practice in criminology. Researchers, including me at times, have assumed that parents can serve as a proxy for their children, or, in other words, that we can understand children through the eyes of their parents.[45] However, as my research studies with my colleagues in the United States and my study in Sweden have shown, children do not always have the same opinions about safety as their parents.[46] Also, children may not always hear the same messages that parents and schools intend to teach them. These findings show the importance of children's agency. If children were merely sponges, they would internalize the exact safety messages presented by their parents. Disguising feelings of fear of crime and teaching others are clear examples of how children have agency in their safety values and behaviors. Whether they hear the correct message from parents or not (in the game of telephone), what children do with these messages and how they incorporate them into their lives needs more research. Also, researchers need to talk more to children about what they think about safety, where they've learned about it, and how safety concerns impact their daily lives. Only through doing so will we understand how we teach fear to children and how children teach other children.

We know that parents can instill safety values that kids can use with agency and confidence. There is an important takeaway here. Parents can change the cycle of succumbing to myths about crime. They do not have to follow the script on safety values; they do not have to teach fear the way they were taught. In the next chapter, we turn to ways we can teach fear better as parents, teachers, and community members.

6
How to Teach Fear Better

In this book, we've covered a lot of ground about gendered crime myths: where they come from, how they impact women in particular, and why such myths persist in society. Myths are fueled by unrealistic victimization fears, notions of boogieman offenders, white women victims, and victim-centered prevention strategies. We teach these fears to others, passing gendered crime myths down from generation to generation. To break the cycle, we need to teach fear differently.

Fear is not necessarily a bad thing. Scientists have found that fear can propel people away from dangers.[1] We do not need to alleviate fear of crime completely, only teach fear more accurately. By teaching (and then normalizing) more appropriate safety values and fear of crime, individuals, armed with correct information, will first and foremost have appropriate images of victims, offenders, and crime. Reality-based images of crime and victimization will give individuals the tools they need to make better decisions about crime prevention.

As we've learned, because crime myths are gendered, fear of crime is often a woman's issue. The gender-fear paradox has been a large part of the discussion in the criminological literature on this topic.[2] Women fear crime at higher levels than is generally warranted when considering victimization chances. Since fear of crime primarily affects women, we need to examine women's fear of crime independent of men. Crimes against women and women's fear of crime are just different from men's victimization and fear of crime experiences. To better understand women's fear of crime and to teach fear better, we need focus on gender-specific theoretical models for women. Further, there are ways that individuals and society can change the image of the crime victim and gendered crime myths.

What Society Can Do

While individuals (both men and women) can debunk gendered crime myths, it is vital to start with the acknowledgement that substantial social forces have supported gendered crime myths. As we discussed in chapter 1, when an issue is considered a social problem (like drugs, crime, global warming), larger institutions (e.g., schools, the criminal justice system) construct issues in specific ways.[3] Groups that hold weight, like legislators, corporations, and the media, sell the constructed images to the public. These groups influence the public and frame the issues in the way they see fit.[4] In the case of women's fear of crime, several institutions hold weight: the media, the criminal justice system, family, and schools have all played a critical role in shaping the image of the crime victim. Society has a responsibility to depict crime accurately, and these institutions are a place to start to change these images.

The Criminal Justice System

The criminal justice system has power to change the image of the woman crime victim. The first way the system can do this is to recognize all victims as worthy victims. The job of the criminal justice system is to solve a crime, reduce victimization, and make society a safer place. Unfortunately, the criminal justice system is too often a place where victims are judged, made to feel invisible, or blamed for victimization.[5] As we've discussed, sexual assault victims are expected to meet the perfect or ideal victim status, but the actual crime victim rarely matches up with the perfect victim: a woman who has no relationship with her assailant, is viewed as having a pristine moral character, and looks like the victims we see on television (white young women).[6] Women victims are judged on their choices (because of the emphasis on victim-centered prevention) both pre- and post-victimization.[7] Thus, women who knew the offender, were at a social event, were out late at night, had a romantic relationship with the offender, or were not white are more likely to be blamed for their victimization.

The ways police officers interact with women crime victims, then, impact how these victims get through a victimization experience. Sexual assault is a highly under-reported crime, and research has continually shown that victims have negative experiences when reporting victimization. Perceptions of police agencies, then, may play a role in the under-reporting of sexual assault partly because of fear of victim blame. The bottom line here is that there is no place in policing for judging victims. It does not help solve cases, catch offenders, or make the world a safer place. Policing agencies can do better by taking the ideal victim metric out of the equation.

Social service agencies also need to be more involved in sexual assault cases. Currently, social service agencies play a small role in sexual assaults reported to the police. Some agencies have sexual assault nurse examiners, victim advocates, or social workers on call.[8] However, social service agencies and police agencies are not seen as equal partners. Victim advocates are there to talk to the victim upon their arrival, but they are not there to be part of the investigation. This makes some sense since victim advocates and nurses are not trained in law enforcement. Even so, more can be done to ensure victim service involvement.[9] Another suggestion would be to make victim services a more significant component of police officer training. Instead of only teaching police officers to catch criminals, we need to do a better job training police officers how to interact with and serve crime victims. Police officers will undoubtedly have better interactions with crime victims if they are taught interpersonal skills, communication skills, and ways to work with people in crisis.

Another way that police agencies can do better is through recruiting people from all demographics. Research has found that having police officers of various backgrounds minimizes mistreatment of victims. By having more racial/ethnic and gender diversity on police forces, police agencies become better. These police forces are better able to serve victims and offenders from various backgrounds and can provide unique perspectives on problem-solving.

These types of changes are not unheard of in policing. For example, agencies have chosen to emphasize community policing at greater levels so that agencies can build relationships within their communities. Community policing happens when police officers spend more time interacting with the community during non-arrests or times of peace.[10] Community policing requires police officers to get to know those in the community who may become or may already be offenders and requires a different skill set than shooting a gun, chasing down an offender, or assessing a dangerous situation. Community policing requires people skills and challenges officers to mediate conflicts in new ways. Similar training, procedures, and protocols could be put into place for working with victims.[11]

Criminal justice programs, typically carried out by local police agencies, also need to focus on societal rather than individual responsibility for victimization. For example, bystander intervention programming is an excellent place to start. "If you see something, say something" educational campaigns have become more common lately. Educational campaigns like bystander intervention programs focus on what we can ALL do to alleviate victimization. For example, bystander prevention teaches women, men, and children to look out for others and act if they see something wrong. Also, by making victim prevention a social problem instead of an individual problem, we will influence how we teach safety values and subsequent fear of crime.

So, police agencies and criminal justice programming can do better in their treatment of victims, training of officers, and victim prevention programming.

The Media

The media is one of the most powerful sources of inaccurate victim images.[12] While the media may not directly cause fear of crime, it most certainly contributes to normalizing gendered crime myths.[13] As discussed in chapter 2, the media over-emphasizes women crime victims and stranger danger and makes the viewer think that crimes can be solved under false conditions and with flawed victim prevention strategies.[14] The media need to be held more accountable for spreading crime myths in society. This is especially the case with the news media, who are supposed to be giving accurate news to viewers. The idea of if "it bleeds, it leads" and "looping," where stories are looped over and over again, make crime seem much worse than it is and increase fear of crime unnecessarily. Some crimes are more attractive to viewers than others (violent crime versus property crime, stranger offender versus known offender), but facts, not fiction, need to prevail here.[15] Viewers need to be more aware of the contextual backstories of cases and be given the outcomes of criminal cases (even if those outcomes are given years later). Additionally, the media also contribute to the gendered nature of crime myths. Whether it be from sexualizing women on television or only showing white women as crime victims, the image of women victims is distorted through the media.[16]

Further, viewers need to understand how the media make decisions when they pick up stories and television shows. A handful of corporations own most networks, so these networks often show what the these corporations deem worthy. Viewers should also understand that various news agencies often recycle the same news story within a corporation. While the media business model will likely never change, public knowledge about how things work would give viewers context. Viewers should understand that white victims are shown more frequently because corporations have deemed these stories worthy.[17] The media, then, can do better in providing accurate information to viewers about crime, victimization, and crime prevention.

Schools

There is a disconnect between criminological research on school safety and what often ends up in federally mandated school safety programs.[18] Federal agencies need to provide accurate knowledge to local school officials on ways to make better decisions. More accurate information at the federal level will trickle down to local school officials. Thus, these federal mandates and programs are the key to revamping victim prevention programming at school. That way, school officials at the local level can also do better by accurately portraying and preventing victimization for staff, faculty, and students.

School shooting prevention programming is a place where federally mandated programs have influenced local-level school districts. It seems illogical that shooting fake blood at actors and putting children in closets while they listen to bullet sounds would significantly decrease school shootings. Further, as discussed earlier, we know that crime prevention programs surrounding safety drills have not been successful at reducing fear of crime.[19] By understanding that school shootings are rare and what crimes are more likely to happen within schools, officials can improve crime prevention efforts. The cost-benefit analysis here is that current school shooter drills may leave kids traumatized, confused, and experiencing more fear of crime.[20] Should schools continue to do drills, more research needs to confirm what impact they have on children.

One suggestion would be for schools to conduct focus groups with children after safety drill exercises. This would give kids the opportunity to talk about how these drills made them feel and provide feedback on school violence prevention plans. The focus groups could conclude with school officials providing accurate information about school shootings to the kids (which would hopefully be sent home to their parents, also). So, while children would be prepared for the potential of a school shooting by doing drills, they would also be given accurate information about the rarity of school shootings, which may alleviate some kids' fear. Further, schools would be incorporating children's feedback on ways to improve safety drills.

Schools also need more of a focus on crime prevention efforts concerning interpersonal violence. In the case of bullying (both cyber and traditional bullying), bullying prevention campaigns seem to be missing the mark, as they are not resonating with students. Because of the nature of Gen Z children, who have a vast knowledge of innovative ways to bully others through social media and in online spaces, a revamp of bullying prevention programs are needed. Simply restricting use of cyber space while at school (e.g., telling children that cell phones cannot be used at school, locking down browsers, and monitoring school assigned chromebooks or iPads) will not curb bullying behavior or create a more welcoming environment for students.

One suggestion is to take a serious look at peer mediation bullying prevention programs. As these programs are being developed, children should be part of the development team. The creation of student-centered programs will ensure that the viewpoint of students are accounted for and will also help with getting children on board when it is time to implement the program. It also holds kids accountable to other kids and gives leaders in the school the opportunity to solve problems (a good skill for resilience). Student-centered programs may have more of an impact on bullying and fear of bullying than we see with current programs.

Schools can also play a more prominent role in preventing family violence. As we've already discussed, the most likely group to hurt children is family members, including parents.[21] Schools are trying to control crime while at school (understandably), but they can also help serve children who need protection from those at home. School officials, including teachers, are mandatory reporters; thus, if they see evidence of family violence, they are required by law to report their suspicions. However, many victims of family violence do not talk to a teacher and go unnoticed by other students because they are fearful of retaliation, perhaps feel shame and embarrassment, and may not know who they can trust. Children victims of family violence may also feel they are somewhat to blame for what is happening to them, even though this is not the case.[22]

Since family violence is more common than school shootings, schools should make family violence a more significant proportion of crime prevention educational campaigns. Again, teaching bystander intervention may be a good strategy. For example, perhaps a child tells a friend something is happening at home, and the friend reaches out to an adult. By doing so, the friend has helped the child in need without causing confrontation between the children. If conversations about family violence prevention are normalized in schools, kids may feel more comfortable coming forward themselves or coming forward on behalf of another person who needs help. These educational programs should also provide specific behavioral indicators of family violence. Adding behavioral statements (behaviors to look out for) to campaigns about physical, emotional, and sexual violence may help children recognize family violence and seek out help—or seek help for others.[23]

Finally, teachers need to be better trained on family violence.[24] The notion that family violence is only a physical form of violence is not an accurate depiction of what family violence looks like in the real world. Teachers are currently trained to notice when students make great efforts to hide bruises, but there are other potential cues teachers should be looking for when interacting with children. For example, children who experience violence in the home may act out in class, may have hygiene issues, may engage in unhealthy behaviors like drugs or smoking, and may struggle academically. It is easy to label these kids as "bad kids" or "problem kids" and write them off, but these behaviors may be from kids who are crying out for help.[25] It is essential that teachers also take the bystander prevention model seriously.

What We Can Do

White Women

I've laid out the case that embedded gendered crime myths cause women to fear crime at higher levels. These gendered crime myths primarily target white women, and one could argue that society has built an empire around the white woman as a crime victim myth. By naming the myths and explaining how they are learned and apply to white women, I hope to break the cycle of this myth.

The focus on white women does not mean that fear of crime is a white woman's issue. We cannot simply believe that women of color, especially Black and Latina women, do not have experiences with fear of crime. An extension of this book must be to try to understand the fears of other racial and ethnic groups of women. For example, why do Black and Latina women not express fear crime even though they are more likely to be crime victims? Is it because they are also sold similar images of the white woman as a crime victim? Is it because society sees victims of color as less worthy of media attention (the missing white woman syndrome)? Is it because researchers (often white, as I am) primarily talk to white participants?

The answers to these questions, the focus of my next project, will give insight into the specific details of what women of color fear, why they fear it, how they teach it, and what they do about it. How important is the combination of gender and race in how they "do fear"? What best explains the women of color fear paradox or why they fear crime less but are more likely to be victims of crime? By changing the research participants, we open the door to understanding women of color, especially Black and Latina women, and their experiences with fear of victimization. Because white women are the primary target audience for victimization prevention campaigns, media stories, and social learning processes studied by researchers, having a solid understanding of these larger institutionalized images will hopefully steer this ship in the right direction. I anticipate doing so in my next research project. But, first, there are some things white women can do to help break gendered and racialized fear of crime socialization.

First, white women need to realize that they are afraid of the wrong things for the wrong reasons. Acknowledging this reality is the first step to debunking crime myths. The men and women of society have been sold snake oil—a false cure for a false illness. It is one thing if a single person believes a fictious claim, but it is another if most people in society also believe it. What this means for white women is that changing internal attitudes, beliefs, and actions is deeply challenging. The white woman crime victim myth is one that will not easily be debunked without a lot of work by a lot of people. One thing white women can do is be gender forward thinking—be change makers when it comes to the rules of gender. As we've learned here, gendered fear of crime, especially for white women, is often based on traditional gender norms. Therefore, by acting in ways that fall outside the norm of gendered crime prevention, white women can take the first step to debunk myths. Among other things, white women, then, can make safety precautions less gendered.

Second, white women must recognize that avoidance is a privilege, and they should not rely on myths when making decisions about where to go and what to do. For example, if you are a white woman and need to go to the grocery store when it is getting dark, don't let fear stop you from doing so. If you want to go for a walk alone but don't have your spouse or a buddy to go with you, go anyway. Throw away that old can of mace. These small changes can make a big impact on thinking about safety precautions in a different manner.

Third, white women, because of their privilege as white people, have more of an ability to make change at the structural level. By acting as good allies and supporting victims, white women may have more power to help spread accurate gendered safety images. Specifically, if you are a white woman, be an ally to those deemed invisible by the criminal justice system, especially women victims of color. Spread accurate information to others about victimization chances (especially that yours are low) and be a good listener and bystander to women of color.[26] For various institutional reasons, women victims of color do not have as many opportunities or help-seeking resources, and having powerful allies can make a difference.

Finally, if you are a white woman, recognize that society uses fear of crime to control women. Your chances of victimization will not be significantly lessened by avoiding public areas, fearing strangers, or taking a dozen precautions each day. If white women can conceptualize fear of crime as a way to control them and put them into little gendered boxes, they may be less likely to tolerate it. Doing so may help teach fear better to white children, who would otherwise grow up to continue the transmission of myth-based fear to others.

Parents

Society has set gendered rules for us. The rules of gender are taken for granted and stem from powerful social institutions that emphasize traditional gender norms.[27] These institutions hold men and women responsible when they fall outside the scope of what is deemed "appropriate" for their gender.[28] When it comes to the family institution, parents are also held accountable for gendered actions and behaviors. We know from the research that moms bear the brunt of parenting tasks, even in the most egalitarian of relationships.[29]

How we teach fear in households is also gendered. Moms are responsible for teaching children about victimization prevention and often do so in traditional ways. They tend to teach daughters to fear crime and teach sons not to fear crime. Moms do so through both verbal safety lessons (e.g., telling daughters "do not go home with someone you do not know after school") and non-verbal cues (e.g. avoiding public spaces at night, avoiding certain areas). Moms also teach sons not to fear crime by allowing them more agency and freedom in unsupervised play because they are boys. These lessons teach boys they are invincible to crime and need not fear it.

Dads, on the other hand, while responsible for protecting the home and family, tend to be very hands-off in teaching their children about crime prevention. Children often see dads doing fear work for the family (e.g., locking doors; owning a weapon; checking on things outside the home, where noises or potential intruders seem to lurk).[30] Children view dads as unafraid of crime and as someone they can turn to if they need protection. Kids, then, eventually grow up to incorporate their views of dads and moms as part of their own safety values.

Both moms and dads can break the cycle by teaching gender-neutral safety values. The advice for dads is to make a conscious effort not to reinforce traditional gender norms or gendered crime myths. For example, do not over-supervise daughters and under-supervise sons in recreational activities. Dads can also give daughters the same opportunities for risk-taking that they give to sons. By seeing daughters as independent and confident beings, dads will ultimately help daughters build resiliency skills. Dads need to teach sons about gendered power dynamics, respect for women, and the importance of consent in relationships. Dads who model this behavior will be more likely to have sons who grow up to have more gender-equal relationships in their own families.

To break the cycle of teaching fear in traditionally gendered ways, moms will first need to think about their own actions and behaviors. By modeling less gendered behavior to daughters and sons, children will be more likely to grow up with egalitarian values. Moms might tell their children not to worry about something happening, but if they constantly take precautions to prevent that something from happening, children may grow up to fear crime anyway. The bottom line here is that children are always watching parents, especially moms. While it is unfair that moms are more responsible for teaching safety values to children, these gendered standards continue to be part of society. Thus, moms will need to really change how they act and what verbal lessons they give their children in order to break the cycle of gendered safety lessons. Both moms and dads can change things by teaching accurate information about crime and safety, allowing children more freedom, teaching kids to take care of each other, and recognizing the unique challenges facing Gen Z kids.

Flip the Script

While parents focus safety talks on stranger danger, the boogieman is a myth.[31] Now that parents know this information, they can teach children about safety and what to fear in a different way. It's most important that parents give their children the tools they need to look out for themselves. Children do not need to be thrown out to the wolves, but we can teach children how to better assess interactions with strangers and how to navigate perceived dangerous situations.

First, rather than teaching children to completely avoid strangers, parents can teach kids to explore their feelings about whether or not strangers are dangerous. Parents might start by allowing their child to talk to people whom parents know but kids do not (in other words, those who are strangers to the child), like a colleague or friend. After the interaction, the parents could discuss what the child thought about the person, whether they liked or disliked them, and how the interaction made them feel. Parents are sometimes guilty of focusing on manners instead of honesty. So, if a child says that they don't like someone or dislikes something about someone, parents' first instinct is often to tell them they are being impolite. By emphasizing politeness over honesty, we unknowingly teach children that when they feel uncomfortable in social interactions, they should not talk about it and should not trust their feelings. Children need to trust their instincts when they enter a situation that makes them feel uncomfortable.

By opening up communication with children about feelings of fear, parents avoid painting all strangers as "bad" or dichotomizing strangers as either good or bad people. Currently, parents teach the message that all strangers are bad, but by teaching children that there are good and bad strangers, children will have more confidence in trusting their feelings. I have found this when speaking with Swedish parents.[32] While these parents also reinforced stranger danger messages, they were more likely to talk about variations in strangers. Swedish parents emphasized that not all strangers were boogiemen. Swedish parents did engage in the same stranger danger messaging for those they deemed "bad" strangers, but they also made it clear there were "good" strangers. Variations in stranger danger for Swedish children might partially explain the lower fear of crime levels we see in Sweden.

Parents' safety lessons should also focus on features rather than only outcomes of crimes. By giving kids the tools they need to be confident in themselves, kids can better decipher the features *and* the outcomes of safety lessons. For example, if a child comes to a parent in the middle of the night after having a bad dream, the parent might tell the child there is nothing to fear and to go back to sleep. When a parent is at a park with a child, they may tell a child to stay away from strangers but not precisely explain why. In both cases, the parent focuses on the outcome, not the features, of the situation. Children are told they should not fear, for example, monsters under the bed, but they should fear strangers in the park. What distinguishes the monster from the boogieman? Open communication between parents and children on features of safety and safety outcomes will ultimately give children the tools they need to understand their fear of crime.

Let Go of Bubble-Wrap, Especially for Daughters

As discussed in chapter 4, helicoptering and bubble-wrapping children are two common parenting styles.[33] Parents need to let go of the bubble-wrap. Of course, this is easier said than done, but as researchers have shown, the biggest issue with these parenting styles is that they do not teach kids resilience.[34] For kids to navigate the world as they age, they need some leeway to make mistakes, solve conflicts, and become good decision-makers. In terms of crime prevention and fear of crime, the best thing we can do for children is to teach confidence and independence. Children who are confident in their ability to manage a situation will be less afraid of it. So, teaching confidence, or at least some self-reliance and independence, will give kids the tools they need to navigate the world during their childhood and later on, when they may not have anyone to take care of them.

Gender-neutral lessons in confidence and independence are also needed. As researchers have shown, boys are more likely to be unafraid of crime because they are more self-assured and self-confident. Girls, on the other hand, are less confident in decision-making and more afraid of crime. One reason for these differences is that boys and girls have separate restrictions and supervision levels for recreational and outdoor play.[35] As children become adolescents, recreational activities continue to be restricted for girls but not boys.[36] Parents, then, see boys as more capable of taking care of themselves and girls as vulnerable and in need of protection. Teen girls who are overly supervised may not trust their ability to protect themselves. Parents who can teach gender-neutral safety beliefs to both boys and girls will have children who can better manage their safety concerns. For example, parents could expect the same level of risk-taking in boys and girls on the playground and in recreational activities. This would eliminate some of the "boys will be boys" mentality, heading off gendered crime myths.

Another thing parents can do is give children more independence in both structured and unstructured recreational activities. As discussed in chapter 4, children's recreational activities without supervision or with limited parental supervision have diminished over time, causing kids to play outdoors less often and at the expense of freedom in recreational spaces. Restricting recreational activities, especially outdoor play, can cause negative health outcomes like obesity, mental health issues, and less resilience. Further, children with more restrictions are actually more afraid of crime and less able to make decisions about potentially dangerous situations. Parents, then, may need to rethink how much they supervise their children in recreational spaces. Over-supervising children in recreational activities has little effect on victimization chances, may cause fear of crime, and also has negative physical and mental health outcomes.

By letting go of the bubble-wrap, then, parents provide the opportunity for children to learn resilience, decision-making, and confidence in navigating outdoor and recreational spaces. The gendered nature of bubble-wrap can have unintended consequences for daughters. Thus, gender-neutral lessons to children about risk-taking and independence also help both daughters and sons grow up to be less afraid of crime.

Have Accurate (But Difficult) Conversations about Crime

This is a hard one for parents. While parents might spend a good deal of time planning for hard conversations with kids as they become teenagers, discussions about crime and victimization are rarely on this list. Many parents understandably do not want to talk to kids about things they think can scare them, like becoming a crime victim. However, having age-appropriate baseline conversations with kids about crime and victimization will give parents a foundation for having more serious, age-appropriate discussions later. One of the best things parents can do is teach accurate information about crime victims to kids and teens. Parents often unknowingly reinforce gendered crime myths through inaccurate conversations—or by avoiding conversations altogether. By accurately explaining the likelihood of victimization for their child's gender, race, and age group, parents can debunk these myths. I recognize that talking about the reality of crime (e.g., it is intraracial and usually happens with known people) may seem scary. Honestly, though, how are these accurate images more frightening than the unrealistic images of strangers jumping out of bushes? Age-appropriate, honest conversations can be a great way to debunk these myths. For example, if a white girl is missing and becomes the source of a lot of media and news stories, we can have a conversation about it over dinner. We can explain that this is horrible for the family and that we hope the child is all right. In doing so, we would be teaching societal responsibility for victim prevention and building a better citizen. We can then also talk about how rare it is that young white girls are victims of this type of crime, making white girls feel less afraid of victimization. We can then discuss why we do not see stories of victims of color, which would allow us to teach about racism, how Black victims are often invisible, and the role of the criminal justice system. Contextualizing crime messages through everyday conversations helps parents teach fear of crime better.

Another meaningful conversation with teenagers has to be about sexual assault. Conversations about sexual assault are again tough to have but are important. Parents do not need to go over graphic details of sexual assault and how this might happen to people. The conversation can again be age appropriate, and these conversations need to occur with both boys and girls.

For boys, in addition to having the "talk" about sexual activity, parents should also have conversations about consent and power dynamics in romantic relationships. Boys who understand that sexual assault is about having power over victims will be more likely to think about power dynamics once they become sexually active. Thus, teaching boys about personal power dynamics in relationships and sexual encounters, and societal gender power dynamics, cannot hurt. While it may do little to curb fear of crime, it may make boys better bystanders later on.

For girls, the messages need to also be about the importance of power dynamics and understanding healthy romantic relationships, including sexual relationships. Girls who have self-worth and confidence in who they are may be less likely to be peer pressured into unhealthy romantic relationships as they get older. Conversations about healthy romantic relationships need to include discussions about both partners being equal in the relationship. Parents should also talk to girls about consent and what that means as part of a more extensive discussion about healthy relationships. Again, girls who are taught to be independent and to have confidence in their own feelings and worries will have better tools to navigate these issues.

Lastly, parents need to talk to girls about victim blame. Even college-aged women who have great relationships with their parents may not feel comfortable talking to them about victimization experiences. They may feel shame, embarrassment, or fear of retaliation. Parents can teach teenage girls the reasons why victims often feel at fault for their victimization experiences and that rape is a societal rather than individual problem. Then, when these teens become college-aged women, they may feel more comfortable reaching out to parents for help if something happens to them or someone they know. If college-aged women feel that their parents will believe them, they are more likely to talk to parents about an assault experience.

Finally, it is essential that parents walk both boys and girls through examples of being a good bystander to others, both friends and unknown people.

Thus, teaching age-appropriate information about victimization to both sons and daughters will help them understand what to fear and what not to fear. It will also give them accurate crime prevention strategies.

Teach Kids to Take Care of Each Other

As we discussed in chapter 5, children are more than sponges that absorb everything they are taught by their parents.[37] Children understand parental lessons about safety but do not always act on these lessons in the same way as their parents. What this tells us is that children, and not just parents, can be agents of change. By listening to children and getting them involved in changing safety beliefs, we are more likely to break the generational cycle of teaching fear in traditionally gendered ways. Such lessons may be particularly relevant to Gen Z children, who seem to be more socially conscious than previous generations.[38] Gen Z children may already want to make the world a better place and be more willing to focus on others rather than themselves as part of their safety values.

Parents should teach children to be good bystanders at an early age. As mentioned above, bystander intervention programs are becoming a popular way to frame victimization prevention, but these programs tend to focus on adults—college students in particular.[39] Age-appropriate lessons for children about being a good bystander would go far in breaking the victim-centered crime prevention myth. These early lessons do not need to focus on crime at all. For example, parents can teach empathy through the importance of being a good friend and being kind to others. Parents can also focus on how individual behaviors affect larger societal issues and others in society. Perhaps these lessons can focus on pollution, food insecurity, or homelessness. Socializing kids to focus on how individual behaviors affect groups of people helps others later. When kids get older, parents can focus on crime prevention by teaching kids how to be good bystanders in situations where they can safely help others. This does not mean that kids should be taught to jump in the middle of a fight at school, but it does mean that when they feel something is wrong or see kids who might be in trouble, they should seek help.

Such an emphasis on taking care of others and being a good bystander cannot only be taught to girls. Boys also need to be taught to think of others, to be good friends, and to understand how individual behaviors affect larger groups. Doing so may mean that as boys grow up, they are more likely to step in when something is wrong. For example, rather than participating in or simply going along with locker room talk, they may tell other guys to stop talking about women as sexual objects and conquests. In other words, boys can grow up to see victimization as a societal rather than an individual problem too. Jackson Katz, a researcher who studies bystander intervention programming, argues that the best prevention for sexual assault victimization is to teach men to be good bystanders.[40] We can imagine that if all kids, both boys and girls, were taught bystander intervention from an early age, they would be more likely to step in to help a friend or someone in need when they grow up.

Another way parents can help children focus on others is by changing how they see safety values in families. Families are often seen as private entities, and what happens in families, especially negative situations, is often not shared with others.[41] The members of a family unit often protect each other at all costs. While this is a good thing in many ways, when it comes to fear of victimization and safety precautions, it is not. Families teach children (unknowingly or knowingly) family-focused protective strategies. Children learn to protect their family above all others, which can lead to feeling that they should only fear for themselves and their family members. As children grow up, they focus on self-protective/family-protective prevention strategies, like protecting the home with security systems or weapons, protecting children in the home, by keeping them away from strangers in public areas, or by taking a variety of preventative strategies to keep their family members safe each day.

An alternative approach is to teach children the importance of societal needs and concerns and to look out for others. In practice, parents will always worry about their children and protect them to the best of their abilities. However, if children feel that they should worry about others in addition to their immediate family unit, they may be more likely to reach out to others in need of help. By teaching kids to be good community citizens, we minimize the power of the victim-centered crime prevention myth.

Recognize How Kids Are Different Today

One last point of advice for parents and researchers alike is to recognize Gen Z kids are not Gen X kids. The world is entirely different from when Gen X kids grew up. Gen Z kids have different dangerous places, fears, crimes, and ways to cope with potential victimization. What I have learned talking to children is entirely different from what I remember growing up and even from what I see other researchers talking about these days in the fear of crime literature. The experiences and viewpoints of children are a missing part of the gendered fear of crime cycle. Parents cannot truly teach the fear of crime better without the help of kids. We need to talk to kids about what they fear and how they cope with that fear. Doing so will continue to give us insight into how to more accurately teach fear to children.

Kids today are plagued with fears surrounding the internet, social media, and a large unknown cyber world.[42] Because of these generational changes, kids' fears of crime are going to be unique. The precautionary measures to alleviate these fears will also be unique. For example, cyberbullying is a crime that the parents of today's children never experienced. Thus, we need to take some time to understand this new-age boogieman. If parents can get educated on these differences, they will better be able to talk to kids about crime prevention. Further, the strategies kids take today to reduce victimization potential, like wearing headphones to avoid conversations with strangers or having friends tell them when a place is unsafe, are not discussed in the literature much.[43] These strategies are going to need to be part of conversations about fear of crime and victimization prevention if we are to move forward in this research area. By understanding the unique experiences of kids today, we can help curb gendered crime myths.

Conclusions

In this book, through my own research, an examination of the studies of others, and a review of what the general public thinks about crime and victimization, I have shown how crime myths form in society. These crime myths are highly gendered, applying only to women, and typically to white women. They are solidified through societal expectations of women's behavior. Most women, then, fear strangers, fear public areas, and take a litany of precautionary measures each day to avoid stranger-induced crime. Intergenerational transmissions of safety values and fear of crime keep gendered crime myths in motion. Through parents, schools, and the media, we learn to fear crime in specific ways and to act on these fears through precautions, and then we teach others the same gendered crime myths we learned growing up. The cycle of teaching fear continues on as children grow up and begin teaching fear to others. These powerful myths, then, are transformed into safety beliefs, safety values, and inaccurate fears of victimization. We can break the cycle by debunking crime myths and more accurately conveying information to others. We have an individual and societal responsibility to do better for future generations. Children of Generation Z and later can be taught to fear in more appropriate ways. We can build resilient and confident children who have the tools they need to navigate the world. All of us—men and women, moms and dads, boys and girls—can flip the script and teach fear of crime better.

Appendix: Research Studies

I am lucky to have found a topic that I have been able to study over 20 years. I have never tired of studying fear of crime and continue in this pursuit because there are still so many questions left unanswered. This book has been informed by my previous qualitative projects and I highlight these study details below.

I completed my doctorate at Southern Illinois University Carbondale in 2005. My dissertation project, titled "Women Doing Fear: Applying the Doing Gender Framework to Women's Fear of Crime," examined how marriage and divorce, two noteworthy life transitions, might affect women's fear of crime. After Institutional Review Board (IRB) approval and using a snowball sampling technique, I conducted qualitative in-depth interviews with 29 women who were recently married (15 women) or recently divorced (14 women). Most interviews were done face to face (with a couple of phone interviews) and took place at a location of the respondent's choosing (often a public but quiet and secluded location). At the beginning of the interview, respondents filled out a brief demographic survey and an informed consent form, and the interview was then audio-recorded and transcribed verbatim. Interviews lasted between 30 minutes and 2 hours. I asked a lot of questions about how respondents "did gender," "did fear," and "did gendered fear of crime." Respondents were primarily white, 21–30 years of age, did not have children, had a higher level of education (bachelor's degree), and made approximately $30,000 per year. The married participants were more likely to have a higher income and more education than the divorced participants.

I found in this work that before women entered into marriage they managed their own fear of crime and subsequent behaviors, but that this changed once they were married. When married, they relied on husbands, who were "in charge" of keeping the household (and the people in it) safe. Their husbands often accompanied them to places late at night and were in charge of locked doors and late-night noises. Divorced participants felt more of a burden for their own safety once divorced, as they were once again in charge of managing this fear of crime, both in the public and private sphere, themselves. The gendered nature of fear of crime was extremely apparent in this study and I also learned the importance of family dynamics in shaping these social processes.

In 2006, after arriving at Mississippi State University, I received funding to conduct a follow-up study. Given the importance of husbands in the "fear work transference" process, I wanted to explore the role of husbands further. After obtaining IRB approval, I used a snowball sampling technique to conduct qualitative in-depth interviews with 21 Southern participants (10 husbands and 11 wives). I asked participants about fear of crime and how they managed safety concerns within their marriage. I also focused more intentionally on how fear of crime and management of fear of crime might have changed once participants were married. At the beginning of the face-to-face interviews, conducted in a public place of the respondents' choosing, respondents filled out a brief demographic survey and an informed consent form, and the interview was then audio-recorded and transcribed verbatim. The interviews lasted between 45 minutes and 2 hours, with the majority in the 1-hour and 15-minute range. The respondents of this study were white and most did not have children, about half had a bachelor's degree or higher, and most made less than $40,000 annually.

The findings of the Southern study again found that wives relied a lot on husbands for precautionary measures and safety concerns. Similar to the Midwestern study, wives relied on husbands to escort them to perceived dangerous places, and they expected husbands to keep the household safe (to lock doors, turn on security systems, check out noises, and handle potential intruders). Husband participants told me that once married, they were aware that they were now responsible for safety precautions for the family and hoped that it helped their partner feel safer. Husband participants felt a lot of pressure to manage or handle safety precautions. For example, one outcome of being responsible for the family's safety was that husbands curbed their personal fear of crime because they felt that they shouldn't be afraid "as men." So, while husbands sometimes did fear crime, they didn't show their fear of crime much to other people. Another finding of importance from the Southern study involved children. The married participants with children told me that they were worried for their children's safety. It was clear from this study that gendered divisions within the family played a part in determining safety responsibilities in the household, and I decided next to study children.

Given the importance of gendered and familial dynamics in fear of crime and safety precautions, my next study did two things. First, I went and did some comparative research in southern Sweden. Sweden consistently ranks as one of the top five countries in the world in terms of gender equality. There are big differences in ranking between the United States and Sweden on gender equality (for example, in 2021, Sweden ranked fifth and the United States ranked thirtieth in the Global Gender Gap Index report produced by the World Economic Forum) and I wanted to see if women in a country with greater gender equality felt differently about crime and safety.[1] I also wondered if gender dynamics within the family, which I'd imagined would be different in a country like Sweden, might also be relevant in terms of safety socialization. Second, I conducted qualitative in-depth interviews with husbands, wives, and their children. For the Sweden project, I interviewed 26 participants (6 husbands, 10 wives and 10 children 8–12 years of age) about fear of crime and management of fear of crime. This study expanded my previous work because I was able to talk to entire families—mom and dad and any children aged 8–12—and also examine the importance of gender in a non-U.S. cultural context. At the beginning of the face-to-face interviews, conducted mainly in the homes of participants, parent participants filled out a brief demographic survey, an informed consent form, and the interview was then audio-recorded and transcribed verbatim. At the conclusion of the parent interviews, if parents were willing to allow their children to be interviewed, they also filled out a consent form, allowing their child or children to participate in the project. I also gave children an assent form and the option to participate in the project or not. There were two interview guides for this project, one for parents and one for children. Parents were more explicitly asked about their fear of crime, safety precautions, and concerns for spouses and children, whereas children were asked more about feeling safe in places and what they learned about safety from parents, schools, and other sources. While most Swedish people are fluent in English and Swedish, I had a Swedish translator during interviews in case the respondents needed assistance with translation. Additionally, some of the Swedish children were not fluent in English, and in that case, they were asked the questions in Swedish, and responses were translated to me in English. The interviews lasted between 45 minutes and 1 and a half hours, and all interviews were transcribed. The parent participants of this study were all white, and the majority were Swedish born, were around 40 years old, and had two children. The average age of the children was ten years old.

I learned that the participants of my study in Sweden were more similar to the participants I had interviewed in the United States than I expected. Although Swedish participants discussed gender equality (e.g., leave policies, political empowerment, financial independence), when it came to fear of crime and management of fear of crime, Swedish participants' gendered divisions of fear work was similar to that of U.S. parents. There were differences between the two groups to be sure (e.g., Swedish children had much more freedom than their American counterparts to ride bikes and go to school without parental supervision), but I was more surprised by the commonalities between the two groups. Interviews with Swedish husbands, wives, and children showcased a socialization process where Swedish parents still taught their children to be fearful of strangers and to manage fear in particular ways. One finding of interest was that Swedish parents were more likely to teach about various types of strangers rather than talking about all strangers as bad. From the Swedish study, I learned that in order to change how we teach fear of crime, we need to understand not only what children hear from their parents but what they see and how they interpret those messages.

These insights led to my most recent qualitative project, which I conducted with Maggie Hagerman and Courtney Heath in the South. The general purpose of this project was to talk to families about some current events and topics of concern. We received IRB approval to conduct qualitative in-depth interviews with parents and their children. We interviewed 28 participants (10 moms, 4 dads, and 14 children) for this project. At the beginning of the face-to-face interviews, conducted in the homes of the participants, parent participants filled out a brief demographic survey and an informed consent form, and the interview was then audio-recorded and transcribed verbatim. At the conclusion of the parent interviews, if parents were willing to allow their children to be interviewed, they also filled out a consent form, allowing their child or children to participate in the project. Children were also given an assent form and the option to participate in the project or not. There were two interview guides for this project, one for parents and one for children. For the safety portion of the interview, parents were more explicitly asked about their fear of crime, safety precautions, and concerns for spouses and children, whereas children were asked more about feeling safe in places and what they learned about safety from parents, schools, and other sources. The interviews lasted between 30 minutes and 1 hour. The parent participants were mainly white and upper middle class and had at least a bachelor's degree, and most had more than one child. The children were between the ages of 10 and 13, with 11 as the average age. The safety concern portion of the interviews were used here to further inform our understanding of the fear of crime socialization process. Our findings highlighted the same socialization process I'd found in Sweden, which showed parents provide specific messages to children about stranger danger in public spaces.

In addition to the studies I have conducted over the years, I think it is important for me to comment on my positionality. I am a white, middle-class, heterosexual woman who married her college sweetheart, and we have two children. I grew up in the eighties and nineties in a suburban portion of St. Louis, MO, where I was part of a blended family. I grew up with working parents and I attended public school for all of my K–12 education. My more advanced degrees come from both small liberal arts private colleges (Central Methodist University, Drury University) and large public institutions (Southern Illinois University Carbondale). I have been lucky to have some of the best professors ever in the areas of criminal justice, criminology, and sociology. I have worked at Mississippi State University for my entire academic career. I have lived in the South almost as long as I've lived in the Midwest, making me a strange blend of these two regional locations.

These identities have shaped who I am, what I study, and how I see the world. As a wife, I am easily able to talk to most other married people. Because I am a mom, I can more easily relate to children and also their parents. These identities have given me the ability to relate to and genuinely be interested in those I hope to understand. These identities have positioned me to talk to others in these categories about their lives, their anxieties, and their safety precautions. As a white, heterosexual woman, I have learned about gendered crime myths from childhood forward. Because of my background in gender studies, criminology, and sociology, I've also been able to critically see the differential application of gendered crime myths to various groups of people. My status as an educated, heterosexual, middle-class, white woman often gives me privilege in society. I try to always be mindful of these privileged positions as I conduct my research, but there are areas where I can do better as a researcher. For example, I acknowledge that my privileged identities may mean that I inadvertently and unintentionally contribute to the pattern in fear of crime research that highlights white participants. Especially in today's environment, where national discussions surrounding policing, racism, and safety are happening, the voices of Black families in our understanding of fear of crime and how we "teach" fear are often absent. My next research study will focus more exclusively on Black mothers and their children, and I hope this avenue of research can be used to help understand the important racial differences in how families talk about safety and teach fear of crime. As a qualitative researcher, I've observed, listened, and understood the importance of giving people the ability to tell their stories, and I hope to continue to do so in the future.

In terms of my own fear of crime and how I myself have navigated safety, I want you to know that I understand the readers of this book because I am very much like you. I, too, have moments where I feel afraid, even knowing I should not. I also take a variety of precautions without noticing and have to make a conscious effort not to do so. My children would likely tell you that I have taught them ways to fear crime and to deal with safety concerns that are more in line with traditional gendered fear of crime norms than I would like. In other words, I am a typical person who also struggles with worries, anxieties, work-life balance, and all the other problems discussed in this book. I have been able to use these experiences to better understand the experiences of others. Further, for all the advice I give, I have to remind myself to take that advice as well. When I say we all need to flip the script, I am not immune to these lessons, either. These experiences, then, along with my qualitative research studies and the studies I've conducted with others over the years, have been a journey and a culmination that has led me to this book, *Teaching Fear.*

Notes

CHAPTER 1

1. Telegraph Reporters, "Master of Media Circus for Madeleine McCann," *The Telegraph*, April 24, 2008, https://www.telegraph.co.uk/news/1902515/Master-of-media-circus-for-Madeleine-McCann.html.
2. Roslyn Muraskin and Shelly Feuer Domash, *Crime and the Media: Headlines vs. Reality* (Upper Saddle River, NJ: Pearson Prentice Hall, 2007).
3. Muraskin and Domash, *Crime and the Media*.
4. Carol M. Liebler, "Me(Di)a Culpa?: The 'Missing White Woman Syndrome' and Media Self-Critique," *Communication, Culture, and Critique* 3, no. 4 (December 1, 2010): 549–65, https://doi.org/10.1111/j.1753-9137.2010.01085.x.
5. Rachel E. Morgan and Jennifer L. Truman, "Criminal Victimization, 2017" (Washington, DC: Office of Justice Programs, The Bureau of Justice Statistics, December 2018), https://bjs.ojp.gov/content/pub/pdf/cv17.pdf.
6. Morgan and Truman, "Criminal Victimization, 2017."
7. Liebler, "Me(Di)a Culpa?"
8. William R. Smith and Marie Tortensson, "Gender Differences in Risk Perception and Neutralizing Fear of Crime: Toward Resolving the Paradoxes," *The British Journal of Criminology* 37, no. 4 (October 1, 1997): 608–34, https://doi.org/10.1093/oxfordjournals.bjc.a014201; David C. May, Nicole E. Rader, and Sarah Goodrum, "A Gendered Assessment of the 'Threat of Victimization': Examining Gender Differences in Fear of Crime, Perceived Risk, Avoidance, and Defensive Behaviors," *Criminal Justice Review* 35, no. 2 (June 2010): 159–82, https://doi.org/10.1177/0734016809349166.
9. Nicole E. Rader and Stacy H. Haynes, "Gendered Fear of Crime Socialization: An Extension of Akers's Social Learning Theory," *Feminist Criminology* 6, no. 4 (October 1, 2011): 291–307, https://doi.org/10.1177/1557085111408278; Lesley Williams Reid and Miriam Konrad, "The Gender Gap in Fear: Assessing the Interactive Effects of Gender

and Perceived Risk on Fear of Crime," *Sociological Spectrum* 24, no. 4 (July 2004): 399–425, https://doi.org/10.1080/02732170490431331; Ferraro, "Women's Fear of Victimization."

10. Cecilia L. Ridgeway, "Framed Before We Know It: How Gender Shapes Social Relations," *Gender and Society* 23, no. 2 (April 2009): 145–60, https://doi.org/10.1177/0891243208330313.

11. Raewyn Connell, *Gender: In World Perspective* (Polity Short Introductions), 4th ed. (Medford, MA: Polity Press, 2021); Candace West and Don H. Zimmerman, "Doing Gender," Gender and Society 1 (1987): 125–51.

12. Małgorzata Lipowska, Mariusz Lipowski, and Paulina Pawlicka, "'Daughter and Son: A Completely Different Story'? Gender as a Moderator of the Relationship between Sexism and Parental Attitudes," *Health Psychology Report* 3 (2016): 224–36, https://doi.org/10.5114/hpr.2016.62221.

13. Ridgeway, "Framed Before We Know It"; Connell, *Gender*.

14. Barrie Thorne, *Gender Play: Girls and Boys in School* (New Brunswick, NJ: Rutgers University Press, 1993).

15. Emily Keener, JoNell Strough, and Lisa DiDonato, "Gender Differences and Similarities in Strategies for Managing Conflict with Friends and Romantic Partners," *Sex Roles* 67, no. 1–2 (July 2012): 83–97, https://doi.org/10.1007/s11199-012-0131-9.

16. Christine Knauss, Susan J. Paxton, and Françoise D. Alsaker, "Body Dissatisfaction in Adolescent Boys and Girls: Objectified Body Consciousness, Internalization of the Media Body Ideal and Perceived Pressure from Media," *Sex Roles* 59, no. 9–10 (November 2008): 633–43, https://doi.org/10.1007/s11199-008-9474-7.

17. Elizabeth A. Daniels, Marlee C. Layh, and Linda K. Porzelius, "Grooming Ten-Year-Olds with Gender Stereotypes? A Content Analysis of Preteen and Teen Girl Magazines," *Body Image* 19 (December 2016): 57–67, https://doi.org/10.1016/j.bodyim.2016.08.011.

18. Rebecca L. Collins, "Content Analysis of Gender Roles in Media: Where Are We Now and Where Should We Go?" *Sex Roles* 64, no. 3–4 (February 2011): 290–98, https://doi.org/10.1007/s11199-010-9929-5; Daniels, Layh, and Porzelius, "Grooming Ten-Year-Olds with Gender Stereotypes?"; Alexander Sink and Dana Mastro, "Depictions of Gender on Primetime Television: A Quantitative Content Analysis," *Mass Communication and Society* 20, no. 1 (January 2, 2017): 3–22, https://doi.org/10.1080/15205436.2016.1212243.

19. Sarah K. Murnen et al., "Thin, Sexy Women and Strong, Muscular Men: Grade-School Children's Responses to Objectified Images of Women and Men," *Sex Roles* 49, no. 9/10 (2003): 427–37, https://doi.org/10.1023/A:1025868320206.

20. Daniels, Layh, and Porzelius, "Grooming Ten-Year-Olds with Gender Stereotypes?"

21. Alexander Sink and Dana Mastro, "Depictions of Gender on Primetime Television: A Quantitative Content Analysis," *Mass Communication and Society* 20, no. 1 (January 2, 2017): 3–22, https://doi.org/10.1080/15205436.2016.1212243.

22. Sink and Mastro, "Depictions of Gender on Primetime Television," 3.

23. Cecilia L. Ridgeway, "Framed Before We Know It."

24. Cecilia L. Ridgeway and Lynn Smith-Lovin, "The Gender System and Interaction," *Annual Review of Sociology* 25 (1999): 191–216; Ridgeway, "Framed Before We Know It."

25. Jill E. Yavorsky, Claire M. Kamp Dush, and Sarah J. Schoppe-Sullivan, "The Production of Inequality: The Gender Division of Labor across the Transition to Parent-

hood," *Journal of Marriage and Family* 77, no. 3 (2015): 662–79, https://doi.org/10.1111/jomf.12189.

26. Connell, *Gender*; Ridgeway, "Framed Before We Know It."

27. Candace West and Don H. Zimmerman, "Doing Gender," *Gender and Society* 1 (1987): 125–51.

28. West and Zimmerman, "Doing Gender"; Nicole E. Rader, "Women Doing Fear: Applying the Doing Gender Framework to Women's Fear of Crime" (Carbondale, IL: Southern Illinois University, 2005).

29. Saskia De Groof, "And My Mama Said: The (Relative) Parental Influence on Fear of Crime among Adolescent Girls and Boys," *Youth and Society* 39, no. 3 (March 2008): 267–93, https://doi.org/10.1177/0044118X07301000; Lisa Hutchinson Wallace and David C. May, "The Impact of Parental Attachment and Feelings of Isolation on Adolescent Fear of Crime at School," *Adolescence (San Diego): An International Quarterly Devoted to the Physiological, Psychological, Psychiatric, Sociological, and Educational Aspects of the Second Decade of Human Life* 40, no. 159 (September 22, 2005): 457; J. Goodey, "Boys Don't Cry: Masculinities, Fear of Crime and Fearlessness," *British Journal of Criminology* 37, no. 3 (January 1, 1997): 401–18, https://doi.org/10.1093/oxfordjournals.bjc.a014177.

30. Nicole E. Rader, "Gendered Fear Strategies: Intersections of Doing Gender and Fear Management Strategies in Married and Divorced Women's Lives," *Sociological Focus* 41, no. 1 (February 2008): 34–52, https://doi.org/10.1080/00380237.2008.10571322; Rader, "Women Doing Fear"; De Groof, "And My Mama Said"; Wallace and May, "The Impact of Parental Attachment and Feelings of Isolation on Adolescent Fear of Crime at School."

31. Wallace and May, "The Impact of Parental Attachment and Feelings of Isolation on Adolescent Fear of Crime at School."

32. De Groof, "And My Mama Said."

33. De Groof, "And My Mama Said," 286.

34. See Smith and Tortensson, "Gender Differences in Risk Perception and Neutralizing Fear of Crime" for a full discussion of these explanations.

35. Esther Madriz, *Nothing Bad Happens to Good Girls: Fear of Crime in Women's Lives* (Berkeley: University of California Press, 1997); Elizabeth A Stanko, "Women, Crime, and Fear," The Annals of the American Academy of Political and Social Science 539, no. 1 (May 1, 1995): 46–58, https://doi.org/10.1177/0002716295539001004; Hannah Scott, "Stranger Danger: Explaining Women's Fear of Crime," *Western Criminology Review* 4, no. 3 (2003): 12.

36. Gwen van Eijk, "Between Risk and Resistance: Gender Socialization, Equality, and Ambiguous Norms in Fear of Crime and Safekeeping," *Feminist Criminology* 12, no. 2 (April 2017): 103–24, https://doi.org/10.1177/1557085115605905; Diederik Cops and Stefaan Pleysier, "'Doing Gender' in Fear of Crime: The Impact of Gender Identity on Reported Levels of Fear of Crime in Adolescents and Young Adults," *The British Journal of Criminology* 51, no. 1 (January 1, 2011): 58–74, https://doi.org/10.1093/bjc/azq065; Nicole E. Rader, "Building Trust in Children: How Parents Talk to Children about Safety Precautions in Sweden," *International Review of Victimology* 23, no. 1 (January 2017): 3–16, https://doi.org/10.1177/0269758016672373.

37. Kevin M. Drakulich, "Concerns for Self or Family? Sources of and Responses to Altruistic Fear," *Journal of Interpersonal Violence* 30, no. 7 (April 1, 2015): 1168–1207, https://doi.org/10.1177/0886260514539842; Scott, "Stranger Danger"; Stanko, "Women, Crime, and Fear."

38. Morgan and Truman, "Criminal Victimization, 2017."

39. Joel Best, *Threatened Children: Rhetoric and Concern about Child-Victims* (Chicago: University of Chicago Press, 1990).

40. T. Smith et al., "General Social Surveys, 1972–2018," National Opinion Research Center, University of Chicago, ed. (Chicago: National Science Foundation, 2018).

41. M. Stokes, "Stranger Danger: Child Protection and Parental Fears in the Risk Society," *Amsterdam Social Science* 1, no. 3 (2009): 8, https://www.semanticscholar.org/paper/Stranger-Danger%3A-Child-Protection-and-Parental-in-Stokes/8605d54a79757ebd36778bd0561aa6b31b5faa16.

42. Ted Chiricos, Kelly Welch, and Marc Gertz, "Racial Typification of Crime and Support for Punitive Measures," *Criminology* 42, no. 2 (May 2004): 358–90, https://doi.org/10.1111/j.1745-9125.2004.tb00523.x.

43. Emmanuel Barthe et al., *Crime Prevention Publicity Campaigns* (Washington, DC: U.S. Dept. of Justice, Office of Community Oriented Policing Services, 2006); Jacinta Francis et al., "'I'll Be Driving You to School for the Rest of Your Life': A Qualitative Study of Parents' Fear of Stranger Danger," *Journal of Environmental Psychology* 53 (November 1, 2017): 112–20, https://doi.org/10.1016/j.jenvp.2017.07.004.

44. Bonnie S. Fisher and John J. Sloan III, "Unraveling the Fear of Victimization among College Women: Is the 'Shadow of Sexual Assault Hypothesis' Supported?" *Justice Quarterly* 20, no. 3 (September 1, 2003): 633–59, https://doi.org/10.1080/07418820300095641; Stokes, "Stranger Danger"; Jocelyn A. Hollander and Katie Rodgers, "Constructing Victims: The Erasure of Women's Resistance to Sexual Assault," *Sociological Forum* 29, no. 2 (2014): 342–64, https://doi.org/10.1111/socf.12087.

45. Karen A. Snedker, "Explaining the Gender Gap in Fear of Crime: Assessments of Risk and Vulnerability among New York City Residents," *Feminist Criminology* 7, no. 2 (April 1, 2012): 75–111, https://doi.org/10.1177/1557085111424405; Jocelyn A. Hollander, "Vulnerability and Dangerousness: The Construction of Gender through Conversation about Violence," *Gender and Society* 15, no. 1 (February 1, 2001): 83–109, https://doi.org/10.1177/089124301015001005; Best, *Threatened Children*.

46. Mark Warr and Christopher G. Ellison, "Rethinking Social Reactions to Crime: Personal and Altruistic Fear in Family Households," *American Journal of Sociology* 106, no. 3 (2001): 551–78, https://doi.org/10.1086/318964; Nicole E. Rader, "Until Death Do Us Part? Husband Perceptions and Responses to Fear of Crime," *Deviant Behavior* 31, no. 1 (December 18, 2009): 33–59, https://doi.org/10.1080/01639620902854704; Karen A. Snedker, "Altruistic and Vicarious Fear of Crime: Fear for Others and Gendered Social Roles," *Sociological Forum* 21, no. 2 (June 1, 2006): 163–95, https://doi.org/10.1007/s11206-006-9019-1.

47. Best, *Threatened Children*.

48. Best, *Threatened Children*, 22.

49. Michael Dimock, "Defining Generations: Where Millennials End and Generation Z Begins" (Washington, DC: Pew Research Center, January 17, 2019), https://www.pewresearch.org/fact-tank/2019/01/17/where-millennials-end-and-generation-z-begins/.

50. Dimock, "Defining Generations."

51. Morgan and Truman, "Criminal Victimization, 2017."

52. Scott, "Stranger Danger," 12.

53. Scott, "Stranger Danger," 211.

54. Kenneth F. Ferraro, "Women's Fear of Victimization."

55. Pamela Wilcox, Carol E. Jordan, and Adam J. Pritchard, "Fear of Acquaintance Versus Stranger Rape as a 'Master Status': Towards Refinement of the 'Shadow of Sexual

Assault,'" *Violence and Victims* 21, no. 3 (June 1, 2006): 355–70, https://doi.org/10.1891/vivi.21.3.355; Fisher and Sloan III, "Unraveling the Fear of Victimization among College Women"; Samantha Riggs and Carrie L. Cook, "The Shadow of Physical Harm? Examining the Unique and Gendered Relationship between Fear of Murder Versus Fear of Sexual Assault on Fear of Violent Crime," *Journal of Interpersonal Violence* 30, no. 14 (2014): 2383–2409, https://doi.org/10.1177/0886260514553117.

56. Morgan and Truman, "Criminal Victimization, 2017"; Ted Chiricos, Michael Hogan, and Marc Gertz, "Racial Composition of Neighborhood and Fear of Crime," *Criminology* 35, no. 1 (1997): 107–32, https://doi.org/10.1111/j.1745-9125.1997.tb00872.x; De Welde, "White Women Beware!"; Liebler, "Me(Di)a Culpa?"

57. Madriz, *Nothing Bad Happens to Good Girls,* 1997; De Welde, "White Women Beware!" 2003

58. Patricia Hill Collins, *Black Feminist Thought: Knowledge, Consciousness, and the Politics of Empowerment*, rev. 10th anniversary ed (New York: Routledge, 2000); Eduardo Bonilla-Silva, "The Structure of Racism in Color-Blind, 'Post-Racial' America," *American Behavioral Scientist* 59, no. 11 (October 2015): 1358–76, https://doi.org/10.1177/0002764215586826; Kimberle Crenshaw, "Mapping the Margins: Intersectionality, Identity Politics, and Violence against Women of Color," *Stanford Law Review* 43, no. 6 (1994): 1241–1299.

59. Amanda Burgess-Proctor, "Intersections of Race, Class, Gender, and Crime: Future Directions for Feminist Criminology," *Feminist Criminology* 1, no. 1 (January 2006): 27–47, https://doi.org/10.1177/1557085105282899.

60. Kristen Day, "Constructing Masculinity and Women's Fear in Public Space in Irvine, California," *Gender, Place, and Culture* 8, no. 2 (June 1, 2001): 114, https://doi.org/10.1080/09663690120050742.

61. Liebler, "Me(Di)a Culpa?"

62. Liebler, "Me(Di)a Culpa?"

63. Liebler, "Me(Di)a Culpa?"

64. De Welde, "White Women Beware!"

65. De Welde, "White Women Beware!," 78.

66. Martha Hodes, "The Sexualization of Reconstruction Politics: White Women and Black Men in the South after the Civil War," *Journal of the History of Sexuality*, Special Issue: African American Culture and Sexuality, 3, no. 3 (1993): 403.

67. Hodes, "The Sexualization of Reconstruction Politics," 409.

68. Leverentz, "Narratives of Crime and Criminals"; Chiricos, Welch, and Gertz, "Racial Typification of Crime and Support for Punitive Measures."

69. Melissa Hickman Barlow, "Race and the Problem of Crime in 'Time' and 'Newsweek' Cover Stories, 1946 to 1995," *Social Justice* 25, no. 2 (1998): 149–83.

70. Michelle Alexander, *The New Jim Crow: Mass Incarceration in the Age of Colorblindness*, 10th anniversary edition (New York: The New Press, 2020).

71. Day, "Constructing Masculinity and Women's Fear in Public Space in Irvine, California"; De Welde, "White Women Beware!"

72. Jennifer E. Cobbina, Jody Miller, and Rod K. Brunson, "Gender, Neighborhood Danger, and Risk-Avoidance Strategies among Urban African-American Youths," *Criminology* 46, no. 3 (2008): 673–709, https://doi.org/10.1111/j.1745-9125.2008.00122.x.

73. Margaret A. Hagerman, *White Kids: Growing Up with Privilege in a Racially Divided America* (New York: New York University Press, 2018).

74. Madriz, *Nothing Bad Happens to Good Girls.*

75. Madriz, *Nothing Bad Happens to Good Girls,* 80.

76. Sydney Cherniawsky and Melanie Morrison, "'You Should Have Known Better': The Social Ramifications of Victimization-Focused Sexual Assault Prevention Tips," *Journal of Interpersonal Violence* (April 29, 2020), https://doi.org/10.1177/0886260520913650.
77. Kathryn M. Ryan, "The Relationship between Rape Myths and Sexual Scripts: The Social Construction of Rape," *Sex Roles* 65, no. 11–12 (December 2011): 774–82, https://doi.org/10.1007/s11199-011-0033-2.
78. Elizabeth A. Stanko, "Warnings to Women: Police Advice and Women's Safety in Britain," *Violence Against Women* 2, no. 1 (March 1996): 5–24, https://doi.org/10.1177/1077801296002001002; Cherniawsky and Morrison, "'You Should Have Known Better.'"
79. Alex Campbell, "Keeping the 'Lady' Safe: The Regulation of Femininity through Crime Prevention Literature," *Critical Criminology* 13, no. 2 (January 2005): 119–40, https://doi.org/10.1007/s10612-005-2390-z.
80. Barthe et al., *Crime Prevention Publicity Campaigns*.
81. Steve Kardian, "The Seven-Second Rule: How to Avoid Being an Easy Target," *NBC News*, August 6, 2017.
82. Kardian, "The Seven-Second Rule," 1.
83. Nicole E. Rader, Jeralynn S. Cossman, and Jeremy R. Porter, "Fear of Crime and Vulnerability: Using a National Sample of Americans to Examine Two Competing Paradigms," *Journal of Criminal Justice* 40, no. 2 (March 1, 2012): 134–41, https://doi.org/10.1016/j.jcrimjus.2012.02.003.
84. Rader, Cossman, and Porter, "Fear of Crime and Vulnerability."
85. Cherniawsky and Morrison, "'You Should Have Known Better.'"
86. Cherniawsky and Morrison, "'You Should Have Known Better.'"
87. Ryan, "The Relationship between Rape Myths and Sexual Scripts"; Megan Stubbs-Richardson, Nicole E. Rader, and Arthur G. Cosby, "Tweeting Rape Culture: Examining Portrayals of Victim Blaming in Discussions of Sexual Assault Cases on Twitter," *Feminism and Psychology* 28, no. 1 (February 2018): 90–108, https://doi.org/10.1177/0959353517715874; Nicole E. Rader, Gayle M. Rhineberger-Dunn, and Lauren Vasquez, "Victim Blame in Fictional Crime Dramas: An Examination of Demographic, Incident-Related, and Behavioral Factors," *Women and Criminal Justice* 26, no. 1 (January 2016): 55–75, https://doi.org/10.1080/08974454.2015.1023487.
88. Eliana Suarez and Tahany M. Gadalla, "Stop Blaming the Victim: A Meta-Analysis on Rape Myths," *Journal of Interpersonal Violence* 25, no. 11 (November 2010): 2010–35, https://doi.org/10.1177/0886260509354503.
89. Suarez and Gadalla, "Stop Blaming the Victim"; Cherniawsky and Morrison, "'You Should Have Known Better.'"
90. Ryan, "The Relationship between Rape Myths and Sexual Scripts."
91. De Welde, "White Women Beware!" 81.

CHAPTER 2

*The participants of my studies may have been given a new pseudonym from those used in previously published or presented work as a way to keep their identities as anonymous as possible.

1. A.L. Baldwin, "Socialization and the Parent-Child Relationship," *Child Development* 19 (1948): 127–36.
2. D. Baumrind, "Effects of Authoritative Parental Control on Child Behavior," *Child Development* 37 (1966): 887–907.

3. Jieqiong Fan and Li-fang Zhang, "The Role of Perceived Parenting Styles in Thinking Styles," *Learning and Individual Differences* 32 (May 1, 2014): 204, https://doi.org/10.1016/j.lindif.2014.03.004.

4. Sang Min Lee, M. Harry Daniels, and Daniel B. Kissinger, "Parental Influences on Adolescent Adjustment: Parenting Styles Versus Parenting Practices," *The Family Journal* 14, no. 3 (July 1, 2006): 253–59, https://doi.org/10.1177/1066480706287654.

5. N. Sorkhabi and J. Mandara, "Are the Effects of Baumrind's Parenting Styles Culturally Specific or Culturally Equivalent?" in *Authoritative Parenting: Synthesizing Nurturance and Discipline for Optimal Child Development*, ed. R.E. Larzelere, A.S. Morris, and A.W. Harrist (Washington, DC: American Psychological Association, 2013), 113–35, https://doi.org/10.1037/13948-006.

6. K. Bayless, "What Is Helicopter Parenting?" *Parents*, December 5, 2019, https://www.parents.com/parenting/better-parenting/what-is-helicopter-parenting/.

7. Marisa Lascala, "Everything You Need to Know about the Free-Range Parenting Method," *Good Housekeeping Magazine*, March 2019.

8. Saskia De Groof, "And My Mama Said: The (Relative) Parental Influence on Fear of Crime among Adolescent Girls and Boys," *Youth and Society* 39, no. 3 (March 2008): 267–293, https://doi.org/10.1177/0044118X07301000.

9. De Groof, "And My Mama Said," 271.

10. Lisa Hutchinson Wallace and David C. May, "The Impact of Parental Attachment and Feelings of Isolation on Adolescent Fear of Crime at School," *Adolescence (San Diego): An International Quarterly Devoted to the Physiological, Psychological, Psychiatric, Sociological, and Educational Aspects of the Second Decade of Human Life* 40, no. 159 (September 22, 2005).

11. Laura Vozmediano et al., "'Watch out, Sweetie': The Impact of Gender and Offence Type on Parents' Altruistic Fear of Crime," *Sex Roles* 77, no. 9 (November 1, 2017): 676–86, https://doi.org/10.1007/s11199-017-0758-7.

12. Sarah Foster et al., "The Impact of Parents' Fear of Strangers and Perceptions of Informal Social Control on Children's Independent Mobility," *Health and Place* 26 (March 1, 2014): 60–68, https://doi.org/10.1016/j.healthplace.2013.11.006.

13. Foster et al., "The Impact of Parents' Fear of Strangers and Perceptions of Informal Social Control on Children's Independent Mobility," 65.

14. Joel Best, *Threatened Children: Rhetoric and Concern about Child-Victims* (Chicago: University of Chicago Press, 1990).

15. Mark Warr and Christopher G. Ellison, "Rethinking Social Reactions to Crime: Personal and Altruistic Fear in Family Households," *American Journal of Sociology* 106, no. 3 (2001): 551–78, https://doi.org/10.1086/318964.

16. Gideon Fishman and Gustavo S. Mesch, "Fear of Crime in Israel: A Multidimensional Approach," *Social Science Quarterly* 77, no. 1 (1996): 76–89.

17. Gustavo S. Mesch, "Women's Fear of Crime: The Role of Fear for the Well-Being of Significant Others," *Violence and Victims* 15, no. 3 (January 1, 2000): 323–36, https://doi.org/10.1891/0886-6708.15.3.323.

18. Mesch, "Women's Fear of Crime," 327.

19. Karen A. Snedker, "Altruistic and Vicarious Fear of Crime: Fear for Others and Gendered Social Roles," *Sociological Forum* 21, no. 2 (June 1, 2006): 163–95, https://doi.org/10.1007/s11206-006-9019-1.

20. Arlie Russell Hochschild and ProQuest (Firm), *The Managed Heart: Commercialization of Human Feeling* (Berkeley: University of California Press, 2012), https://ebookcentral.proquest.com/lib/qut/detail.action?docID=870020.

21. Snedker, "Altruistic and Vicarious Fear of Crime," 169.

22. Sara Raley and Suzanne Bianchi, "Sons, Daughters, and Family Processes: Does Gender of Children Matter?" *Annual Review of Sociology* 32, no. 1 (2006): 401–21, https://doi.org/10.1146/annurev.soc.32.061604.123106.

23. Nicole E. Rader, "Building Trust in Children: How Parents Talk to Children about Safety Precautions in Sweden," *International Review of Victimology* 23, no. 1 (January 2017): 3–16, https://doi.org/10.1177/0269758016672373; Barbara A. Morrongiello and Tess Dawber, "Mothers' Responses to Sons and Daughters Engaging in Injury-Risk Behaviors on a Playground: Implications for Sex Differences in Injury Rates," *Journal of Experimental Child Psychology* 76, no. 2 (June 1, 2000): 89–103, https://doi.org/10.1006/jecp.2000.2572; Elizabeth E. O'Neal and Jodie M. Plumert, "Mother–Child Conversations about Safety: Implications for Socializing Safety Values in Children," *Journal of Pediatric Psychology* 39, no. 4 (May 1, 2014): 481–91, https://doi.org/10.1093/jpepsy/jsu005.

24. Abby Ohlheiser, "'Don't Leave Campus': Parents Are Now Using Tracking Apps to Watch Their Kids at College," *Washington Post*, October 22, 2019, https://www.washingtonpost.com/technology/2019/10/22/dont-leave-campus-parents-are-now-using-tracking-apps-watch-their-kids-college/.

25. Hille Koskela, "'Bold Walk and Breakings': Women's Spatial Confidence versus Fear of Violence," *Gender, Place, and Culture* 4, no. 3 (November 1, 1997): 301–20, https://doi.org/10.1080/09663699725369; Gwen van Eijk, "Between Risk and Resistance: Gender Socialization, Equality, and Ambiguous Norms in Fear of Crime and Safekeeping," *Feminist Criminology* 12, no. 2 (April 2017): 103–24, https://doi.org/10.1177/1557085115605905; Nicole E. Rader, "Women Doing Fear: Applying the Doing Gender Framework to Women's Fear of Crime" (Carbondale, IL: Southern Illinois University, 2005).

26. Nicole E. Rader, "Gendered Fear Strategies: Intersections of Doing Gender and Fear Management Strategies in Married and Divorced Women's Lives," *Sociological Focus* 41, no. 1 (February 2008): 34–52, https://doi.org/10.1080/00380237.2008.10571322; Rader, "Women Doing Fear."

27. O'Neal and Plumert, "Mother–Child Conversations about Safety"; Morrongiello and Dawber, "Mothers' Responses to Sons and Daughters Engaging in Injury-Risk Behaviors on a Playground."

28. Vozmediano et al., "'Watch out, Sweetie'"; De Groof, "And My Mama Said."

29. Warr and Ellison, "Rethinking Social Reactions to Crime."

30. Rader, "Women Doing Fear."

31. Nicole E. Rader, "Until Death Do Us Part? Husband Perceptions and Responses to Fear of Crime," *Deviant Behavior* 31, no. 1 (December 18, 2009): 33–59, https://doi.org/10.1080/01639620902854704.

32. O'Neal and Plumert, "Mother–Child Conversations about Safety"; Raley and Bianchi, "Sons, Daughters, and Family Processes."

33. Gill Valentine, "'Oh Yes I Can.' 'Oh No You Can't': Children and Parents' Understandings of Kids' Competence to Negotiate Public Space Safely," *Antipode* 29, no. 1 (1997): 65–89, https://doi.org/10.1111/1467-8330.00035.

34. Jennifer L. Turner, "Black Mothering in Action: The Racial-Class Socialization Practices of Low-Income Black Single Mothers," *Sociology of Race and Ethnicity* 6, no. 2 (April 2020): 242–53, https://doi.org/10.1177/2332649219899683.

35. Shannon Malone Gonzalez, "Making It Home: An Intersectional Analysis of the Police Talk," *Gender and Society* 33, no. 3 (June 2019): 363–86, https://doi.org/10.1177/0891243219828340.

36. Turner, "Black Mothering in Action."
37. John A. Rich and Courtney M. Grey, "Pathways to Recurrent Trauma among Young Black Men: Traumatic Stress, Substance Use, and the 'Code of the Street,'" *American Journal of Public Health* 95, no. 5 (May 2005): 816–24, https://doi.org/10.2105/AJPH.2004.044560.
38. Dawn Marie Dow, "The Deadly Challenges of Raising African American Boys: Navigating the Controlling Image of the 'Thug,'" *Gender and Society* 30, no. 2 (April 2016): 161–88, https://doi.org/10.1177/0891243216629928.
39. Malone Gonzalez, "Making It Home."
40. Malone Gonzalez, "Making It Home," 371.
41. Jocelyn R. Smith Lee and Michael A. Robinson, "'That's My Number One Fear in Life. It's the Police': Examining Young Black Men's Exposures to Trauma and Loss Resulting from Police Violence and Police Killings," *Journal of Black Psychology* 45, no. 3 (April 2019): 143–84, https://doi.org/10.1177/0095798419865152.
42. Elijah Anderson, *Code of the Street: Decency, Violence, and the Moral Life of the Inner City*, 1st ed. (New York: W.W Norton, 1999).
43. Kristin Turney, "The Mental Health Consequences of Vicarious Adolescent Police Exposure," *Social Forces* 100, no. 3 (2022): 1142–69.
44. Rich and Grey, "Pathways to Recurrent Trauma among Young Black Men."
45. Rich and Grey, "Pathways to Recurrent Trauma among Young Black Men," 818.
46. NCES, "Students' Relationships in School and Feelings about Personal Safety at School," *U.S. Department of Education*, n.d., 2.
47. James Allen Fox and Emma E. Fridel, "The Menace of School Shootings in America," in *The Wiley Handbook on Violence in Education: Forms, Factors, and Preventions*, 1st ed. (John Wiley and Sons, Inc, 2018), 15–35.
48. National Center for Education Statistics, "Violent Deaths at School and Away From School and School Shootings," *Condition of Education*, U.S. Department of Education, Institute of Education Sciences, 2022, https://nces.ed.gov/programs/coe/indicator/a01.
49. M.B. Robinson, *Media Coverage of Crime and Criminal Justice* (Durham, NC: Carolina Academic Press, 2018), 103.
50. "Bullying at School and Electronic Bullying," Indicators of School Crime and Safety: 2019 (National Center for Education Statistics: U.S. Department of Education, 2019), https://nces.ed.gov/programs/coe/indicator/a10.
51. Megan Brenan, "Parents' Concern about School Safety Remains Elevated," Gallup Poll, 2019, https://news.gallup.com/poll/265868/parents-concern-school-safety-remains-elevated.aspx
52. Megan Brenan, "Parents' Concern about School Safety Remains Elevated."
53. Hsiang Iris Chyi and Maxwell McCombs, "Media Salience and the Process of Framing: Coverage of the Columbine School Shootings," *Journalism and Mass Communication Quarterly* 81, no. 1 (March 2004): 22–35, https://doi.org/10.1177/107769900408100103; J.H. Schildkraut, J. Elsass, and C. Stafford, "Could It Happen Here? Moral Panic, School Shootings, and Fear of Crime among College Students," *Crime, Law, and Social Change* 63 (2015): 91–110.
54. Stephen Hilgartner and Charles L. Bosk, "The Rise and Fall of Social Problems: A Public Arenas Model," *American Journal of Sociology* 94, no. 1 (1988): 53–78; Joseph W. Schneider, "Defining the Definitional Perspective on Social Problems," *Social Problems* 32 (n.d.): 232–240; Best, *Threatened Children*.

55. Peter L. Berger and Thomas Luckmann, *The Social Construction of Reality: A Treatise in the Sociology of Knowledge* (London: Penguin Books, 1966; reprint Garden City, NY: Penguin Books, Penguin Social Sciences).

56. Jennifer Paff Ogle, Molly Eckman, and Catherine Amoroso Leslie, "Appearance Cues and the Shootings at Columbine High: Construction of a Social Problem in Print Media," *Sociological Inquiry* 73, no. 1 (2003): 1–27; Chyi and McCombs, "Media Salience and the Process of Framing."

57. M. Brock, N. Kriger, and R. Miro, "School Safety Policies and Programs Administered by the U.S. Federal Government: 1990–2016" (Federal Research Division, Library of Congress: Office of Justice Programs, National Criminal Justice Reference Service, 2018).

58. Brock et al., "School Safety Policies and Programs Administered by the U.S. Federal Government," 50.

59. Christopher J. Schreck and Mitchell J. Miller, "Sources of Fear of Crime at School," *Journal of School Violence* 2, no. 4 (December 12, 2003): 57–79, https://doi.org/10.1300/J202v02n04_04.

60. P. Kaufman et al., "Indicators of School Crime and Safety, 1998" (Washington, DC: U.S. Departments of Education and Justice, 1998), https://ojjdp.ojp.gov/library/publications/annual-report-school-safety-1998.

61. Kaufman et al., "Indicators of School Crime and Safety, 1998."

62. NCES, "Students' Relationships in School and Feelings about Personal Safety at School."

63. DHS, "Final Report of the Federal Commission on School Safety" (United States. Department of Education; United States. Department of Justice; United States. Department of Health and Human Services; United States Department of Homeland Security, December 18, 2018), https://www.hsdl.org/?abstract&did=.

64. DHS, "Final Report of the Federal Commission on School Safety."

65. "Teaching: Respect but Dwindling Appeal." The 50th Annual PDK Poll of the Public's Attitudes toward the Public Schools. September 2018. A supplement to *Kappan Magazine*.

66. Department of Homeland Security, "School and Workplace Violence," https://www.dhs.gov/school-and-workplace-violence.

67. Council of State Governments Justice Center, "School Safety Plans: A Snapshot of Legislative Action" (New York: Council of State Governments Justice Center, February 2014).

68. Stephen Hilgartner and Charles L. Bosk, "The Rise and Fall of Social Problems: A Public Arenas Model," *American Journal of Sociology* 94, no. 1 (1988): 53–78.

69. Allen Fox and Emma E. Fridel, "The Menace of School Shootings in America," in *The Wiley Handbook on Violence in Education: Forms, Factors, and Preventions*, 1st ed. (John Wiley and Sons, Inc, 2018), 15–35.

70. Schreck and Miller, "Sources of Fear of Crime at School," 2003.

71. *The Oprah Winfrey Show*, "How to Protect Yourself Against an Attacker," Harpo Productions, 1991, https://www.oprah.com/.

72. *The Oprah Winfrey Show: The Podcast*, "How to Protect Yourself Against an Attacker," https://omny.fm/shows/the-oprah-winfrey-show-the-podcast/the-oprah-winfrey-show-how-to-protect-yourself-aga#description.

73. Elizabeth A. Stanko, "Women, Crime, and Fear," *The Annals of the American Academy of Political and Social Science* 539, no. 1 (May 1, 1995): 46–58, https://doi.org/10.1177/0002716295539001004.

74. Janet L. Lauritsen et al., "Gender and Violent Victimization, 1973–2005," U.S. Department of Justice, 2009.

75. Jonathan Intravia et al., "Investigating the Relationship between Social Media Consumption and Fear of Crime: A Partial Analysis of Mostly Young Adults," *Computers in Human Behavior* 77 (December 1, 2017): 158–68, https://doi.org/10.1016/j.chb.2017.08.047; Daniel Romer, Kathleen Hall Jamieson, and Sean Aday, "Television News and the Cultivation of Fear of Crime," *Journal of Communication* 53, no. 1 (2003): 88–104, https://doi.org/10.1111/j.1460-2466.2003.tb03007.x.

76. Ronald Weitzer and Charis E. Kubrin, "Breaking News: How Local TV News and Real-World Conditions Affect Fear of Crime," *Justice Quarterly* 21, no. 3 (September 1, 2004): 497–520, https://doi.org/10.1080/07418820400095881; Robinson, *Media Coverage of Crime and Criminal Justice*.

77. Gregg Barak, "Doing Newsmaking Criminology from within the Academy," *Theoretical Criminology* 11, no. 2 (May 2007): 191–207, https://doi.org/10.1177/1362480607075847; Victor E. Kappeler and Gary W. Potter, eds., *Constructing Crime: Perspectives on Making News and Social Problems*, 2nd ed. (Long Grove, IL: Waveland Press, 2006); Ray Surette, *Media, Crime, and Criminal Justice: Images, Realities, and Policies*, 4th ed. (Belmont, CA: Wadsworth, 2011).

78. Surette, *Media, Crime, and Criminal Justice*; Valerie J. Callanan, "Media Consumption, Perceptions of Crime Risk and Fear of Crime: Examining Race/Ethnic Differences," *Sociological Perspectives* 55, no. 1 (March 1, 2012): 93–115, https://doi.org/10.1525/sop.2012.55.1.93.

79. Bernard C. Cohen, *Press and Foreign Policy* (Princeton, NJ: Princeton University Press, 1963).

80. George Gerbner and Larry Gross, "Living with Television: The Violence Profile," *Journal of Communication* 26, no. 2 (June 1, 1976): 172–99, https://doi.org/10.1111/j.1460-2466.1976.tb01397.x.

81. Patrick E. Jamieson and Daniel Romer, "Violence in Popular U.S. Prime Time TV Dramas and the Cultivation of Fear: A Time Series Analysis," *Media and Communication* 2, no. 2 (2014): 31–41.

82. Sydney Cherniawsky and Melanie Morrison, "'You Should Have Known Better': The Social Ramifications of Victimization-Focused Sexual Assault Prevention Tips," *Journal of Interpersonal Violence* (April 29, 2020), https://doi.org/10.1177/0886260520913650.

83. Sarah Britto et al., "Does 'Special' Mean Young, White, and Female? Deconstructing the Meaning of 'Special' in *Law and Order: Special Victims Unit*," *Journal of Criminal Justice and Popular Culture* 14, no. 1 (2007): 39–96; Valerie J. Callanan and Brent Teasdale, "An Exploration of Gender Differences in Measurement of Fear of Crime," *Feminist Criminology* 4, no. 4 (October 1, 2009): 359–76, https://doi.org/10.1177/1557085109345462; Callanan, "Media Consumption, Perceptions of Crime Risk and Fear of Crime."

84. Cherniawsky and Morrison, "'You Should Have Known Better'"; Nicole E. Rader, Gayle M. Rhineberger-Dunn, and Lauren Vasquez, "Victim Blame in Fictional Crime Dramas: An Examination of Demographic, Incident-Related, and Behavioral Factors," *Women and Criminal Justice* 26, no. 1 (January 2016): 55–75, https://doi.org/10.1080/08974454.2015.1023487.

85. Valerie J. Callanan and J.T. Rosenberger, "Media, Gender, and Fear of Crime," *Criminal Justice Review* 40, no. 3 (2015): 322–39.

86. Weitzer and Kubrin, "Breaking News"; Barak, "Doing Newsmaking Criminology from within the Academy."

87. Callanan, "Media Consumption, Perceptions of Crime Risk and Fear of Crime"; Jodi Lane and James W. Meeker, "Ethnicity, Information Sources, and Fear of Crime," *Deviant Behavior* 24, no. 1 (January 1, 2003): 1–26, https://doi.org/10.1080/10639620390117165.

88. Robinson, *Media Coverage of Crime and Criminal Justice*.

89. Cherniawsky and Morrison, "'You Should Have Known Better.'"

90. Kappeler and Potter, *Constructing Crime*; Barak, "Doing Newsmaking Criminology from within the Academy"; Surette, *Media, Crime, and Criminal Justice*.

91. Robinson, *Media Coverage of Crime and Criminal Justice*.

92. Callanan, "Media Consumption, Perceptions of Crime Risk and Fear of Crime"; Weitzer and Kubrin, "Breaking News."

93. Robinson, *Media Coverage of Crime and Criminal Justice*.

94. Britto et al., "Does 'Special' Mean Young, White, and Female? Deconstructing the Meaning of 'Special' in *Law and Order: Special Victims Unit*."

95. Britto et al., "Does 'Special' Mean Young, White, and Female? Deconstructing the Meaning of 'Special' in *Law and Order: Special Victims Unit*."

96. Gregory G. Justis and Steven Chermak, "Framing the Scene: Presentations of Forensics Programming in the News," in *Sociology of Crime, Law and Deviance*, ed. Mathieu Deflem (Bingley, West Yorkshire, England: Emerald Group Publishing Limited, 2010), 221, https://doi.org/10.1108/S1521-6136(2010)0000014013.

97. Gayle Rhineberger-Dunn, Steven J. Briggs, and Nicole E. Rader, "The CSI Effect, DNA Discourse, and Popular Crime Dramas," *Social Science Quarterly* 98, no. 2 (June 2017): 532–47, https://doi.org/10.1111/ssqu.12289; Justis and Chermak, "Framing the Scene."

98. Rader, Rhineberger-Dunn, and Vasquez, "Victim Blame in Fictional Crime Dramas."

99. Britto et al., "Does 'Special' Mean Young, White, and Female? Deconstructing the Meaning of 'Special' in *Law and Order: Special Victims Unit*."

100. Robinson, *Media Coverage of Crime and Criminal Justice*; Rhineberger-Dunn, Briggs, and Rader, "The CSI Effect, DNA Discourse, and Popular Crime Dramas."

101. Esther Madriz, *Nothing Bad Happens to Good Girls: Fear of Crime in Women's Lives* (Berkeley: University of California Press, 1997).

CHAPTER 3

1. J.E. Cobbina, J. Miller, and R.K. Brunson, "Gender, Neighborhood Danger, and Risk-Avoidance Strategies among Urban African-American Youths," *Criminology* 46, no. 3 (2008): 673–709.

2. Jodi Lane, Nicole Rader, Billy Henson, David May, and Bonnie Fisher, *Fear of Crime: Causes, Consequences, and Contradictions* (Durham, NC: Carolina Academic Press, 2014); Chris Hale, "Fear of Crime: A Review of the Literature," *International Review of Victimology* 4, no. 2 (January 1, 1996): 79–150, https://doi.org/10.1177/026975809600400201.

3. Nicole E. Rader and Stacy H. Haynes, "Avoidance, Protective, and Weapons Behaviors: An Examination of Constrained Behaviors and Their Impact on Concerns about Crime," *Journal of Crime and Justice* 37, no. 2 (2014): 197–213.

4. Christopher W. Mullins and Sou Lee, "'Like Make Up on a Man': The Gendered Nature of Gun Norms," *Deviant Behavior* 41, no. 3 (March 3, 2020): 294–310, https://doi.org/10.1080/01639625.2019.1565515; Gary Kleck et al., "The Effect of Perceived Risk

and Victimization on Plans to Purchase a Gun for Self-Protection," *Journal of Criminal Justice* 39, no. 4 (2010): 312–19, https://doi.org/10.1016/j.jcrimjus.2011.03.002.

5. Matthew R. Lee, Timothy C. Hayes, and Shaun A. Thomas, "Revisiting the Southern Culture of Violence," *The Sociological Quarterly* 48 (2007): 253–75.

6. Men are more likely to own guns than women: Mullins and Lee, "'Like Make Up on a Man.'" Whites are more likely to own guns than non-Whites: Lane et al., *Fear of Crime*. See Kleck et al., "The Effect of Perceived Risk and Victimization on Plans to Purchase a Gun for Self-Protection," and Mullins and Lee, "'Like Make Up on a Man'" for a more detailed discussion of gun ownership, fear of crime, and race/gender differences.

7. Kleck et al., "The Effect of Perceived Risk and Victimization on Plans to Purchase a Gun for Self-Protection."

8. Mullins and Lee, "'Like Make Up on a Man.'"

9. Kleck et al., "The Effect of Perceived Risk and Victimization on Plans to Purchase a Gun for Self-Protection."

10. Carrying mace/pepper spray is a more common precautionary behavior for women: Pamela Wilcox, Carol E. Jordan, and Adam J. Pritchard, "A Multidimensional Examination of Campus Safety: Victimization, Perceptions of Danger, Worry about Crime, and Precautionary Behavior among College Women in the Post-Clery Era," *Crime and Delinquency* 53, no. 2 (April 2007): 219–54, https://doi.org/10.1177/0097700405283664; Rader and Haynes, "Avoidance, Protective, and Weapons Behaviors." Studies that talk to college students (especially women) have focused on preventive behavior: Wesley G. Jennings, Angela R. Gover, and Dagmar Pudrzynska, "Are Institutions of Higher Learning Safe? A Descriptive Study of Campus Safety Issues and Self-Reported Campus Victimization among Male and Female College Students," *Journal of Criminal Justice Education* 18, no. 2 (July 2007): 191–208, https://doi.org/10.1080/10511250701383327; Wilcox, Jordan, and Pritchard, "A Multidimensional Examination of Campus Safety"; Bonnie S. Fisher and David May, "College Students' Crime-Related Fears on Campus: Are Fear-Provoking Cues Gendered?" *Journal of Contemporary Criminal Justice* 25, no. 3 (August 2009): 300–321, https://doi.org/10.1177/1043986209335013.

11. Lance R. Hignite, Shantal Marshall, and Laura Naumann, "The Ivory Tower Meets the Inner City: Student Protective and Avoidance Behaviors on an Urban University Campus," *College Student Journal* 52, no. 1 (March 1, 2018).

12. Kristine De Welde, "White Women Beware!: Whiteness, Fear of Crime, and Self-Defense," *Race, Gender and Class* 10, no. 4 (2003): 75–91; Rader and Haynes, "Avoidance, Protective, and Weapons Behaviors."

13. Alex Campbell, "Keeping the 'Lady' Safe: The Regulation of Femininity through Crime Prevention Literature," *Critical Criminology* 13, no. 2 (January 2005): 119–40, https://doi.org/10.1007/s10612-005-2390-z; De Welde, "White Women Beware!"

14. "Rape Aggression Defense System Programs (R.A.D.)" (Denham Springs, LA: R.A.D. Systems International Headquarters, n.d.), http://www.rad-systems.com/rad_programs.html.

15. "Rape Aggression Defense System Programs (R.A.D.)."

16. "Rape Aggression Defense System Programs (R.A.D.)."

17. Campbell, "Keeping the 'Lady' Safe."

18. CrossFit, n.d., https://www.crossfit.com/.

19. De Welde, "White Women Beware!"

20. De Welde, "White Women Beware!"

21. Aliza Vigderman, "Do I Need a Security System?" Security.org, August 23, 2021, https://www.security.org/home-security-systems/do-i-need-one/.

22. Carlos J. Vilalta, "Fear of Crime and Home Security Systems," *Police Practice and Research* 13, no. 1 (February 1, 2012): 4–14, https://doi.org/10.1080/15614263.2011.607651.

23. Allen E. Liska, Andrew Sanchirico, and Mark D. Reed, "Fear of Crime and Constrained Behavior Specifying and Estimating a Reciprocal Effects Model," *Social Forces* 66, no. 3 (1988): 827–837.

24. David C. May, Nicole E. Rader, and Sarah Goodrum, "A Gendered Assessment of the 'Threat of Victimization': Examining Gender Differences in Fear of Crime, Perceived Risk, Avoidance, and Defensive Behaviors," *Criminal Justice Review* 35, no. 2 (June 2010): 159–82, https://doi.org/10.1177/0734016809349166; Lane et al., *Fear of Crime*; Vilalta, "Fear of Crime and Home Security Systems"; Hannah Scott, "Stranger Danger: Explaining Women's Fear of Crime," *Western Criminology Review* 4, no. 3 (2003): 203–214.

25. ADT, n.d., https://www.macrotrends.net/stocks/charts/ADT/adt/revenue.

26. https://www.ispot.tv/ad/7Rdg/adt-before-something-bad-happens.

27. De Welde, "White Women Beware!"; Esther Madriz, "Images of Criminals and Victims: A Study of Women's Fear and Social Control," *Gender and Society* 11 (1997): 342–56; Scott, "Stranger Danger"; Elizabeth A. Stanko, "Women, Crime, and Fear," *The Annals of the American Academy of Political and Social Science* 539, no. 1 (May 1, 1995): 46–58, https://doi.org/10.1177/0002716295539001004.

28. May, Rader, and Goodrum, "A Gendered Assessment of the 'Threat of Victimization.'"

29. Hale, "Fear of Crime"; May, Rader, and Goodrum, "A Gendered Assessment of the 'Threat of Victimization'"; Lane et al., *Fear of Crime*.

30. Scott, "Stranger Danger," 12.

31. Scott, "Stranger Danger," 212.

32. Carl Keane, "Evaluating the Influence of Fear of Crime as an Environmental Mobility Restrictor on Women's Routine Activities," *Environment and Behavior* 30, no. 1 (January 1, 1998): 60–74, https://doi.org/10.1177/0013916598301003.

33. Keane, "Evaluating the Influence of Fear of Crime as an Environmental Mobility Restrictor on Women's Routine Activities," 70.

34. Jocelyn A. Hollander, "Vulnerability and Dangerousness: The Construction of Gender through Conversation about Violence," *Gender and Society* 15, no. 1 (February 1, 2001): 105, https://doi.org/10.1177/089124301015001005.

35. Gustavo S. Mesch, "Women's Fear of Crime: The Role of Fear for the Well-Being of Significant Others," *Violence and Victims* 15, no. 3 (January 1, 2000): 323–36, https://doi.org/10.1891/0886-6708.15.3.323.

36. Andres F. Rengifo and Amanda Bolton, "Routine Activities and Fear of Crime: Specifying Individual-Level Mechanisms," *European Journal of Criminology* 9, no. 2 (2012): 99–119.

37. Alec Brownlow, "A Geography of Men's Fear," *Geoforum* 36 (2005): 581–92.

38. Esther Madriz, *Nothing Bad Happens to Good Girls: Fear of Crime in Women's Lives* (Berkeley: University of California Press, 1997), 117.

39. Madriz, *Nothing Bad Happens to Good Girls*, 123.

40. John Creamer, "Inequalities Persist Despite Decline in Poverty for All Major Race and Hispanic Origin Groups" (Washington, DC: U.S. Census Bureau, April 14, 2021), https://www.census.gov/library/stories/2020/09/poverty-rates-for-blacks-and-hispanics-reached-historic-lows-in-2019.html.

41. Kristen Day, "Constructing Masculinity and Women's Fear in Public Space in Irvine, California," *Gender, Place, and Culture* 8, no. 2 (June 1, 2001): 114, https://doi.org/10.1080/09663690120050742.; Madriz, "Images of Criminals and Victims"; De Welde, "White Women Beware!"

42. Cobbina, Miller, and Brunson, "Gender, neighborhood danger, and risk-avoidance strategies among urban African-American youths."

43. Hille Koskela, "'Bold Walk and Breakings': Women's Spatial Confidence versus Fear of Violence," *Gender, Place, and Culture* 4, no. 3 (November 1, 1997): 301–20, https://doi.org/10.1080/09663699725369; Gwen van Eijk, "Between Risk and Resistance: Gender Socialization, Equality, and Ambiguous Norms in Fear of Crime and Safekeeping," *Feminist Criminology* 12, no. 2 (April 2017): 103–24, https://doi.org/10.1177/1557085115605905; Diederik Cops and Stefaan Pleysier, "'Doing Gender' in Fear of Crime: The Impact of Gender Identity on Reported Levels of Fear of Crime in Adolescents and Young Adults," *The British Journal of Criminology* 51, no. 1 (January 1, 2011): 58–74, https://doi.org/10.1093/bjc/azq065.

44. Oona Brooks, "'Guys! Stop Doing It!': Young Women's Adoption and Rejection of Safety Advice When Socializing in Bars, Pubs, and Clubs," *The British Journal of Criminology* 51, no. 4 (July 1, 2011): 635–51, https://doi.org/10.1093/bjc/azr011.

45. Reviewed by *Psychology Today* staff, "Self-Talk," psychologytoday.com, November 10, 2017, https://www.psychologytoday.com/us/basics/self-talk#:~:text=Many%20people%20are%20conscious%20of,interpret%20and%20process%20daily%20experiences.

46. Piotr K. Oles, Thomas M. Brinthaupt, Rachel Dier, and Dominka Polak, "Types of Inner Dialogues and Functions of Self-Talk: Comparisons and Implications," *Frontiers in Psychology*, published online March 6, 2020, doi: 10.3389/fpsyg.2020.00227.

47. Nicole E. Rader, "Women Doing Fear: Applying the Doing Gender Framework to Women's Fear of Crime" (Carbondale, IL: Southern Illinois University, 2005).

48. Nicole E. Rader, "Gendered Fear Strategies: Intersections of Doing Gender and Fear Management Strategies in Married and Divorced Women's Lives," *Sociological Focus* 41, no. 1 (February 2008): 34–52, https://doi.org/10.1080/00380237.2008.10571322.

49. Rader, "Gendered Fear Strategies"; Nicole E. Rader, "Until Death Do Us Part? Husband Perceptions and Responses to Fear of Crime," *Deviant Behavior* 31, no. 1 (December 18, 2009): 33–59, https://doi.org/10.1080/01639620902854704. Nicole E. Rader, "Until Death Do Us Part? Husband Perceptions and Responses to Fear of Crime," *Deviant Behavior* 31, no. 1 (December 18, 2009): 33–59, https://doi.org/10.1080/01639620902854704.

50. Rader, "Women Doing Fear."

51. Sydney Cherniawsky and Melanie Morrison, "'You Should Have Known Better': The Social Ramifications of Victimization-Focused Sexual Assault Prevention Tips," *Journal of Interpersonal Violence* (April 29, 2020): 3, https://doi.org/10.1177/0886260520913650.

52. Michael Norris, "Campus Safety and Security: A Team Effort," National Association of Student Personnel Administrators (NASPA): Student Affairs Administrators in Higher Education, n.d., https://www.naspa.org/blog/campus-safety-and-security-a-team-effort.

53. Norris, "Campus Safety and Security: A Team Effort."

54. J. Hibdon, Joseph A. Schafer, and M. Summers, "Avoidance Behaviors in a Campus Residential Environment," *Criminology, Criminal Justice Law and Society* 17, no. 3 (2016): 74–89; Rader and Haynes, "Avoidance, Protective, and Weapons Behaviors";

Hollander, "Vulnerability And Dangerousness"; Stanko, "Women, Crime, and Fear"; Lane et al., *Fear of Crime.*

55. Gwen van Eijk, "Between Risk and Resistance: Gender Socialization, Equality, and Ambiguous Norms in Fear of Crime and Safekeeping," *Feminist Criminology* 12, no. 2 (April 2017): 103–24, https://doi.org/10.1177/1557085115605905.

56. Van Eijk, "Between Risk and Resistance," 107.

57. Van Eijk, "Between Risk and Resistance," 117.

58. Van Eijk, "Between Risk and Resistance"; Rader, "Women Doing Fear"; Rader, "Gendered Fear Strategies."

59. Day, "Constructing Masculinity and Women's Fear in Public Space in Irvine, California"; Carol Brooks Gardner, "Analyzing Gender in Public Places: Rethinking Goffman's Vision of Everyday Life," *The American Sociologist* 20, no. 1 (March 1, 1989): 42, https://doi.org/10.1007/BF02697786; Stanko, "Women, Crime, and Fear."

60. Stanko, "Women, Crime, and Fear"; Hollander and Rodgers, "Constructing Victims"; Cherniawsky and Morrison, "'You Should Have Known Better.'"

61. Stanko, "Women, Crime, and Fear," 51.

62. Shannan Catalano et al., "Female Victims of Violence," *U.S. Department of Justice Publications and Materials*, October 1, 2009, https://digitalcommons.unl.edu/usjusticematls/7.

63. De Welde, "White Women Beware!"; Gardner, "Analyzing Gender in Public Places"; Rader, "Gendered Fear Strategies."

64. Stanko, "Women, Crime, and Fear"; Madriz, "Images of Criminals and Victims."

65. Scott, "Stranger Danger"; van Eijk, "Between Risk and Resistance."

66. Madriz, "Images of Criminals and Victims"; Stanko, "Women, Crime, and Fear"; Gardner, "Analyzing Gender in Public Places"; Hollander and Rodgers, "Constructing Victims."

CHAPTER 4

1. Elizabeth E. O'Neal and Jodie M. Plumert, "Mother–Child Conversations about Safety: Implications for Socializing Safety Values in Children," *Journal of Pediatric Psychology* 39, no. 4 (May 1, 2014): 481–91, https://doi.org/10.1093/jpepsy/jsu005; Saskia De Groof, "And My Mama Said: The (Relative) Parental Influence on Fear of Crime among Adolescent Girls and Boys," *Youth and Society* 39, no. 3 (March 2008): 267–93, https://doi.org/10.1177/0044118X07301000; Nicole E. Rader, "Building Trust in Children: How Parents Talk to Children about Safety Precautions in Sweden," *International Review of Victimology* 23, no. 1 (January 2017): 3–16, https://doi.org/10.1177/0269758016672373.

2. Evan Altar, Malica Nikolic, and Susan M. Bogels, "Environmental Transmission of Generalized Anxiety Disorder from Parents to Children: Worries, Experiential Avoidance, and Intolerance of Uncertainty," *Dialogues Clinical Neurosciences* 19 (2017): 137.

3. Mark Warr and Christopher G. Ellison, "Rethinking Social Reactions to Crime: Personal and Altruistic Fear in Family Households," *American Journal of Sociology* 106, no. 3 (2001): 551–78, https://doi.org/10.1086/318964.

4. Warr and Ellison, "Rethinking Social Reactions to Crime."

5. Jacinta Francis et al., "'I'll Be Driving You to School for the Rest of Your Life': A Qualitative Study of Parents' Fear of Stranger Danger," *Journal of Environmental Psychology* 53 (November 1, 2017): 112–20, https://doi.org/10.1016/j.jenvp.2017.07.004.

6. Francis et al., "'I'll Be Driving You to School for the Rest of Your Life.'"

7. Francis et al., "'I'll Be Driving You to School for the Rest of Your Life,'" 112.
8. Joel Best, *Threatened Children: Rhetoric and Concern about Child-Victims* (Chicago: University of Chicago Press, 1990).
9. Rachel Pain, "Paranoid Parenting? Rematerializing Risk and Fear for Children," *Social and Cultural Geography* 7, no. 2 (April 1, 2006): 221–43, https://doi.org/10.1080/14649360600600585.
10. M. Stokes, "Stranger Danger: Child Protection and Parental Fears in the Risk Society," *Undefined*, 2009, 18, https://www.semanticscholar.org/paper/Stranger-Danger%3A-Child-Protection-and-Parental-in-Stokes/8605d54a79757ebd36778bd0561aa6b31b5faa16.
11. Karen Malone, "The Bubble-Wrap Generation: Children Growing Up in Walled Gardens," *Environmental Education Research* 13, no. 4 (September 1, 2007): 513–27, https://doi.org/10.1080/13504620701581612.
12. Malone, "The Bubble-Wrap Generation," 516.
13. Malone, "The Bubble-Wrap Generation."
14. Laura M. Padilla-Walker and Larry J. Nelson, "Black Hawk Down?: Establishing Helicopter Parenting as a Distinct Construct from Other Forms of Parental Control during Emerging Adulthood," *Journal of Adolescence* 35, no. 5 (October 2012): 1177–90, https://doi.org/10.1016/j.adolescence.2012.03.007; Chrystyna D. Kouros et al., "Helicopter Parenting, Autonomy Support, and College Students' Mental Health and Well-Being: The Moderating Role of Sex and Ethnicity," *Journal of Child and Family Studies* 26, no. 3 (March 2017): 939–49, https://doi.org/10.1007/s10826-016-0614-3.
15. Elizabeth E. O'Neal and Jodie M. Plumert, "Mother–Child Conversations about Safety: Implications for Socializing Safety Values in Children," *Journal of Pediatric Psychology* 39, no. 4 (May 1, 2014): 481–91, https://doi.org/10.1093/jpepsy/jsu005.
16. Altar, Nikolic, and Bogels, "Environmental Transmission of Generalized Anxiety Disorder from Parents to Children"; De Groof, "And My Mama Said."
17. Daniel Larsson, "Fear of Crime among the Poor in Britain and Sweden," *International Review of Victimology* 15, no. 3 (January 1, 2009): 223–54, https://doi.org/10.1177/026975800901500302; Rader, "Building Trust in Children."
18. Stokes, "Stranger Danger"; Hannah Scott, "Stranger Danger: Explaining Women's Fear of Crime," *Criminology Review* 4, no. 3 (2003): 203–213.
19. Roslyn Muraskin and Shelly Feuer Domash, *Crime and the Media: Headlines vs. Reality* (Upper Saddle River, NJ: Pearson Prentice Hall, 2007).
20. For more information on this kit, see: childidprogram.com.the-id-kit/2021.
21. National Child Identification Program, "Prevention Tips," 2021, https://childidprogram.com/prevention-tips/.
22. National Child Identification Program, "Prevention Tips."
23. Barbara A. Morrongiello and Tess Dawber, "Mothers' Responses to Sons and Daughters Engaging in Injury-Risk Behaviors on a Playground: Implications for Sex Differences in Injury Rates," *Journal of Experimental Child Psychology* 76, no. 2 (June 1, 2000): 89–103, https://doi.org/10.1006/jecp.2000.2572
24. Morrongiello and Dawber, "Mothers' Responses to Sons and Daughters Engaging in Injury-Risk Behaviors on a Playground," 91.
25. Morrongiello and Dawber, "Mothers' Responses to Sons and Daughters Engaging in Injury-Risk Behaviors on a Playground," 100.
26. Sara Raley and Suzanne Bianchi, "Sons, Daughters, and Family Processes: Does Gender of Children Matter?" *Annual Review of Sociology* 32, no. 1 (2006): 401–21, https://doi.org/10.1146/annurev.soc.32.061604.123106; O'Neal and Plumert, "Mother–Child

Conversations about Safety"; Morrongiello and Dawber, "Mothers' Responses to Sons and Daughters Engaging in Injury-Risk Behaviors on a Playground."

27. Raley and Bianchi, "Sons, Daughters, and Family Processes"; Lisa Hutchinson Wallace and David C. May, "The Impact of Parental Attachment and Feelings of Isolation on Adolescent Fear of Crime at School," *Adolescence (San Diego): An International Quarterly Devoted to the Physiological, Psychological, Psychiatric, Sociological, and Educational Aspects of the Second Decade of Human Life* 40, no. 159 (September 22, 2005).

28. Kevin M. Drakulich, "Concerns for Self or Family? Sources of and Responses to Altruistic Fear," *Journal of Interpersonal Violence* 30, no. 7 (April 1, 2015): 1168–1207, https://doi.org/10.1177/0886260514539842.

29. Susan M. McHale, Ann C. Crouter, and Shawn D. Whiteman, "The Family Contexts of Gender Development in Childhood and Adolescence," *Social Development* 12, no. 1 (2003): 125–48, https://doi.org/10.1111/1467-9507.00225.

30. Sara Raley and Suzanne Bianchi, "Sons, Daughters, and Family Processes: Does Gender of Children Matter?" *Annual Review of Sociology* 32, no. 1 (2006): 401–21, https://doi.org/10.1146/annurev.soc.32.061604.123106.

31. Daniel Paquette, "Theorizing the Father-Child Relationship: Mechanisms and Developmental Outcomes," *Human Development* 47, no. 4 (2004): 193–219, https://doi.org/10.1159/000078723.

32. Mick Cunningham, "The Influence of Parental Attitudes and Behaviors on Children's Attitudes toward Gender and Household Labor in Early Adulthood," *Journal of Marriage and Family* 63, no. 1 (February 2001): 111–22, https://doi.org/10.1111/j.1741-3737.2001.00111.x.

33. Katie M. Lawson, Ann C. Crouter, and Susan M. McHale, "Links between Family Gender Socialization Experiences in Childhood and Gendered Occupational Attainment in Young Adulthood," *Journal of Vocational Behavior* 90 (October 1, 2015): 26–35, https://doi.org/10.1016/j.jvb.2015.07.003.

34. Lawson, Crouter, and McHale, "Links between Family Gender Socialization Experiences in Childhood and Gendered Occupational Attainment in Young Adulthood," 24.

35. Lawson, Crouter, and McHale, "Links between Family Gender Socialization Experiences in Childhood and Gendered Occupational Attainment in Young Adulthood"; Laura Vozmediano et al., "'Watch out, Sweetie': The Impact of Gender and Offence Type on Parents' Altruistic Fear of Crime," *Sex Roles* 77, no. 9 (November 1, 2017): 676–86, https://doi.org/10.1007/s11199-017-0758-7.; O'Neal and Plumert, "Mother–Child Conversations about Safety."

36. Rachel Pain, "Paranoid Parenting? Rematerializing Risk and Fear for Children," *Social and Cultural Geography* 7, no. 2 (April 1, 2006): 221–43, https://doi.org/10.1080/14649360600600585. Pain quoting from S. Jackson and S. Scott, "Risk Anxiety and the Social Construction of Childhood," in *Risk and Sociocultural Theory: New Directions and Perspectives*, edited by D. Lupton (Cambridge: Cambridge University Press, 1999).

37. Pain, "Paranoid Parenting?"; Malone, "The Bubble-Wrap Generation."

38. Mary Jane Kehily, "Childhood in Crisis? Tracing the Contours of 'Crisis' and Its Impact upon Contemporary Parenting Practices," *Media, Culture, and Society* 32, no. 2 (March 2010): 171–85, https://doi.org/10.1177/0163443709355605.

39. De Groof, "And My Mama Said"; Zuzana Podaná and Eva Krulichová, "The Impact of Parenting Style on Fear of Crime among Adolescent Girls and Boys," *Journal of*

Youth Studies 21, no. 8 (September 14, 2018): 1077–94, https://doi.org/10.1080/13676261.2018.1449945.

40. Francis et al., "'I'll Be Driving You to School for the Rest of Your Life'"; Justen O'Connor and Alice Brown, "A Qualitative Study of 'Fear' as a Regulator of Children's Independent Physical Activity in the Suburbs," *Health and Place* 24 (November 1, 2013): 157–64, https://doi.org/10.1016/j.healthplace.2013.09.002.

41. Mariana Brussoni et al., "A Qualitative Investigation of Unsupervised Outdoor Activities for 10- to 13-Year-Old Children: 'I like Adventuring but I Don't like Adventuring without Being Careful,'" *Journal of Environmental Psychology* 70 (August 2020): 101460, https://doi.org/10.1016/j.jenvp.2020.101460; David C. May, Lesa Rae Vartanian, and Keri Virgo, "The Impact of Parental Attachment and Supervision on Fear of Crime among Adolescent Males," *Adolescence* 37, no. 146 (2002): 267–87.

42. May, Vartanian, and Virgo, "The Impact of Parental Attachment and Supervision on Fear of Crime among Adolescent Males"; Brussoni et al., "A Qualitative Investigation of Unsupervised Outdoor Activities for 10- to 13-Year-Old Children"; Morrongiello and Dawber, "Mothers' Responses to Sons and Daughters Engaging in Injury-Risk Behaviors on a Playground."

43. Malone, "The Bubble-Wrap Generation."

44. Ding et al., "Is Fear of Strangers Related to Physical Activity among Youth?" *American Journal of Health Promotion* 26, no. 3 (January 2012): 189–95, https://doi.org/10.4278/ajhp.100701-QUAN-224.

45. O'Connor and Brown, "A Qualitative Study of 'Fear' as a Regulator of Children's Independent Physical Activity in the Suburbs"; Sarah Foster et al., "The Impact of Parents' Fear of Strangers and Perceptions of Informal Social Control on Children's Independent Mobility," *Health and Place* 26 (March 1, 2014): 60–68, https://doi.org/10.1016/j.healthplace.2013.11.006.

46. Foster et al., "The Impact of Parents' Fear of Strangers and Perceptions of Informal Social Control on Children's Independent Mobility"; Ding et al., "Is Fear of Strangers Related to Physical Activity among Youth?"; O'Connor and Brown, "A Qualitative Study of 'Fear' as a Regulator of Children's Independent Physical Activity in the Suburbs."

47. Altar, Nikolic, and Bogels, "Environmental Transmission of Generalized Anxiety Disorder from Parents to Children: Worries, Experiential Avoidance, and Intolerance of Uncertainty."

48. Lisa Hutchinson Wallace and David C. May, "The Impact of Parental Attachment and Feelings of Isolation on Adolescent Fear of Crime at School," *Adolescence (San Diego): An International Quarterly Devoted to the Physiological, Psychological, Psychiatric, Sociological, and Educational Aspects of the Second Decade of Human Life* 40, no. 159 (September 22, 2005): 457.

49. Nicole E. Rader, "Building Trust in Children."

50. Malone, "The Bubble-Wrap Generation."

51. Stokes, "Stranger Danger."

52. Malone, "The Bubble-Wrap Generation."

53. David Finkelhor et al., "Youth Internet Safety Education: Aligning Programs with the Evidence Base," *Trauma, Violence, and Abuse*, April 3, 2020, https://doi.org/10.1177/1524838020916257; Kehily, "Childhood in Crisis?"

54. M. Valcke et al., "Internet Parenting Styles and the Impact on Internet Use of Primary School Children," *Computers and Education* 55, no. 2 (September 2010): 454–64, https://doi.org/10.1016/j.compedu.2010.02.009.

55. Finkelhor et al., "Youth Internet Safety Education"; Valcke et al., "Internet Parenting Styles and the Impact on Internet Use of Primary School Children."

56. Valcke et al., "Internet Parenting Styles and the Impact on Internet Use of Primary School Children."

57. Sonia Livingstone et al., "Maximizing Opportunities and Minimizing Risks for Children Online: The Role of Digital Skills in Emerging Strategies of Parental Mediation: Maximizing Opportunities and Minimizing Risks," *Journal of Communication* 67, no. 1 (February 2017): 82–105, https://doi.org/10.1111/jcom.12277.

58. Livingstone et al., "Maximizing Opportunities and Minimizing Risks for Children Online," 99.

59. Brooke Auxier and Monica Anderson, "Social Media Use in 2021" (Pew Research Center, 2021).

60. Auxier and Anderson, "Social Media Use in 2021."

61. Marian I. Tulloch, "Parental Fear of Crime: A Discursive Analysis," *Journal of Sociology* 40, no. 4 (December 1, 2004): 362–77, https://doi.org/10.1177/1440783304048380.

62. Francis et al., "'I'll Be Driving You to School for the Rest of Your Life.'"

63. Livingstone et al., "Maximizing Opportunities and Minimizing Risks for Children Online"; Francis et al., "'I'll Be Driving You to School for the Rest of Your Life'"; Malone, "The Bubble-Wrap Generation."

64. Malone, "The Bubble-Wrap Generation."

65. Finkelhor et al., "Youth Internet Safety Education"; Penn State University and Michelle Wright, "Cyberbullying Victimization through Social Networking Sites and Adjustment Difficulties: The Role of Parental Mediation," *Journal of the Association for Information Systems* 19 (August 2018): 113–23, https://doi.org/10.17705/1jais.00486; Valcke et al., "Internet Parenting Styles and the Impact on Internet Use of Primary School Children."

66. Brian Simpson, "Tracking Children, Constructing Fear: GPS and the Manufacture of Family Safety," *Information and Communications Technology Law* 23, no. 3 (September 2, 2014): 273–85, https://doi.org/10.1080/13600834.2014.970377.

67. Simpson, "Tracking Children, Constructing Fear"; Amy Adele Hasinoff, "Where Are You? Location Tracking and the Promise of Child Safety," *Television and New Media* 18, no. 6 (September 2017): 496–512, https://doi.org/10.1177/1527476416680450.

68. Abby Ohlheiser, "'Don't Leave Campus': Parents Are Now Using Tracking Apps to Watch Their Kids at College," *Washington Post*, October 22, 2019, https://www.washingtonpost.com/technology/2019/10/22/dont-leave-campus-parents-are-now-using-tracking-apps-watch-their-kids-college/.

69. Brett Singer, "11 Best Apps for Parents to Monitor Their Kids," *Parents*, June 11, 2020, https://www.parents.com/parenting/technology/best-apps-for-paranoid-parents/.

70. https://www.life360.com/.

71. Allen E. Liska, Andrew Sanchirico, and Mark D. Reed, "Fear of Crime and Constrained Behavior: Specifying and Estimating a Reciprocal Effects Model," *Social Forces* 66, no. 3 (1988): 827–37.

72. M. Valcke et al., "Internet Parenting Styles and the Impact on Internet Use of Primary School Children," *Computers and Education* 55, no. 2 (September 2010): 454–64, https://doi.org/10.1016/j.compedu.2010.02.009.

73. Brian Simpson, "Tracking Children, Constructing Fear: GPS and the Manufacture of Family Safety," *Information and Communications Technology Law* 23, no. 3 (September 2, 2014): 273–85, https://doi.org/10.1080/13600834.2014.970377.

74. Tommy K.H. Chan, Christy M.K. Cheung, and Zach W.Y. Lee, "Cyberbullying on Social Networking Sites: A Literature Review and Future Research Directions," *Information and Management* 58, no. 2 (March 2021): 103411, https://doi.org/10.1016/j.im.2020.103411.

75. Michelle Wright, "Cyberbullying Victimization through Social Networking Sites and Adjustment Difficulties: The Role of Parental Mediation," *Journal of the Association for Information Systems* 19 (August 2018): 113–23, https://doi.org/10.17705/1jais.00486.

76. Chan, Cheung, and Lee, "Cyberbullying on Social Networking Sites"; Danah Boyd and Eszter Hargittai, "Connected and Concerned: Variatin in Parents' Online Safety Concerns," *Policy and Internet* 5, no. 3 (2013).

77. "Cyberbullying—What Is It?" (Washington, DC: U.S. Department of Health and Human Services, 2021), https://www.stopbullying.gov/cyberbullying/what-is-it.

78. "Bullying at School and Electronic Bullying," Indicators of School Crime and Safety: 2019 (National Center for Education Statistics: U.S. Department of Education, 2019), https://nces.ed.gov/programs/coe/indicator/a10.

79. "Cyberbullying—What Is It?"

80. Auxier and Anderson, "Social Media Use in 2021"; Maeve Duggan et al., "Parents and Social Media" (Pew Research Center, July 16, 2015), https://www.pewresearch.org/internet/2015/07/16/parents-and-social-media/.

81. "Cyberbullying—What Is It?"

82. Because cyberbullying is more common among girls: "Bullying at School and Electronic Bullying." White girls report this behavior more than non-White girls: Kathleen C. Basile et al., "Interpersonal Violence Victimization among High School Students—Youth Risk Behavior Survey, United States, 2019," *Morbidity and Mortality Weekly Report*, U.S. Department of Health and Human Services/Centers for Disease Control and Prevention, 69, no. 1 (August 1, 2020): 28–37.Additionally, some research shows girls who identify as two or more races are also likely to experience cyberbullying victimization at higher rates than other groups of girls.

83. Pain, "Paranoid Parenting?"; Stokes, "Stranger Danger."

84. Megan Brenan, "Parents' Concern about School Safety Remains Elevated," Gallup Poll, 2019, https://news.gallup.com/poll/265868/parents-concern-school-safety-remains-elevated.aspx.

85. Michael G. Huskey and Nadine M. Connell, "Preparation or Provocation? Student Perceptions of Active Shooter Drills," *Criminal Justice Policy Review* 32, no. 1 (February 1, 2021): 3–26, https://doi.org/10.1177/0887403419900316.

86. Huskey and Connell, "Preparation or Provocation?"

87. James Allen Fox and Emma E. Fridel, "The Menace of School Shootings in America," in *The Wiley Handbook on Violence in Education: Forms, Factors, and Preventions*, 1st ed. (John Wiley and Sons, Inc, 2018), 15–35.

88. Fox and Fridel, "The Menace of School Shootings in America."

89. Jaclyn Schildkraut and Glenn W. Muschert, "Media Salience and the Framing of Mass Murder in Schools: A Comparison of the Columbine and Sandy Hook Massacres," *Homicide Studies* 18, no. 1 (February 2014): 24, https://doi.org/10.1177/1088767913511458.

90. Hsiang Iris Chyi and Maxwell McCombs, "Media Salience and the Process of Framing: Coverage of the Columbine School Shootings," *Journalism and Mass Communication Quarterly* 81, no. 1 (March 2004): 22–35, https://doi.org/10.1177/107769900408100103; David L. Altheide, "The Columbine Shootings and the Discourse of Fear," *American Behavioral Scientist* 52, no. 10 (June 2009): 8, https://doi.org/10.1177/0002764209332552.

91. Schildkraut and Muschert, "Media Salience and the Framing of Mass Murder in Schools," 37.

92. Chyi and McCombs, "Media Salience and the Process of Framing."

93. Christopher J. Ferguson, "Sandy Hook Shooting: Why Did Lanza Target a School?" *Time*, December 15, 2012, https://ideas.time.com/2012/12/15/sandy-hook-shooting-why-did-lanza-target-a-school/.

94. While not a completely inaccurate picture of school shooters: DHS, "Final Report of the Federal Commission on School Safety," U.S. Department of Education, U.S. Department of Justice, U.S. Department of Health and Human Services, U.S. Department of Homeland Security, December 18, 2018, https://www.hsdl.org/?abstractanddid=. Kids with these traits make up only a tiny fraction of school shooters: Kristin M. Holland et al., "Characteristics of School-Associated Youth Homicides—United States, 1994–2018," *Morbidity and Mortality Weekly Report* 68, no. 3 (January 25, 2019): 53–60, https://doi.org/10.15585/mmwr.mm6803a1.

95. Brenan, "Parents' Concern about School Safety Remains Elevated."

CHAPTER 5

1. Mariana Brussoni et al., "A Qualitative Investigation of Unsupervised Outdoor Activities for 10- to 13-Year-Old Children: 'I like Adventuring but I Don't like Adventuring without Being Careful,'" *Journal of Environmental Psychology* 70 (August 2020): 101460, https://doi.org/10.1016/j.jenvp.2020.101460; J. Goodey, "Boys Don't Cry: Masculinities, Fear of Crime and Fearlessness," *British Journal of Criminology* 37, no. 3 (January 1, 1997): 401–18, https://doi.org/10.1093/oxfordjournals.bjc.a014177; Danielle Van der Burgt, "Spatial Avoidance or Spatial Confidence? Young People's Agency in the Active Negotiation of Risk and Safety in Public Space," *Children's Geographies* 13, no. 2 (March 4, 2015): 181–95, https://doi.org/10.1080/14733285.2013.828455; Pia Haudrup Christensen, "Children's Participation in Ethnographic Research: Issues of Power and Representation," *Children and Society* 18, no. 2 (April 2004): 165–76, https://doi.org/10.1002/chi.823.

2. Susan M. McHale, Ann C. Crouter, and Shawn D. Whiteman, "The Family Contexts of Gender Development in Childhood and Adolescence," *Social Development* 12, no. 1 (2003): 125–48, https://doi.org/10.1111/1467-9507.00225; William A. Corsaro, *The Sociology of Childhood*, 5th ed. (Los Angeles, CA: Sage, 2018).

3. Allison James, "Agency," in *The Palgrave Handbook of Childhood Studies*, ed. Jens Qvortrup, William A. Corsaro, and Michael-Sebastian Honig (London: Palgrave Macmillan UK, 2009), 34–45, https://doi.org/10.1007/978-0-230-27468-6_3.

4. James, "Agency"; Allison James and Alan Prout, eds., *Constructing and Reconstructing Childhood: Contemporary Issues in the Sociological Study of Childhood*, Routledge Education Classic Edition Series (Abingdon: Routledge, Taylor and Francis Group, 2015).

5. Anoop Nayak, "'Through Children's Eyes': Childhood, Place, and the Fear of Crime," *Geoforum* 34 (2003): 303/315; Brussoni et al., "A Qualitative Investigation of Unsupervised Outdoor Activities for 10- to 13-Year-Old Children"; Christensen, "Children's Participation in Ethnographic Research."

6. Saskia De Groof, "And My Mama Said: The (Relative) Parental Influence on Fear of Crime among Adolescent Girls and Boys," *Youth and Society* 39, no. 3 (March 2008): 267–93, https://doi.org/10.1177/0044118X07301000; Jo Goodey, "Fear of Crime: What Can Children Tell Us?" *International Review of Victimology* 3, no. 3 (September 1, 1994): 195–210, https://doi.org/10.1177/026975809400300302.

7. Gustavo S. Mesch, "Women's Fear of Crime: The Role of Fear for the Well-Being of Significant Others," *Violence and Victims* 15, no. 3 (January 1, 2000): 323–36, https://doi.org/10.1891/0886-6708.15.3.323; Nicole E. Rader, "Building Trust in Children: How Parents Talk to Children about Safety Precautions in Sweden," *International Review of Victimology* 23, no. 1 (January 2017): 3–16, https://doi.org/10.1177/0269758016672373; Mark Warr and Christopher G. Ellison, "Rethinking Social Reactions to Crime: Personal and Altruistic Fear in Family Households," *American Journal of Sociology* 106 (n.d.): 551–78.

8. Warr and Ellison, "Rethinking Social Reactions to Crime"; Kevin M. Drakulich, "Concerns for Self or Family? Sources of and Responses to Altruistic Fear," *Journal of Interpersonal Violence* 30, no. 7 (April 1, 2015): 1168–1207, https://doi.org/10.1177/0886260514539842; Mesch, "Women's Fear of Crime."

9. Danielle Van der Burgt, "Spatial Avoidance or Spatial Confidence? Young People's Agency in the Active Negotiation of Risk and Safety in Public Space," *Children's Geographies* 13, no. 2 (March 4, 2015): 181–95, https://doi.org/10.1080/14733285.2013.828455.

10. Diederik Cops, "Socializing into Fear: The Impact of Socializing Institutions on Adolescents' Fear of Crime," *Young* 18, no. 4 (November 1, 2010): 385–402, https://doi.org/10.1177/110330881001800402; David C. May, Lesa Rae Vartanian, and Keri Virgo, "The Impact of Parental Attachment and Supervision on Fear of Crime among Adolescent Males," *Adolescence* 37, no. 146 (2002): 267–87; De Groof, "And My Mama Said."

11. Barrie Thorne, *Gender Play: Girls and Boys in School* (New Brunswick, NJ: Rutgers University Press, 1993); Goodey, "Fear of Crime."

12. Van der Burgt, "Spatial Avoidance or Spatial Confidence?"; De Groof, "And My Mama Said."

13. Mariana Brussoni et al., "A Qualitative Investigation of Unsupervised Outdoor Activities for 10- to 13-Year-Old Children."

14. Brussoni et al., "A Qualitative Investigation of Unsupervised Outdoor Activities for 10- to 13-Year-Old Children."

15. Van der Burgt, "Spatial Avoidance or Spatial Confidence?"

16. Van der Burgt, "Spatial Avoidance or Spatial Confidence?"

17. Van der Burgt, "Spatial Avoidance or Spatial Confidence?"

18. Hille Koskela, "'Bold Walk and Breakings': Women's Spatial Confidence versus Fear of Violence," *Gender, Place, and Culture* 4, no. 3 (November 1, 1997): 301–20, https://doi.org/10.1080/09663699725369.

19. Van der Burgt, "Spatial Avoidance or Spatial Confidence?" 183.

20. Christopher J. Schreck and Mitchell J. Miller, "Sources of Fear of Crime at School," *Journal of School Violence* 2, no. 4 (December 12, 2003): 57–79, https://doi.org/10.1300/J202v02n04_04.

21. A. Zhang, L. Musu-Gillette, and B.A. Oudekerk, "Indicators of School Crime and Safety: 2015," U.S. Department of Education and U.S. Department of Justice, National Center for Education Statistics and Bureau of Justice Statistics, 2016; Nadine Frederique, "What Do the Data Reveal about Violence in Schools?" *National Institute of Justice Journal* (2020), https://nij.ojp.gov/topics/articles/what-do-data-reveal-about-violence-schools.

22. Deborah Lessne and Christine Yanez, "Student's Relationships in School and Feelings about Personal Safety at School," U.S. Department of Education, National Center for Education Statistics, 2018.

23. David C. May and R. Gregory Dunaway, "Predictors of Fear of Criminal Victimization at School among Adolescents," *Sociological Spectrum* 20, no. 2 (April 2000): 149–68, https://doi.org/10.1080/027321700279938.

24. May and Dunaway, "Predictors of Fear of Criminal Victimization at School among Adolescents."

25. Schreck and Miller, "Sources of Fear of Crime at School."

26. Whereas most kids feel safe at school: M.B. Robinson, *Media Coverage of Crime and Criminal Justice* (Durham, NC: Carolina Academic Press, 2018), 103. Kids in schools with more security measures: Kristin Swartz et al., "Fear of In-School Victimization: Contextual, Gendered, and Developmental Considerations," *Youth Violence and Juvenile Justice* 9, no. 1 (January 1, 2011): 59–78, https://doi.org/10.1177/1541204010374606; Pamela Wilcox, David C. May, and Staci D. Roberts, "Student Weapon Possession and the 'Fear and Victimization Hypothesis': Unraveling the Temporal Order," *Justice Quarterly* 23, no. 4 (December 1, 2006): 502–29, https://doi.org/10.1080/07418820600985362; Schreck and Miller, "Sources of Fear of Crime at School." Those from perceived vulnerable populations (girls, racial minorities): May and Dunaway, "Predictors of Fear of Criminal Victimization at School among Adolescents"; Swartz et al., "Fear of In-School Victimization."

27. Council of State Governments Justice Center, "School Safety Plans: A Snapshot of Legislative Action" (New York: Council of State Governments Justice Center, 2014); U.S. Department of Homeland Security, "K-12 School Security: A Guide for Preventing and Protecting Against Gun Violence" (Washington, DC: U.S. Department of Homeland Security, 2018), https://www.cisa.gov/publication/k-12-school-security-guide.

28. Schreck and Miller, "Sources of Fear of Crime at School."

29. Schildkraut, Elsass, and Stafford, "Could It Happen Here? Moral Panic, School Shootings, and Fear of Crime among College Students."

30. Schreck and Miller, "Sources of Fear of Crime at School"; Rafael Heller, "The 50th Annual PDK Poll of the Public's Attitudes toward the Public Schools," Teaching: Respect but Dwindling Appeal (Arlington, VA: PDK International, 2018); Wilcox, May, and Roberts, "Student Weapon Possession and the 'Fear and Victimization Hypothesis.'"

31. Rader, "Building Trust in Children."

32. R. Pendola and S. Gen, "Does 'Main Street' Promote Sense of Community? A Comparison of San Francisco Neighborhoods," *Environment and Behavior* 40, no. 4 (2008): 545–74; R.D. Putnam, *Bowling Alone: The Collapse and Revival of American Community* (New York: Simon and Schuster, 2000); M. Shields, "Community Belonging and Self-Perceived Health," *Health Reports*, Statistics Canada, Catalogue, 19, no. 2 (2008): 82–103.

33. Peter Kitchen, Allison Williams, and James Chowhan, "Sense of Community Belonging and Health in Canada: A Regional Analysis," *Social Indicators Research* 107, no. 1 (May 2012): 103–26, https://doi.org/10.1007/s11205-011-9830-9.

34. Putnam, *Bowling Alone*.

35. Lessne and Yanez, "Student's Relationships in School and Feelings about Personal Safety at School."

36. Alex Campbell, "Keeping the 'Lady' Safe: The Regulation of Femininity through Crime Prevention Literature," *Critical Criminology* 13, no. 2 (January 2005): 119–40, https://doi.org/10.1007/s10612-005-2390-z; Esther Madriz, "Images of Criminals and Victims: A Study of Women's Fear and Social Control," *Gender and Society* 11 (1997): 342–56; Lance R. Hignite, Shantal Marshall, and Laura Naumann, "The Ivory Tower Meets the Inner City: Student Protective and Avoidance Behaviors on an Urban University Campus," *College Student Journal* 52, no. 1 (March 1, 2018).

37. Schreck and Miller, "Sources of Fear of Crime at School."

38. Courtney Heath, Nicole E. Rader, and Margaret Ann Hagerman, "Decision-Making in Families Project," unpublished, 2020; Rader, "Building Trust in Children."

39. Allen E. Liska, Andrew Sanchirico, and Mark D. Reed, "Fear of Crime and Constrained Behavior Specifying and Estimating a Reciprocal Effects Model," *Social Forces* 66, no. 3 (1988): 827–837; Nicole E. Rader and Stacy H. Haynes, "Avoidance, Protective, and Weapons Behaviors: An Examination of Constrained Behaviors and Their Impact on Concerns about Crime," *Journal of Crime and Justice* 37, no. 2 (2014): 197–213; David C. May, "Scared Kids, Unattached Kids, or Peer Pressure: Why Do Students Carry Firearms to School?" *Youth and Society* 31, no. 1 (September 1, 1999): 100–127, https://doi.org/10.1177/0044118X99031001005.

40. J. Goodey, "Boys Don't Cry: Masculinities, Fear of Crime and Fearlessness," *British Journal of Criminology* 37, no. 3 (January 1, 1997): 401–18, https://doi.org/10.1093/oxfordjournals.bjc.a014177.

41. Nicole E. Rader, "Until Death Do Us Part? Husband Perceptions and Responses to Fear of Crime," *Deviant Behavior* 31, no. 1 (December 18, 2009): 33–59, https://doi.org/10.1080/01639620902854704; Kathleen A. Fox, Matt R. Nobles, and Alex R. Piquero, "Gender, Crime Victimization, and Fear of Crime," *Security Journal* 22, no. 1 (February 2009): 24–39, https://doi.org/10.1057/sj.2008.13; Karen A. Snedker, "Explaining the Gender Gap in Fear of Crime: Assessments of Risk and Vulnerability among New York City Residents," *Feminist Criminology* 7, no. 2 (April 1, 2012): 75–111, https://doi.org/10.1177/1557085111424405.

42. M. Stokes, "Stranger Danger: Child Protection and Parental Fears in the Risk Society," *Undefined*, 2009, p. 8, https://www.semanticscholar.org/paper/Stranger-Danger%3A-Child-Protection-and-Parental-in-Stokes/8605d54a79757ebd36778bd0561aa6b31b5faa16; Rader, "Building Trust in Children"; Nayak, "'Through Children's Eyes.'"

43. Kristen L. Stives et al., "Strategies to Combat Bullying: Parental Responses to Bullies, Bystanders, and Victims," *Youth and Society* 51, no. 3 (April 2019): 358–76, https://doi.org/10.1177/0044118X18756491.

44. Stives et al., "Strategies to Combat Bullying."

45. De Groof, "And My Mama Said"; Nayak, "'Through Children's Eyes'"; Barbara A. Morrongiello and Tess Dawber, "Mothers' Responses to Sons and Daughters Engaging in Injury-Risk Behaviors on a Playground: Implications for Sex Differences in Injury Rates," *Journal of Experimental Child Psychology* 76, no. 2 (June 1, 2000): 89–103, https://doi.org/10.1006/jecp.2000.2572.

46. For United States, see Heath, Rader, and Hagerman, "Decision-Making in Families Project"; for Sweden, see Rader, "Building Trust in Children."

CHAPTER 6

1. Lane et al., *Fear of Crime: Causes, Consequences, and Contradictions* (Durham, NC: Carolina Academic Press, 2014).

2. William R. Smith and Marie Tortensson, "Gender Differences in Risk Perception and Neutralizing Fear of Crime: Toward Resolving the Paradoxes," *The British Journal of Criminology* 37, no. 4 (October 1, 1997): 608–34, https://doi.org/10.1093/oxfordjournals.bjc.a014201; Cortney A. Franklin and Travis W. Franklin, "Predicting Fear of Crime: Considering Differences across Gender," *Feminist Criminology* 4, no. 1 (January 1, 2009): 83–106, https://doi.org/10.1177/1557085108325196; Nicole E. Rader, "Women Doing Fear: Applying the Doing Gender Framework to Women's Fear of Crime" (Carbondale, IL: Southern Illinois University, 2005).

3. Joel Best, *Threatened Children: Rhetoric and Concern about Child-Victims* (Chicago: University of Chicago Press, 1990); Victor E. Kappeler and Gary W. Potter, eds.,

Constructing Crime: Perspectives on Making News and Social Problems, 2nd ed. (Long Grove, IL: Waveland Press, 2006); Jennifer Paff Ogle, Molly Eckman, and Catherine Amoroso Leslie, "Appearance Cues and the Shootings at Columbine High: Construction of a Social Problem in Print Media," *Sociological Inquiry* 73, no. 1 (2003): 1–27.

4. Peter L. Berger and Thomas Luckmann, *The Social Construction of Reality: A Treatise in the Sociology of Knowledge* (London: Penguin Books, 1966; reprint Garden City, NY: Penguin Books, Penguin Social Sciences).

5. Megan Stubbs-Richardson, Nicole E. Rader, and Arthur G. Cosby, "Tweeting Rape Culture: Examining Portrayals of Victim Blaming in Discussions of Sexual Assault Cases on Twitter," *Feminism and Psychology* 28, no. 1 (February 2018): 90–108, https://doi.org/10.1177/0959353517715874; Sydney Cherniawsky and Melanie Morrison, "'You Should Have Known Better': The Social Ramifications of Victimization-Focused Sexual Assault Prevention Tips," *Journal of Interpersonal Violence* (April 29, 2020): 088626052091365, https://doi.org/10.1177/0886260520913650.

6. Carol M. Liebler, "Me(Di)a Culpa?: The 'Missing White Woman Syndrome' and Media Self-Critique," *Communication, Culture, and Critique* 3, no. 4 (December 1, 2010): 549–65, https://doi.org/10.1111/j.1753-9137.2010.01085.x; Cherniawsky and Morrison, "'You Should Have Known Better.'"

7. Nicole E. Rader, Gayle M. Rhineberger-Dunn, and Lauren Vasquez, "Victim Blame in Fictional Crime Dramas: An Examination of Demographic, Incident-Related, and Behavioral Factors," *Women and Criminal Justice* 26, no. 1 (January 2016): 55–75, https://doi.org/10.1080/08974454.2015.1023487; Stubbs-Richardson, Rader, and Cosby, "Tweeting Rape Culture."

8. Shana L. Maier, "'I Have Heard Horrible Stories . . .' : Rape Victim Advocates' Perceptions of the Revictimization of Rape Victims by the Police and Medical System," *Violence Against Women* 14, no. 7 (July 2008): 786–808, https://doi.org/10.1177/1077801208320245.

9. Maier, "'I Have Heard Horrible Stories . . .'"

10. Wesley G. Skogan and Susan M. Hartnett, *Community Policing, Chicago Style* (New York: Oxford University Press, 2000), http://www.dawsonera.com/depp/reader/protected/external/AbstractView/S9780195350449.

11. Michael D. Reisig and Roger B. Parks, "Can Community Policing Help the Truly Disadvantaged?" *Crime and Delinquency* 50, no. 2 (April 2004): 139–67, https://doi.org/10.1177/0011128703253157.

12. M.B. Robinson, *Media Coverage of Crime and Criminal Justice* (Durham, NC: Carolina Academic Press, 2018).

13. Liebler, "Me(Di)a Culpa?"

14. Valerie J. Callanan and J.T. Rosenberger, "Media, Gender, and Fear of Crime," *Criminal Justice Review* 40, no. 3 (2015): 322–39; Ray Surette, *Media, Crime, and Criminal Justice: Images, Realities, and Policies*, 4th ed. (Belmont, CA: Wadsworth, 2011).

15. Robinson, *Media Coverage of Crime and Criminal Justice*.

16. Liebler, "Me(Di)a Culpa?"

17. Liebler, "Me(Di)a Culpa?"

18. Jaclyn Schildkraut and Glenn W. Muschert, "Media Salience and the Framing of Mass Murder in Schools: A Comparison of the Columbine and Sandy Hook Massacres," *Homicide Studies* 18, no. 1 (February 2014): 24, https://doi.org/10.1177/1088767913511458.

19. Deborah Lessne and Christine Yanez, "Student's Relationships in School and Feelings about Personal Safety at School," U.S. Department of Education, National Center for Education Statistics, 2018.

20. J.H. Schildkraut, J. Elsass, and C. Stafford, "Could It Happen Here? Moral Panic, School Shootings, and Fear of Crime among College Students," *Crime, Law, and Social Change* 63 (2015): 91–110.

21. Rafael Heller, "The 50th Annual PDK Poll of the Public's Attitudes toward the Public Schools," Teaching: Respect but Dwindling Appeal (Arlington, VA: PDK International, 2018).

22. Sherry L. Hamby, David Finkelhor, Heather Turner, and Richard Ormrod, "Children's Exposure to Intimate Partner Violence and Other Family Violence: Nationally Representative Rates among US Youth," OJJDP Juvenile Justice Bulletin (Washington, DC: U.S. Government Printing Office, 2011).

23. Hamby et al., "Children's Exposure to Intimate Partner Violence and Other Family Violence."

24. Hanna L. Young, Alfred F. Mancuso, Ellen Faherty, Sally A. Dorman, and Jessica R. Umbrell, "Helping Child Victims of Family Violence through School Personnel: An Evaluation of a Training Program," *Journal of Aggression, Maltreatment, and Trauma* 16, no. 2 (June 2, 2008): 144–63, https://doi.org/10.1080/10926770801921386.

25. Young et al., "Helping Child Victims of Family Violence through School Personnel"; Hamby et al., "Children's Exposure to Intimate Partner Violence and Other Family Violence."

26. Janet L. Lauritsen et al., "Gender and Violent Victimization, 1973–2005," U.S. Department of Justice, 2009.

27. Cecilia L. Ridgeway, "Framed Before We Know It: How Gender Shapes Social Relations," *Gender and Society* 23, no. 2 (April 2009): 145–60, https://doi.org/10.1177/0891243208330313.

28. Candace West and Don H. Zimmerman, "Doing Gender," *Gender and Society* 1 (1987): 125–51.

29. Jill E. Yavorsky, Claire M. Kamp Dush, and Sarah J. Schoppe-Sullivan, "The Production of Inequality: The Gender Division of Labor Across the Transition to Parenthood," *Journal of Marriage and Family* 77, no. 3 (2015): 662–79, https://doi.org/10.1111/jomf.12189; Mick Cunningham, "The Influence of Parental Attitudes and Behaviors on Children's Attitudes toward Gender and Household Labor in Early Adulthood," *Journal of Marriage and Family* 63, no. 1 (February 2001): 111–22, https://doi.org/10.1111/j.1741-3737.2001.00111.x.

30. Nicole E. Rader, "Until Death Do Us Part? Husband Perceptions and Responses to Fear of Crime," *Deviant Behavior* 31, no. 1 (December 18, 2009): 33–59, https://doi.org/10.1080/01639620902854704.

31. M. Stokes, "Stranger Danger: Child Protection and Parental Fears in the Risk Society," *Undefined*, 2009, p. 8, https://www.semanticscholar.org/paper/Stranger-Danger%3A-Child-Protection-and-Parental-in-Stokes/8605d54a79757ebd36778bd0561aa6b31b5faa16.

32. Nicole E. Rader, "Building Trust in Children: How Parents Talk to Children about Safety Precautions in Sweden," *International Review of Victimology* 23, no. 1 (January 2017): 3–16, https://doi.org/10.1177/0269758016672373

33. Karen Malone, "The Bubble-Wrap Generation: Children Growing Up in Walled Gardens," *Environmental Education Research* 13, no. 4 (September 1, 2007): 513–27, https://doi.org/10.1080/13504620701581612; Chrystyna D. Kouros et al., "Helicopter Parenting, Autonomy Support, and College Students' Mental Health and Well-Being: The Moderating Role of Sex and Ethnicity," *Journal of Child and Family Studies* 26, no. 3 (March 2017): 939–49, https://doi.org/10.1007/s10826-016-0614-3.

34. Malone, "The Bubble-Wrap Generation."

35. Gill Valentine and John McKendrick, "Children's Outdoor Play: Exploring Parental Concerns about Children's Safety and the Changing Nature of Childhood," *Geoforum* 28, no. 2 (May 1, 1997): 219–35, https://doi.org/10.1016/S0016-7185(97)00010-9.

36. Lisa Hutchinson Wallace and David C. May, "The Impact of Parental Attachment and Feelings of Isolation on Adolescent Fear of Crime at School," *Adolescence (San Diego): An International Quarterly Devoted to the Physiological, Psychological, Psychiatric, Sociological, and Educational Aspects of the Second Decade of Human Life* 40, no. 159 (September 22, 2005): 457; Saskia De Groof, "And My Mama Said: The (Relative) Parental Influence on Fear of Crime among Adolescent Girls and Boys," *Youth and Society* 39, no. 3 (March 2008): 267–93, https://doi.org/10.1177/0044118X07301000.

37. Allison James, "Agency," in *The Palgrave Handbook of Childhood Studies*, ed. Jens Qvortrup, William A. Corsaro, and Michael-Sebastian Honig (London: Palgrave Macmillan UK, 2009), 34–45, https://doi.org/10.1007/978-0-230-27468-6_3.

38. Malinvisa Sakdiyakorn, Maria Golubovskaya, and David Solnet, "Understanding Generation Z through Collective Consciousness: Impacts for Hospitality Work and Employment," *International Journal of Hospitality Management* 94 (April 2021): 102822, https://doi.org/10.1016/j.ijhm.2020.102822.

39. Ann L. Coker, Heather M. Bush, Bonnie S. Fisher, Suzanne C. Swan, Corrine M. Williams, Emily R. Clear, and Sarah DeGrue, "Multi-College Bystander Intervention Evaluation for Violence Prevention," *American Journal of Preventive Medicine* 50, no. 3 (March 2016): 295–302, https://doi.org/10.1016/j.amepre.2015.08.034.

40. Jackson Katz, "Bystander Training as Leadership Training: Notes on the Origins, Philosophy, and Pedagogy of the Mentors in Violence Prevention Model," *Violence Against Women* 24, no. 15 (December 2018): 1755–76, https://doi.org/10.1177/1077801217753322.

41. Hamby et al., "Children's Exposure to Intimate Partner Violence and Other Family Violence."

42. M. Valcke et al., "Internet Parenting Styles and the Impact on Internet Use of Primary School Children," *Computers and Education* 55, no. 2 (September 2010): 454–64, https://doi.org/10.1016/j.compedu.2010.02.009.

43. For an exception, see Danielle Van der Burgt, "Spatial Avoidance or Spatial Confidence? Young People's Agency in the Active Negotiation of Risk and Safety in Public Space," *Children's Geographies* 13, no. 2 (March 4, 2015): 181–95, https://doi.org/10.1080/14733285.2013.828455.

APPENDIX

1. World Economic Forum, "Global Gender Gap Report 2021," Geneva, Switzerland, March 2021, https://www3.weforum.org/docs/WEF_GGGR_2021.pdf.

References

ADT, n.d. https://www.adtsecurity.com/.
Alexander, Michelle. *The New Jim Crow: Mass Incarceration in the Age of Colorblindness.* Tenth anniversary edition. New York London: The New Press, 2020.
Altar, Evan, Malica Nikolic, and Susan M. Bogels. "Environmental Transmission of Generalized Anxiety Disorder from Parents to Children: Worries, Experiential Avoidance, and Intolerance of Uncertainty." *Dialogues Clinical Neurosciences* 19 (2017): 137–47.
Altheide, David L. "The Columbine Shootings and the Discourse of Fear." *American Behavioral Scientist* 52, no. 10 (June 2009): 1354–70. https://doi.org/10.1177/0002764209332552.
Anderson, Elijah. *Code of the Street: Decency, Violence, and the Moral Life of the Inner City.* 1st ed. New York: W.W Norton, 1999.
Auxier, Brooke, and Monica Anderson. "Social Media Use in 2021." Pew Research Center, 2021.
Baldwin, A.L. "Socialization and the Parent-Child Relationship." *Child Development* 19 (1948): 127–36.
Barak, Gregg. "Doing Newsmaking Criminology from within the Academy." *Theoretical Criminology* 11, no. 2 (May 2007): 191–207. https://doi.org/10.1177/1362480607075847.
Barlow, Melissa Hickman. "Race and the Problem of Crime in 'Time' and 'Newsweek' Cover Stories, 1946 to 1995." *Social Justice* 25, no. 2 (1998): 149–83.
Barthe, Emmanuel, *Crime Prevention Publicity Campaigns.* Washington, DC: U.S. Dept. of Justice, Office of Community Oriented Policing Services, 2006.
Basile, Kathleen C., Heather Clayton, Sarah DeGue, John W. Gilford, Kevin J. Vagi, Nicholas A. Suarez, Marissa L. Zwald, and Richard Lowry. "Interpersonal Violence Victimization among High School Students—Youth Risk Behavior Survey, United States, 2019." *Morbidity and Mortality Weekly Report*, U.S. Department of Health

and Human Services/Centers for Disease Control and Prevention, 69, no. 1 (August 1, 2020): 28–37.

Baumrind, D. "Effects of Authoritative Parental Control on Child Behavior." *Child Development* 37 (1966): 887–907.

Bayless, K. "What Is Helicopter Parenting?" *Parents*, 2019. https://www.parents.com/parenting/better-parenting/what-is-helicopter-parenting/.

Berger, Peter L., and Thomas Luckmann. *The Social Construction of Reality: A Treatise in the Sociology of Knowledge*. Reprint Penguin Books. Penguin Social Sciences, 1967. London: Penguin Books, 1966.

Best, Joel. *Threatened Children: Rhetoric and Concern about Child-Victims*. Chicago: University of Chicago Press, 1990.

Bonilla-Silva, Eduardo. "The Structure of Racism in Color-Blind, 'Post-Racial' America." *American Behavioral Scientist* 59, no. 11 (October 2015): 1358–76. https://doi.org/10.1177/0002764215586826.

Boyd, Danah, and Eszter Hargittai. "Connected and Concerned: Variation in Parents' Online Safety Concerns." *Policy and Internet* 5, no. 3 (2013).

Brenan, Megan. "Parents' Concern about School Safety Remains Elevated." Gallup Poll, 2019. https://news.gallup.com/poll/265868/parents-concern-school-safety-remains-elevated.aspx.

Britto, Sarah, T. Hughes, K. Saltzman, and C. Stoh. "Does 'Special' Mean Young, White, and Female? Deconstructing the Meaning of 'Special' in *Law and Order: Special Victims Unit*." *Journal of Criminal Justice and Popular Culture* 14, no. 1 (2007): 39–96.

Brock, M., N. Kriger, and R. Miro. "School Safety Policies and Programs Administered by the U.S. Federal Government: 1990–2016." Federal Research Division, Library of Congress: Office of Justice Programs, National Criminal Justice Reference Service, 2018.

Brooks, Oona. "'Guys! Stop Doing It!': Young Women's Adoption and Rejection of Safety Advice When Socializing in Bars, Pubs, and Clubs." *The British Journal of Criminology* 51, no. 4 (July 1, 2011): 635–51. https://doi.org/10.1093/bjc/azr011.

Brownlow, Alec. "A Geography of Men's Fear." *Geoforum* 36 (2005): 581–92.

Brussoni, Mariana, Yingyi Lin, Christina Han, Ian Janssen, Nadine Schuurman, Randy Boyes, David Swanlund, and Louise C. Mâsse. "A Qualitative Investigation of Unsupervised Outdoor Activities for 10- to 13-Year-Old Children: 'I like Adventuring but I Don't like Adventuring without Being Careful.'" *Journal of Environmental Psychology* 70 (August 2020): 101460. https://doi.org/10.1016/j.jenvp.2020.101460.

"Bullying at School and Electronic Bullying." Indicators of School Crime and Safety: 2019. National Center for Education Statistics: U.S. Department of Education, 2019. https://nces.ed.gov/programs/coe/indicator/a10.

Burgess-Proctor, Amanda. "Intersections of Race, Class, Gender, and Crime: Future Directions for Feminist Criminology." *Feminist Criminology* 1, no. 1 (January 2006): 27–47. https://doi.org/10.1177/1557085105282899.

Callanan, Valerie J. "Media Consumption, Perceptions of Crime Risk and Fear of Crime: Examining Race/Ethnic Differences." *Sociological Perspectives* 55, no. 1 (March 1, 2012): 93–115. https://doi.org/10.1525/sop.2012.55.1.93.

Callanan, Valerie J., and J.T. Rosenberger. "Media, Gender, and Fear of Crime." *Criminal Justice Review* 40, no. 3 (2015): 322–39.

Callanan, Valerie J., and Brent Teasdale. "An Exploration of Gender Differences in Measurement of Fear of Crime." *Feminist Criminology* 4, no. 4 (October 1, 2009): 359–76. https://doi.org/10.1177/1557085109345462.

Campbell, Alex. "Keeping the 'Lady' Safe: The Regulation of Femininity through Crime Prevention Literature." *Critical Criminology* 13, no. 2 (January 2005): 119–40. https://doi.org/10.1007/s10612-005-2390-z.

Catalano, Shannan, Erica Smith, Howard Snyder, and Michael Rand. "Female Victims of Violence." *U.S. Department of Justice Publications and Materials*, October 1, 2009. https://digitalcommons.unl.edu/usjusticematls/7.

Chan, Tommy K.H., Christy M.K. Cheung, and Zach W.Y. Lee. "Cyberbullying on Social Networking Sites: A Literature Review and Future Research Directions." *Information and Management* 58, no. 2 (March 2021): 103411. https://doi.org/10.1016/j.im.2020.103411.

Cherniawsky, Sydney, and Melanie Morrison. "'You Should Have Known Better': The Social Ramifications of Victimization-Focused Sexual Assault Prevention Tips." *Journal of Interpersonal Violence*, April 29, 2020, 088626052091365. https://doi.org/10.1177/0886260520913650.

Chiricos, Ted, Michael Hogan, and Marc Gertz. "Racial Composition of Neighborhood and Fear of Crime." *Criminology* 35, no. 1 (1997): 107–32. https://doi.org/10.1111/j.1745-9125.1997.tb00872.x.

Chiricos, Ted, Kelly Welch, and Marc Gertz. "Racial Typification of Crime and Support for Punitive Measures." *Criminology* 42, no. 2 (May 2004): 358–90. https://doi.org/10.1111/j.1745-9125.2004.tb00523.x.

Christensen, Pia Haudrup. "Children's Participation in Ethnographic Research: Issues of Power and Representation." *Children and Society* 18, no. 2 (April 2004): 165–76. https://doi.org/10.1002/chi.823.

Chyi, Hsiang Iris, and Maxwell McCombs. "Media Salience and the Process of Framing: Coverage of the Columbine School Shootings." *Journalism and Mass Communication Quarterly* 81, no. 1 (March 2004): 22–35. https://doi.org/10.1177/107769900408100103.

Cobbina, Jennifer E., Jody Miller, and Rod K. Brunson. "Gender, Neighborhood Danger, and Risk-Avoidance Strategies among Urban African-American Youths." *Criminology* 46, no. 3 (2008): 673–709. https://doi.org/10.1111/j.1745-9125.2008.00122.x.

Coker, Ann L., Heather M. Bush, Bonnie S. Fisher, Suzanne C. Swan, Corrine M. Williams, Emily R. Clear, and Sarah DeGue. "Multi - College Bystander Intervention Evaluation for Violence Prevention." *American Journal of Preventive Medicine* 50, no. 3 (March 2016): 295–302. https://doi.org/10.1016/j.amepre.2015.08.034.

Collins, Rebecca L. "Content Analysis of Gender Roles in Media: Where Are We Now and Where Should We Go?" *Sex Roles* 64, no. 3–4 (February 2011): 290–98. https://doi.org/10.1007/s11199-010-9929-5.

Connell, Raewyn. *Gender: In World Perspective* (Polity Short Introductions), 4th ed. Medford, MA: Polity Press, 2021.

Cops, Diederik. "Socializing into Fear: The Impact of Socializing Institutions on Adolescents' Fear of Crime." *Young* 18, no. 4 (November 1, 2010): 385–402. https://doi.org/10.1177/110330881001800402.

Cops, Diederik, and Stefaan Pleysier. "'Doing Gender' in Fear of Crime: The Impact of Gender Identity on Reported Levels of Fear of Crime in Adolescents and Young Adults." *The British Journal of Criminology* 51, no. 1 (January 1, 2011): 58–74. https://doi.org/10.1093/bjc/azq065.

Corsaro, William A. *The Sociology of Childhood*. 5th ed. Los Angeles, CA: Sage, 2018.

Council of State Governments Justice Center. "School Safety Plans: A Snapshot of Legislative Action." New York: Council of State Governments Justice Center, 2014.

Creamer, John. "Inequalities Persist Despite Decline in Poverty for All Major Race and Hispanic Origin Groups." Washington, DC: U.S. Census Bureau, April 14, 2021. https://www.census.gov/library/stories/2020/09/poverty-rates-for-blacks-and-hispanics-reached-historic-lows-in-2019.html.

Crenshaw, Kimberle. "Mapping the Margins: Intersectionality, Identity Politics, and Violence against Women of Color." *Stanford Law Review* 43, no. 6 (1994):1241–1299.

CrossFit, n.d. https://www.crossfit.com/.

Cunningham, Mick. "The Influence of Parental Attitudes and Behaviors on Children's Attitudes toward Gender and Household Labor in Early Adulthood." *Journal of Marriage and Family* 63, no. 1 (February 2001): 111–22. https://doi.org/10.1111/j.1741-3737.2001.00111.x.

"Cyberbullying—What Is It?" U.S. Department of Health and Human Services, Washington, DC, 2021. https://www.stopbullying.gov/cyberbullying/what-is-it.

Daniels, Elizabeth A., Marlee C. Layh, and Linda K. Porzelius. "Grooming Ten-Year-Olds with Gender Stereotypes? A Content Analysis of Preteen and Teen Girl Magazines." *Body Image* 19 (December 2016): 57–67. https://doi.org/10.1016/j.bodyim.2016.08.011.

Day, Kristen. "Constructing Masculinity and Women's Fear in Public Space in Irvine, California." *Gender, Place, and Culture* 8, no. 2 (June 1, 2001): 109–27. https://doi.org/10.1080/09663690120050742.

De Groof, Saskia. "And My Mama Said: The (Relative) Parental Influence on Fear of Crime among Adolescent Girls and Boys." *Youth and Society* 39, no. 3 (March 2008): 267–93. https://doi.org/10.1177/0044118X07301000.

De Welde, Kristine. "White Women Beware!: Whiteness, Fear of Crime, and Self-Defense." *Race, Gender, and Class* 10, no. 4 (2003): 75–91.

DHS. "Final Report of the Federal Commission on School Safety." U.S. Department of Education, U.S. Department of Justice, U.S. Department of Health and Human Services, U.S. Department of Homeland Security, December 18, 2018. https://www.hsdl.org/?abstract&did=.

Dimock, Michael. "Defining Generations: Where Millennials End and Generation Z Begins." Washington, DC: Pew Research Center, January 17, 2019. https://www.pewresearch.org/fact-tank/2019/01/17/where-millennials-end-and-generation-z-begins/.

Ding, Ding, Nicole L. Bracy, James F. Sallis, Brian E. Saelens, Gregory J. Norman, Sion Kim Harris, Nefertiti Durant, Dori Rosenberg, and Jacqueline Kerr. "Is Fear of Strangers Related to Physical Activity among Youth?" *American Journal of Health Promotion* 26, no. 3 (January 2012): 189–95. https://doi.org/10.4278/ajhp.100701-QUAN-224.

Dow, Dawn Marie. "The Deadly Challenges of Raising African American Boys: Navigating the Controlling Image of the 'Thug.'" *Gender and Society* 30, no. 2 (April 2016): 161–88. https://doi.org/10.1177/0891243216629928.

Drakulich, Kevin M. "Concerns for Self or Family? Sources of and Responses to Altruistic Fear." *Journal of Interpersonal Violence* 30, no. 7 (April 1, 2015): 1168–1207. https://doi.org/10.1177/0886260514539842.

Duggan, Maeve, Amanda Lenhart, Cliff Lampe, and Nicole B. Ellison. "Parents and Social Media." Pew Research Center, July 16, 2015. https://www.pewresearch.org/internet/2015/07/16/parents-and-social-media/.

Eijk, Gwen van. "Between Risk and Resistance: Gender Socialization, Equality, and Ambiguous Norms in Fear of Crime and Safekeeping." *Feminist Criminology* 12, no. 2 (April 2017): 103–24. https://doi.org/10.1177/1557085115605905.

Fan, Jieqiong, and Li-fang Zhang. "The Role of Perceived Parenting Styles in Thinking Styles." *Learning and Individual Differences* 32 (May 1, 2014): 204–11. https://doi.org/10.1016/j.lindif.2014.03.004.

Ferguson, Christopher J. "Sandy Hook Shooting: Why Did Lanza Target a School?" *Time*, December 15, 2012. https://ideas.time.com/2012/12/15/sandy-hook-shooting-why-did-lanza-target-a-school/.

Ferraro, Kenneth F. "Women's Fear of Victimization: Shadow of Sexual Assault?" *Social Forces* 75, no. 2 (December 1, 1996): 667–90. https://doi.org/10.1093/sf/75.2.667.

Finkelhor, David, Kerryann Walsh, Lisa Jones, Kimberly Mitchell, and Anne Collier. "Youth Internet Safety Education: Aligning Programs with the Evidence Base." *Trauma, Violence, and Abuse*, April 3, 2020, 152483802091625. https://doi.org/10.1177/1524838020916257.

Fisher, Bonnie S., and David May. "College Students' Crime-Related Fears on Campus: Are Fear-Provoking Cues Gendered?" *Journal of Contemporary Criminal Justice* 25, no. 3 (August 2009): 300–321. https://doi.org/10.1177/1043986209335013.

Fisher, Bonnie S., and John J. Sloan III. "Unraveling the Fear of Victimization among College Women: Is the 'Shadow of Sexual Assault Hypothesis' Supported?" *Justice Quarterly* 20, no. 3 (September 1, 2003): 633–59. https://doi.org/10.1080/07418820300095641.

Fishman, Gideon, and Gustavo S. Mesch. "Fear of Crime in Israel: A Multidimensional Approach." *Social Science Quarterly* 77, no. 1 (1996): 76–89.

Foster, Sarah, Karen Villanueva, Lisa Wood, Hayley Christian, and Billie Giles-Corti. "The Impact of Parents' Fear of Strangers and Perceptions of Informal Social Control on Children's Independent Mobility." *Health and Place* 26 (March 1, 2014): 60–68. https://doi.org/10.1016/j.healthplace.2013.11.006.

Fox, James Allen, and Emma E. Fridel. "The Menace of School Shootings in America." In *The Wiley Handbook on Violence in Education: Forms, Factors, and Preventions*, 1st ed. Hoboken, NJ: John Wiley and Sons, Inc, 2018.

Fox, Kathleen A., Matt R. Nobles, and Alex R. Piquero. "Gender, Crime Victimization, and Fear of Crime." *Security Journal* 22, no. 1 (February 2009): 24–39. https://doi.org/10.1057/sj.2008.13.

Francis, Jacinta, Karen Martin, Lisa Wood, and Sarah Foster. "'I'll Be Driving You to School for the Rest of Your Life': A Qualitative Study of Parents' Fear of Stranger Danger." *Journal of Environmental Psychology* 53 (November 1, 2017): 112–20. https://doi.org/10.1016/j.jenvp.2017.07.004.

Franklin, Cortney A., and Travis W. Franklin. "Predicting Fear of Crime: Considering Differences across Gender." *Feminist Criminology* 4, no. 1 (January 1, 2009): 83–106. https://doi.org/10.1177/1557085108325196.

Frederique, Nadine. "What Do the Data Reveal about Violence in Schools?" National Institute of Justice Journal. National Institute of Justice, 2020. https://nij.ojp.gov/topics/articles/what-do-data-reveal-about-violence-schools.

Gardner, Carol Brooks. "Analyzing Gender in Public Places: Rethinking Goffman's Vision of Everyday Life." *The American Sociologist* 20, no. 1 (March 1, 1989): 42. https://doi.org/10.1007/BF02697786.

Gerbner, George, and Larry Gross. "Living with Television: The Violence Profile." *Journal of Communication* 26, no. 2 (June 1, 1976): 172–99. https://doi.org/10.1111/j.1460-2466.1976.tb01397.x.

Goodey, Jo. "Boys Don't Cry: Masculinities, Fear of Crime, and Fearlessness." *British Journal of Criminology* 37, no. 3 (January 1, 1997): 401–18. https://doi.org/10.1093/oxfordjournals.bjc.a014177.

———. "Fear of Crime: What Can Children Tell Us?" *International Review of Victimology* 3, no. 3 (September 1, 1994): 195–210. https://doi.org/10.1177/026975809400300302.

Hagerman, Margaret A. *White Kids: Growing Up with Privilege in a Racially Divided America*. New York: New York University Press, 2018.

Hale, C. "Fear of Crime: A Review of the Literature." *International Review of Victimology* 4, no. 2 (January 1, 1996): 79–150. https://doi.org/10.1177/026975809600400201.

Hamby, Sherry L., David Finkelhor, Heather Turner, and Richard Ormrod. "Children's Exposure to Intimate Partner Violence and Other Family Violence: Nationally Representative Rates among U.S. Youth." Office of Juvenile Justice and Delinquency Prevention. Juvenile Justice Bulletin. Washington, DC: U.S. Government Printing Office, 2011.

Hasinoff, Amy Adele. "Where Are You? Location Tracking and the Promise of Child Safety." *Television and New Media* 18, no. 6 (September 2017): 496–512. https://doi.org/10.1177/1527476416680450.

Heller, Rafael. "The 50th Annual PDK Poll of the Public's Attitudes toward the Public Schools." Teaching: Respect but Dwindling Appeal. Arlington, VA: PDK International, 2018.

Hibdon, J., Joseph A. Schafer, and M. Summers. "Avoidance Behaviors in a Campus Residential Environment." *Criminology, Criminal Justice Law, and Society* 17, no. 3 (2016): 74–89.

Hignite, Lance R., Shantal Marshall, and Laura Naumann. "The Ivory Tower Meets the Inner City: Student Protective and Avoidance Behaviors on an Urban University Campus." *College Student Journal* 52, no. 1 (March 1, 2018).

Hilgartner, Stephen, and Charles L. Bosk. "The Rise and Fall of Social Problems: A Public Arenas Model." *American Journal of Sociology* 94, no. 1 (1988): 53–78.

Hill Collins, Patricia. *Black Feminist Thought: Knowledge, Consciousness, and the Politics of Empowerment*. Rev. 10th anniversary ed. New York: Routledge, 2000.

Hochschild, Arlie Russell and ProQuest (Firm). *The Managed Heart: Commercialization of Human Feeling*. Berkeley: University of California Press, 2012. https://ebookcentral.proquest.com/lib/qut/detail.action?docID=870020.

Hodes, Martha. "The Sexualization of Reconstruction Politics: White Women and Black Men in the South after the Civil War." *Journal of the History of Sexuality*, Special Issue: African American Culture and Sexuality, 3, no. 3 (1993): 402–17.

Holland, Kristin M., Jeffrey E. Hall, Jing Wang, Elizabeth M. Gaylor, Linda L. Johnson, Daniel Shelby, Thomas R. Simon, and School-Associated Violent Deaths Study Group. "Characteristics of School-Associated Youth Homicides – United States, 1994–2018." *Morbidity and Mortality Weekly Report* 68, no. 3 (January 25, 2019): 53–60. https://doi.org/10.15585/mmwr.mm6803a1.

Hollander, Jocelyn A. "Vulnerability and Dangerousness: The Construction of Gender through Conversation about Violence." *Gender and Society* 15, no. 1 (February 1, 2001): 83–109. https://doi.org/10.1177/089124301015001005.

Hollander, Jocelyn A., and Katie Rodgers. "Constructing Victims: The Erasure of Women's Resistance to Sexual Assault." *Sociological Forum* 29, no. 2 (2014): 342–64. https://doi.org/10.1111/socf.12087.

Huskey, Michael G., and Nadine M. Connell. "Preparation or Provocation? Student Perceptions of Active Shooter Drills." *Criminal Justice Policy Review* 32, no. 1 (February 1, 2021): 3–26. https://doi.org/10.1177/0887403419900316.

Intravia, Jonathan, Kevin T. Wolff, Rocio Paez, and Benjamin R. Gibbs. "Investigating the Relationship between Social Media Consumption and Fear of Crime: A Partial Analysis of Mostly Young Adults." *Computers in Human Behavior* 77 (December 1, 2017): 158–68. https://doi.org/10.1016/j.chb.2017.08.047.

Jackson, Stevi, and Sue Scott. "Risk Anxiety and the Social Construction of Childhood." In *Risk and Sociocultural Theory: New Directions and Perspectives*, edited by Deborah Lupton. Cambridge: Cambridge University Press, 1999.

James, Allison. "Agency." In *The Palgrave Handbook of Childhood Studies*, edited by Jens Qvortrup, William A. Corsaro, and Michael-Sebastian Honig, 34–45. London: Palgrave Macmillan UK, 2009. https://doi.org/10.1007/978-0-230-27468-6_3.

James, Allison, and Alan Prout, eds. *Constructing and Reconstructing Childhood: Contemporary Issues in the Sociological Study of Childhood*. Routledge Education Classic Edition Series. New York: Routledge, Taylor, and Francis Group, 2015.

Jamieson, Patrick E., and Daniel Romer. "Violence in Popular U.S. Prime Time TV Dramas and the Cultivation of Fear: A Time Series Analysis." *Media and Communication* 2, no. 2 (2014): 31–41.

Jennings, Wesley G., Angela R. Gover, and Dagmar Pudrzynska. "Are Institutions of Higher Learning Safe? A Descriptive Study of Campus Safety Issues and Self-Reported Campus Victimization among Male and Female College Students." *Journal of Criminal Justice Education* 18, no. 2 (July 2007): 191–208. https://doi.org/10.1080/10511250701383327.

Justis, Gregory G., and Steven Chermak. "Framing the Scene: Presentations of Forensics Programming in the News." In *Sociology of Crime, Law, and Deviance*. Edited by Mathieu Deflem. Bingley, West Yorkshire: Emerald Group Publishing Limited, 2010. https://doi.org/10.1108/S1521-6136(2010)0000014013.

Kappeler, Victor E., and Gary W. Potter, eds. *Constructing Crime: Perspectives on Making News and Social Problems*. 2nd ed. Long Grove, IL: Waveland Press, 2006.

Kardian, Steve. "The Seven-Second Rule: How to Avoid Being an Easy Target. A Criminal Decides in Just Seven Seconds If You Will Be Their Next Victim." *NBC News*, August 6, 2017.

Katz, Jackson. "Bystander Training as Leadership Training: Notes on the Origins, Philosophy, and Pedagogy of the Mentors in Violence Prevention Model." *Violence against Women* 24, no. 15 (December 2018): 1755–76. https://doi.org/10.1177/1077801217753322.

Kaufman, P., X. Chen, S. Choy, K. Chandler, C. Chapman, M. Rand, and C. Ringel. "Indicators of School Crime and Safety, 1998." Washington, DC: U.S. Departments of Education and Justice, 1998. https://ojjdp.ojp.gov/library/publications/annual-report-school-safety-1998.

Keane, Carl. "Evaluating the Influence of Fear of Crime as an Environmental Mobility Restrictor on Women's Routine Activities." *Environment and Behavior* 30, no. 1 (January 1, 1998): 60–74. https://doi.org/10.1177/0013916598301003.

Keener, Emily, JoNell Strough, and Lisa DiDonato. "Gender Differences and Similarities in Strategies for Managing Conflict with Friends and Romantic Partners." *Sex Roles* 67, no. 1–2 (July 2012): 83–97. https://doi.org/10.1007/s11199-012-0131-9.

Kehily, Mary Jane. "Childhood in Crisis? Tracing the Contours of 'Crisis' and Its Impact upon Contemporary Parenting Practices." *Media, Culture, and Society* 32, no. 2 (March 2010): 171–85. https://doi.org/10.1177/0163443709355605.
Kitchen, Peter, Allison Williams, and James Chowhan. "Sense of Community Belonging and Health in Canada: A Regional Analysis." *Social Indicators Research* 107, no. 1 (May 2012): 103–26. https://doi.org/10.1007/s11205-011-9830-9.
Kleck, Gary, Tomislav Kovandzic, Mark Saber, and Will Hauser. "The Effect of Perceived Risk and Victimization on Plans to Purchase a Gun for Self-Protection." *Journal of Criminal Justice* 39, no. 4 (2010): 312–19. https://doi.org/10.1016/j.jcrimjus.2011.03.002.
Knauss, Christine, Susan J. Paxton, and Françoise D. Alsaker. "Body Dissatisfaction in Adolescent Boys and Girls: Objectified Body Consciousness, Internalization of the Media Body Ideal, and Perceived Pressure from Media." *Sex Roles* 59, no. 9–10 (November 2008): 633–43. https://doi.org/10.1007/s11199-008-9474-7.
Koskela, Hille. "'Bold Walk and Breakings': Women's Spatial Confidence versus Fear of Violence." *Gender, Place, and Culture* 4, no. 3 (November 1, 1997): 301–20. https://doi.org/10.1080/09663699725369.
Kouros, Chrystyna D., Megan M. Pruitt, Naomi V. Ekas, Romilyn Kiriaki, and Megan Sunderland. "Helicopter Parenting, Autonomy Support, and College Students' Mental Health and Well-Being: The Moderating Role of Sex and Ethnicity." *Journal of Child and Family Studies* 26, no. 3 (March 2017): 939–49. https://doi.org/10.1007/s10826-016-0614-3.
Lane, Jodi, and James W. Meeker. "Ethnicity, Information Sources, and Fear of Crime." *Deviant Behavior* 24, no. 1 (January 1, 2003): 1–26. https://doi.org/10.1080/10639620390117165.
Lane, Jodi, Nicole E. Rader, Billy Henson, Bonnie S. Fisher, and David C. May. *Fear of Crime: Causes, Consequences, and Contradictions*. Durham, NC: Carolina Academic Press, 2014.
Larsson, Daniel. "Fear of Crime among the Poor in Britain and Sweden." *International Review of Victimology* 15, no. 3 (January 1, 2009): 223–54. https://doi.org/10.1177/026975800901500302.
Lascala, Marisa. "Everything You Need to Know about the Free-Range Parenting Method." *Good Housekeeping Magazine*, March 2019.
Lauritsen, Janet L., Karen Heimer, and Janet L. Lauritsen. "Gender and Violent Victimization, 1973–2005." *U.S. Department of Justice*, 2009.
Lawson, Katie M., Ann C. Crouter, and Susan M. McHale. "Links between Family Gender Socialization Experiences in Childhood and Gendered Occupational Attainment in Young Adulthood." *Journal of Vocational Behavior* 90 (October 1, 2015): 26–35. https://doi.org/10.1016/j.jvb.2015.07.003.
Lee, Matthew R., Timothy C. Hayes, and Shaun A. Thomas. "Revisiting the Southern Culture of Violence." *The Sociological Quarterly* 48 (2007): 253–75.
Lee, Sang Min, M. Harry Daniels, and Daniel B. Kissinger. "Parental Influences on Adolescent Adjustment: Parenting Styles Versus Parenting Practices." *The Family Journal* 14, no. 3 (July 1, 2006): 253–59. https://doi.org/10.1177/1066480706287654.
Lessne, Deborah, and Christine Yanez. "Student's Relationships in School and Feelings about Personal Safety at School." Data Point. National Center for Education Statistics: U.S. Department of Education, 2018.
Leverentz, Andrea. "Narratives of Crime and Criminals: How Places Socially Construct the Crime Problem." *Sociological Forum* 27, no. 2 (2012): 348–71. https://doi.org/10.1111/j.1573-7861.2012.01321.x.

Liebler, Carol M. "Me(Di)a Culpa?: The 'Missing White Woman Syndrome' and Media Self-Critique." *Communication, Culture, and Critique* 3, no. 4 (December 1, 2010): 549–65. https://doi.org/10.1111/j.1753-9137.2010.01085.x.

Life360, n.d. https://www.life360.com/.

Lipowska, Małgorzata, Mariusz Lipowski, and Paulina Pawlicka. "'Daughter and Son: A Completely Different Story'? Gender as a Moderator of the Relationship between Sexism and Parental Attitudes." *Health Psychology Report* 3 (2016): 224–36. https://doi.org/10.5114/hpr.2016.62221.

Liska, Allen E., Andrew Sanchirico, and Mark D. Reed. "Fear of Crime and Constrained Behavior: Specifying and Estimating a Reciprocal Effects Model." *Social Forces* 66, no. 3 (1988): 827–37.

Livingstone, Sonia, Kjartan Ólafsson, Ellen J. Helsper, Francisco Lupiáñez-Villanueva, Giuseppe A. Veltri, and Frans Folkvord. "Maximizing Opportunities and Minimizing Risks for Children Online: The Role of Digital Skills in Emerging Strategies of Parental Mediation: Maximizing Opportunities and Minimizing Risks." *Journal of Communication* 67, no. 1 (February 2017): 82–105. https://doi.org/10.1111/jcom.12277.

Madriz, Esther. "Images of Criminals and Victims: A Study of Women's Fear and Social Control." *Gender and Society* 11 (1997): 342–56.

———. *Nothing Bad Happens to Good Girls: Fear of Crime in Women's Lives.* Berkeley, CA: University of California Press, 1997.

Maier, Shana L. "'I Have Heard Horrible Stories . . . ': Rape Victim Advocates' Perceptions of the Revictimization of Rape Victims by the Police and Medical System." *Violence against Women* 14, no. 7 (July 2008): 786–808. https://doi.org/10.1177/1077801208320245.

Malone, Karen. "The Bubble-Wrap Generation: Children Growing Up in Walled Gardens." *Environmental Education Research* 13, no. 4 (September 1, 2007): 513–27. https://doi.org/10.1080/13504620701581612.

Malone Gonzalez, Shannon. "Making It Home: An Intersectional Analysis of the Police Talk." *Gender and Society* 33, no. 3 (June 2019): 363–86. https://doi.org/10.1177/0891243219828340.

May, David C. "Scared Kids, Unattached Kids, or Peer Pressure: Why Do Students Carry Firearms to School?" *Youth and Society* 31, no. 1 (September 1, 1999): 100–127. https://doi.org/10.1177/0044118X99031001005.

May, David C., and R. Gregory Dunaway. "Predictors of Fear of Criminal Victimization at School among Adolescents." *Sociological Spectrum* 20, no. 2 (April 2000): 149–68. https://doi.org/10.1080/027321700279938.

May, David C., Nicole E. Rader, and Sarah Goodrum. "A Gendered Assessment of the 'Threat of Victimization': Examining Gender Differences in Fear of Crime, Perceived Risk, Avoidance, and Defensive Behaviors." *Criminal Justice Review* 35, no. 2 (June 2010): 159–82. https://doi.org/10.1177/0734016809349166.

May, David C., Lesa Rae Vartanian, and Keri Virgo. "The Impact of Parental Attachment and Supervision on Fear of Crime among Adolescent Males." *Adolescence* 37, no. 146 (2002): 267–87.

McHale, Susan M., Ann C. Crouter, and Shawn D. Whiteman. "The Family Contexts of Gender Development in Childhood and Adolescence." *Social Development* 12, no. 1 (2003): 125–48. https://doi.org/10.1111/1467-9507.00225.

Merton, Robert K. *Social Theory and Social Structure.* 6th ed. Glencoe, IL: Free Press, 1968.

Mesch, Gustavo S. "Women's Fear of Crime: The Role of Fear for the Well-Being of Significant Others." *Violence and Victims* 15, no. 3 (January 1, 2000): 323–36. https://doi.org/10.1891/0886-6708.15.3.323.

Morgan, Rachel E., and Jennifer L. Truman. "Criminal Victimization, 2017." Washington, DC: Office of Justice Programs, The Bureau of Justice Statistics, December 2018. https://bjs.ojp.gov/content/pub/pdf/cv17.pdf.

Morrongiello, Barbara A., and Tess Dawber. "Mothers' Responses to Sons and Daughters Engaging in Injury-Risk Behaviors on a Playground: Implications for Sex Differences in Injury Rates." *Journal of Experimental Child Psychology* 76, no. 2 (June 1, 2000): 89–103. https://doi.org/10.1006/jecp.2000.2572.

Mullins, Christopher W., and Sou Lee. "'Like Make Up on a Man': The Gendered Nature of Gun Norms." *Deviant Behavior* 41, no. 3 (March 3, 2020): 294–310. https://doi.org/10.1080/01639625.2019.1565515.

Muraskin, Roslyn, and Shelly Feuer Domash. *Crime and the Media: Headlines vs. Reality*. Upper Saddle River, NJ: Pearson Prentice Hall, 2007.

Murnen, Sarah K., Linda Smolak, J. Andrew Mills, and Lindsey Good. "Thin, Sexy Women and Strong, Muscular Men: Grade-School Children's Responses to Objectified Images of Women and Men." *Sex Roles* 49, no. 9/10 (2003): 427–37. https://doi.org/10.1023/A:1025868320206.

National Child Identification Program. "Prevention Tips," 2021. https://childidprogram.com/prevention-tips/.

Nayak, Anoop. "'Through Children's Eyes': Childhood, Place, and the Fear of Crime." *Geoforum* 34 (2003): 303–315.

O'Connor, Justen, and Alice Brown. "A Qualitative Study of 'Fear' as a Regulator of Children's Independent Physical Activity in the Suburbs." *Health and Place* 24 (November 1, 2013): 157–64. https://doi.org/10.1016/j.healthplace.2013.09.002.

Ogle, Jennifer Paff, Molly Eckman, and Catherine Amoroso Leslie. "Appearance Cues and the Shootings at Columbine High: Construction of a Social Problem in Print Media." *Sociological Inquiry* 73, no. 1 (2003): 1–27.

Ohlheiser, Abby. "'Don't Leave Campus': Parents Are Now Using Tracking Apps to Watch Their Kids at College." *Washington Post*, October 22, 2019. https://www.washingtonpost.com/technology/2019/10/22/dont-leave-campus-parents-are-now-using-tracking-apps-watch-their-kids-college/.

O'Neal, Elizabeth E., and Jodie M. Plumert. "Mother–Child Conversations about Safety: Implications for Socializing Safety Values in Children." *Journal of Pediatric Psychology* 39, no. 4 (May 1, 2014): 481–91. https://doi.org/10.1093/jpepsy/jsu005.

Padilla-Walker, Laura M., and Larry J. Nelson. "Black Hawk Down?: Establishing Helicopter Parenting as a Distinct Construct from Other Forms of Parental Control during Emerging Adulthood." *Journal of Adolescence* 35, no. 5 (October 2012): 1177–90. https://doi.org/10.1016/j.adolescence.2012.03.007.

Pain, Rachel. "Paranoid Parenting? Rematerializing Risk and Fear for Children." *Social and Cultural Geography* 7, no. 2 (April 1, 2006): 221–43. https://doi.org/10.1080/14649360600600585.

Paquette, Daniel. "Theorizing the Father-Child Relationship: Mechanisms and Developmental Outcomes." *Human Development* 47, no. 4 (2004): 193–219. https://doi.org/10.1159/000078723.

Pendola, R., and S. Gen. "Does 'Main Street' Promote Sense of Community? A Comparison of San Francisco Neighborhoods." *Environment and Behavior* 40, no. 4 (2008): 545–74.

Penn State University and Michelle Wright. "Cyberbullying Victimization through Social Networking Sites and Adjustment Difficulties: The Role of Parental Mediation." *Journal of the Association for Information Systems* 19 (August 2018): 113–23. https://doi.org/10.17705/1jais.00486.

Podaná, Zuzana, and Eva Krulichová. "The Impact of Parenting Style on Fear of Crime among Adolescent Girls and Boys." *Journal of Youth Studies* 21, no. 8 (September 14, 2018): 1077–94. https://doi.org/10.1080/13676261.2018.1449945.

Putnam, R.D. *Bowling Alone: The Collapse and Revival of American Community.* New York, NY: Simon and Schuster, 2000.

Rader, Nicole E. "Building Trust in Children: How Parents Talk to Children about Safety Precautions in Sweden." *International Review of Victimology* 23, no. 1 (January 2017): 3–16. https://doi.org/10.1177/0269758016672373.

———. "Gendered Fear Strategies: Intersections of Doing Gender and Fear Management Strategies in Married and Divorced Women's Lives." *Sociological Focus* 41, no. 1 (February 2008): 34–52. https://doi.org/10.1080/00380237.2008.10571322.

———. "Until Death Do Us Part? Husband Perceptions and Responses to Fear of Crime." *Deviant Behavior* 31, no. 1 (December 18, 2009): 33–59. https://doi.org/10.1080/01639620902854704.

———. "Women Doing Fear: Applying the Doing Gender Framework to Women's Fear of Crime." Doctoral dissertation, Southern Illinois University, 2005.

Rader, Nicole E., and Stacy H. Haynes. "Avoidance, Protective, and Weapons Behaviors: An Examination of Constrained Behaviors and Their Impact on Concerns about Crime." *Journal of Crime and Justice* 37, no. 2 (2012): 197–213. https://doi.org/10.1080/0735648X.2012.723358.

———. "Gendered Fear of Crime Socialization: An Extension of Akers's Social Learning Theory." *Feminist Criminology* 6, no. 4 (October 1, 2011): 291–307. https://doi.org/10.1177/1557085111408278.

Rader, Nicole E., Gayle M. Rhineberger-Dunn, and Lauren Vasquez. "Victim Blame in Fictional Crime Dramas: An Examination of Demographic, Incident-Related, and Behavioral Factors." *Women and Criminal Justice* 26, no. 1 (January 2016): 55–75. https://doi.org/10.1080/08974454.2015.1023487.

Raley, Sara, and Suzanne Bianchi. "Sons, Daughters, and Family Processes: Does Gender of Children Matter?" *Annual Review of Sociology* 32, no. 1 (2006): 401–21. https://doi.org/10.1146/annurev.soc.32.061604.123106.

"Rape Aggression Defense System Programs (R.A.D.)." Denham Springs, LA: R.A.D. Systems International Headquarters, n.d. http://www.rad-systems.com/rad_programs.html.

Reid, Lesley Williams, and Miriam Konrad. "The Gender Gap in Fear: Assessing the Interactive Effects of Gender and Perceived Risk on Fear of Crime." *Sociological Spectrum* 24, no. 4 (July 2004): 399–425. https://doi.org/10.1080/02732170490431331.

Reisig, Michael D., and Roger B. Parks. "Can Community Policing Help the Truly Disadvantaged?" *Crime and Delinquency* 50, no. 2 (April 2004): 139–67. https://doi.org/10.1177/0011128703253157.

Rhineberger-Dunn, Gayle, Steven J. Briggs, and Nicole E. Rader. "The CSI Effect, DNA Discourse, and Popular Crime Dramas." *Social Science Quarterly* 98, no. 2 (June 2017): 532–47. https://doi.org/10.1111/ssqu.12289.

Rich, John A., and Courtney M. Grey. "Pathways to Recurrent Trauma among Young Black Men: Traumatic Stress, Substance Use, and the 'Code of the Street.'" *American*

Journal of Public Health 95, no. 5 (May 2005): 816–24. https://doi.org/10.2105/AJPH.2004.044560.

Ridgeway, Cecilia L. "Framed Before We Know It: How Gender Shapes Social Relations." *Gender and Society* 23, no. 2 (April 2009): 145–60. https://doi.org/10.1177/0891243208330313.

Ridgeway, Cecilia L., and Lynn Smith-Lovin. "The Gender System and Interaction." *Annual Review of Sociology* 25 (1999): 191–216.

Riggs, Samantha, and Carrie L. Cook. "The Shadow of Physical Harm? Examining the Unique and Gendered Relationship between Fear of Murder Versus Fear of Sexual Assault on Fear of Violent Crime." *Journal of Interpersonal Violence* 30, no. 14 (2014): 2383–2409. https://doi.org/10.1177/0886260514553117.

Robinson, M.B. *Media Coverage of Crime and Criminal Justice*. Durham, NC: Carolina Academic Press, 2018.

Romer, Daniel, Kathleen Hall Jamieson, and Sean Aday. "Television News and the Cultivation of Fear of Crime." *Journal of Communication* 53, no. 1 (2003): 88–104. https://doi.org/10.1111/j.1460-2466.2003.tb03007.x.

Ryan, Kathryn M. "The Relationship between Rape Myths and Sexual Scripts: The Social Construction of Rape." *Sex Roles* 65, no. 11–12 (December 2011): 774–82. https://doi.org/10.1007/s11199-011-0033-2.

Sakdiyakorn, Malinvisa, Maria Golubovskaya, and David Solnet. "Understanding Generation Z through Collective Consciousness: Impacts for Hospitality Work and Employment." *International Journal of Hospitality Management* 94 (April 2021): 102822. https://doi.org/10.1016/j.ijhm.2020.102822.

Schildkraut, Jaclyn, and Glenn W. Muschert. "Media Salience and the Framing of Mass Murder in Schools: A Comparison of the Columbine and Sandy Hook Massacres." *Homicide Studies* 18, no. 1 (February 2014): 23–43. https://doi.org/10.1177/1088767913511458.

Schildkraut, J.H., J. Elsass, and C. Stafford. "Could It Happen Here? Moral Panic, School Shootings, and Fear of Crime among College Students." *Crime, Law, and Social Change* 63 (2015): 91–110.

Schneider, Joseph W. "Defining the Definitional Perspective on Social Problems." *Social Problems* 32 (1985): 232–240.

Schreck, Christopher J, and Mitchell J Miller. "Sources of Fear of Crime at School." *Journal of School Violence* 2, no. 4 (December 12, 2003): 57–79. https://doi.org/10.1300/J202v02n04_04.

Scott, Hannah. "Stranger Danger: Explaining Women's Fear of Crime," *Western Criminology Review* 4, no. 3 (2003): 203–214.

Shields, M. "Community Belonging and Self-Perceived Health." *Health Reports*, Statistics Canada, Catalogue, 19, no. 2 (2008): 82–103.

Simpson, Brian. "Tracking Children, Constructing Fear: GPS and the Manufacture of Family Safety." *Information and Communications Technology Law* 23, no. 3 (September 2, 2014): 273–85. https://doi.org/10.1080/13600834.2014.970377.

Singer, Brett. "11 Best Apps for Parents to Monitor Their Kids." *Parents*, 2020. https://www.parents.com/parenting/technology/best-apps-for-paranoid-parents/.

Sink, Alexander, and Dana Mastro. "Depictions of Gender on Primetime Television: A Quantitative Content Analysis." *Mass Communication and Society* 20, no. 1 (January 2, 2017): 3–22. https://doi.org/10.1080/15205436.2016.1212243.

Skogan, Wesley G, and Susan M Hartnett. *Community Policing, Chicago Style.* New York: Oxford University Press, 2000. http://www.dawsonera.com/depp/reader/protected/external/AbstractView/S9780195350449.

Smith, T., M. Davern, J. Freese, and S. Morgan. "General Social Surveys, 1972–2018." Chicago: National Opinion Research Center, 2018.

Smith, William R., and Marie Tortensson. "Gender Differences in Risk Perception and Neutralizing Fear of Crime: Toward Resolving the Paradoxes." *The British Journal of Criminology* 37, no. 4 (October 1, 1997): 608–34. https://doi.org/10.1093/oxfordjournals.bjc.a014201.

Smith Lee, Jocelyn R., and Michael A. Robinson. "'That's My Number One Fear in Life. It's the Police': Examining Young Black Men's Exposures to Trauma and Loss Resulting from Police Violence and Police Killings." *Journal of Black Psychology* 45, no. 3 (April 2019): 143–84. https://doi.org/10.1177/0095798419865152.

Snedker, Karen A. "Altruistic and Vicarious Fear of Crime: Fear for Others and Gendered Social Roles." *Sociological Forum* 21, no. 2 (June 1, 2006): 163–95. https://doi.org/10.1007/s11206-006-9019-1.

———. "Explaining the Gender Gap in Fear of Crime: Assessments of Risk and Vulnerability among New York City Residents." *Feminist Criminology* 7, no. 2 (April 1, 2012): 75–111. https://doi.org/10.1177/1557085111424405.

Sorkhabi, N., and J. Mandara. "Are the Effects of Baumrind's Parenting Styles Culturally Specific or Culturally Equivalent?" In *Authoritative Parenting: Synthesizing Nurturance and Discipline for Optimal Child Development,* edited by Robert Larzelere, Amanda Sheffield Morris, and Amanda Harrist. Washington, DC: American Psychological Association, 2012.

Stanko, Elizabeth A. "Warnings to Women: Police Advice and Women's Safety in Britain." *Violence against Women* 2, no. 1 (March 1996): 5–24. https://doi.org/10.1177/1077801296002001002.

———. "Women, Crime, and Fear." *The Annals of the American Academy of Political and Social Science* 539, no. 1 (May 1, 1995): 46–58. https://doi.org/10.1177/0002716295539001004.

Stives, Kristen L., David C. May, Melinda Pilkinton, Cindy L. Bethel, and Deborah K. Eakin. "Strategies to Combat Bullying: Parental Responses to Bullies, Bystanders, and Victims." *Youth and Society* 51, no. 3 (April 2019): 358–76. https://doi.org/10.1177/0044118X18756491.

Stokes, M. "Stranger Danger: Child Protection and Parental Fears in the Risk Society." *Amsterdam Social Science* 1, no. 3 (2009): 6–24. https://www.semanticscholar.org/paper/Stranger-Danger%3A-Child-Protection-and-Parental-in-Stokes/8605d54a79757ebd36778bd0561aa6b31b5faa16.

Stubbs-Richardson, Megan, Nicole E. Rader, and Arthur G. Cosby. "Tweeting Rape Culture: Examining Portrayals of Victim Blaming in Discussions of Sexual Assault Cases on Twitter." *Feminism and Psychology* 28, no. 1 (February 2018): 90–108. https://doi.org/10.1177/0959353517715874.

Suarez, Eliana, and Tahany M. Gadalla. "Stop Blaming the Victim: A Meta-Analysis on Rape Myths." *Journal of Interpersonal Violence* 25, no. 11 (November 2010): 2010–35. https://doi.org/10.1177/0886260509354503.

Surette, Ray. *Media, Crime, and Criminal Justice: Images, Realities, and Policies.* 4th ed. Belmont, CA: Wadsworth, 2011.

Swartz, Kristin, Bradford W. Reyns, Billy Henson, and Pamela Wilcox. "Fear of In-School Victimization: Contextual, Gendered, and Developmental Considerations." *Youth Violence and Juvenile Justice* 9, no. 1 (January 1, 2011): 59–78. https://doi.org/10.1177/1541204010374606.

Telegraph Reporters. "Master of Media Circus for Madeleine McCann." *The Telegraph*, April 24, 2008. https://www.telegraph.co.uk/news/1902515/Master-of-media-circus-for-Madeleine-McCann.html.

"The ID Kit: Inkless Fingerprint I.D. Kit." The National Child Identification Program, n.d. childidprogram.com.the-id-kit/2021.

The National Association for Student Affairs Administration in Higher Education, n.d. https://naspa.org/.

Thorne, Barrie. *Gender Play: Girls and Boys in School*. New Brunswick, NJ: Rutgers University Press, 1993.

Tulloch, Marian I. "Parental Fear of Crime: A Discursive Analysis." *Journal of Sociology* 40, no. 4 (December 1, 2004): 362–77. https://doi.org/10.1177/1440783304048380.

Turner, Jennifer L. "Black Mothering in Action: The Racial-Class Socialization Practices of Low-Income Black Single Mothers." *Sociology of Race and Ethnicity* 6, no. 2 (April 2020): 242–53. https://doi.org/10.1177/2332649219899683.

Turney, Kristin. "The Mental Health Consequences of Vicarious Adolescent Police Exposure." *Social Forces* 100, no. 3 (2022): 1142–69.

U.S. Department of Homeland Security. "K-12 School Security: A Guide for Preventing and Protecting against Gun Violence." Washington, DC: U.S. Department of Homeland Security, 2018. https://www.cisa.gov/publication/k-12-school-security-guide.

Valcke, M., S. Bonte, B. De Wever, and I. Rots. "Internet Parenting Styles and the Impact on Internet Use of Primary School Children." *Computers and Education* 55, no. 2 (September 2010): 454–64. https://doi.org/10.1016/j.compedu.2010.02.009.

Valentine, Gill. "'Oh Yes I Can.' 'Oh No You Can't': Children and Parents' Understandings of Kids' Competence to Negotiate Public Space Safely." *Antipode* 29, no. 1 (1997): 65–89. https://doi.org/10.1111/1467-8330.00035.

Valentine, Gill, and John McKendrick. "Children's Outdoor Play: Exploring Parental Concerns about Children's Safety and the Changing Nature of Childhood." *Geoforum* 28, no. 2 (May 1, 1997): 219–35. https://doi.org/10.1016/S0016-7185(97)00010-9.

Van der Burgt, Danielle. "Spatial Avoidance or Spatial Confidence? Young People's Agency in the Active Negotiation of Risk and Safety in Public Space." *Children's Geographies* 13, no. 2 (March 4, 2015): 181–95. https://doi.org/10.1080/14733285.2013.828455.

Vigderman, Aliza. "Do I Need a Security System?" security.org, August 23, 2021. https://www.security.org/home-security-systems/do-i-need-one/.

Vilalta, Carlos J. "Fear of Crime and Home Security Systems." *Police Practice and Research* 13, no. 1 (February 1, 2012): 4–14. https://doi.org/10.1080/15614263.2011.607651.

Vozmediano, Laura, César San-Juan, Ana I. Vergara, and Natalia Alonso-Alberca. "'Watch out, Sweetie': The Impact of Gender and Offence Type on Parents' Altruistic Fear of Crime." *Sex Roles* 77, no. 9 (November 1, 2017): 676–86. https://doi.org/10.1007/s11199-017-0758-7.

Wallace, Lisa Hutchinson, and David C. May. "The Impact of Parental Attachment and Feelings of Isolation on Adolescent Fear of Crime at School." *Adolescence* 40, no. 159 (September 22, 2005): 457.

Warr, Mark, and Christopher G. Ellison. "Rethinking Social Reactions to Crime: Personal and Altruistic Fear in Family Households." *American Journal of Sociology* 106, no. 3 (2001): 551–78. https://doi.org/10.1086/318964.

Weitzer, Ronald, and Charis E. Kubrin. "Breaking News: How Local TV News and Real-World Conditions Affect Fear of Crime." *Justice Quarterly* 21, no. 3 (September 1, 2004): 497–520. https://doi.org/10.1080/07418820400095881.

West, Candace, and Don H. Zimmerman. "Doing Gender." *Gender and Society* 1 (1987): 125–51.

Wilcox, Pamela, Carol E. Jordan, and Adam J. Pritchard. "Fear of Acquaintance Versus Stranger Rape as a 'Master Status': Towards Refinement of the 'Shadow of Sexual Assault.'" *Violence and Victims* 21, no. 3 (June 1, 2006): 355–70. https://doi.org/10.1891/vivi.21.3.355.

———. "A Multidimensional Examination of Campus Safety: Victimization, Perceptions of Danger, Worry about Crime, and Precautionary Behavior among College Women in the Post-Clery Era." *Crime and Delinquency* 53, no. 2 (April 2007): 219–54. https://doi.org/10.1177/0097700405283664.

Wilcox, Pamela, David C. May, and Staci D. Roberts. "Student Weapon Possession and the 'Fear and Victimization Hypothesis': Unraveling the Temporal Order." *Justice Quarterly* 23, no. 4 (December 1, 2006): 502–29. https://doi.org/10.1080/07418820600985362.

Windhorn, Courtney Heath, Nicole E. Rader, and Margaret Ann Hagerman. "Decision-Making in Families Project." Unpublished, 2020.

Winfrey, Oprah. "How to Protect Yourself against an Attacker." *The Oprah Winfrey Show: The Podcast*. https://omny.fm/shows/the-oprah-winfrey-show-the-podcast/the-oprah-winfrey-show-how-to-protect-yourself-aga#description.

———. *The Oprah Winfrey Show*. Harpo Productions, n.d. https://www.oprah.com/.

Yavorsky, Jill E., Claire M. Kamp Dush, and Sarah J. Schoppe-Sullivan. "The Production of Inequality: The Gender Division of Labor across the Transition to Parenthood." *Journal of Marriage and Family* 77, no. 3 (2015): 662–79. https://doi.org/10.1111/jomf.12189.

Young, Hannah L., Alfred F. Mancuso, Ellen Faherty, Sally A. Dorman, and Jessica R. Umbrell. "Helping Child Victims of Family Violence through School Personnel: An Evaluation of a Training Program." *Journal of Aggression, Maltreatment, and Trauma* 16, no. 2 (June 2, 2008): 144–63. https://doi.org/10.1080/10926770801921386.

Zhang, A., L. Musu-Gillette, and B.A. Oudekerk. "Indicators of School Crime and Safety: 2015." U.S. Department of Education and U.S. Department of Justice: National Center for Education Statistics and Bureau of Justice Statistics, 2016.

Index

ADT (home security company), 59–60
Altar, Evan, 81
American Civil War, racialized fears of rape, 12
Anderson, Elijah, 32
Authoritarian parenting, 18, 20
Authoritative parenting, 18, 20
Authority figures: asking for help from, 129–130; learning fear from, 33–34
Avoidance behaviors, 60–68; avoiding places, 61–63; avoiding public spaces, 9, 11, 13, 15–16, 61–63, 66; voluntary versus involuntary activities, 65
Avoidance privilege, 67–68, 139

Beauty standards, 3
Best, Joel, 8
Bogels, Susan, 81
Bolton, Amanda, 65
Brownlow, Alec, 65–66
Brussoni, Mariana, 113
Bubble-wrap generation, 83, 96
Bubble-wrap parenting, 83–84, 87, 96, 142–143
Buddy system, as precautionary behavior, 14, 64, 73–75
Bullying: cyberbullying, 36–37, 101–103, 147; peer mediation programs, 128–129, 137; prevention and intervention programs, 117–118, 120–121, 128–129, 136–137; risk-perception of, 97; statistics, school-related, 34
Bystander, being a good, 129, 130, 139, 144–146
Bystander intervention programs, 134–135, 137, 138, 145–146

Campbell, Alex, 14, 57
Cherniawsky, Sydney, 73
Children and teens: auditory bubble, as fear management strategy, 114–115; empowerment and boldness strategies, 115; fear of crime, disguising, 125–127; fear of crime, fluctuation of, 119–120; fear of crime, parental safety messaging and, 112–116; feeling safe, effective messaging, 122–125; parental safety messaging, what youth hear, 109–112; risk-confrontation strategies, 114–115; safety messaging, to other youth, 128–131; school safety messaging, what youth hear, 116–121
Cobbina, Jennifer, 13
Community, sense of, 113, 123
Community policing, 134
Connell, Nadine, 38, 103
Cossman, Lynne, 15
COVID-19 pandemic, prevention measures, 49–50

Crime myths, 6. *See also* Stranger danger myth; Victim-centered crime prevention myth; White woman crime victim myth

Crime prevention, precautionary behaviors: action-based, 50–60; adaptation, 68–77; avoidance-oriented, 60–68; avoiding places, 61–63; buddy system, 73–75; changing routine activities, 63–67; consequences of, 77–79; escorts, male romantic partners as, 71–73; guns, 50–53; home security systems, 58–60; independent women and, 77; mace/pepper spray, 53–54; resistance, adapting through, 75–77; self-defense courses, 54–58; self-talk, 69–71; social control of women, 58, 78–79; types of, 50

Criminal justice system, 133–135; Black parents and families, impact on, 31–33; bystander intervention programming, 134–135; community policing, 134; media depictions of, 47; police officers, interactions with women crime victims, 133–134; police recruitment, 134; social service agencies, 134; victim-centered prevention myth, 14–15

Cyberbullying, 101–103, 147; crime myths and, 102–103; as criminal behavior, 101–102; definition, 101; statistics, 102

Daniels, Elizabeth, 3
Day, Kristen, 11
De Groof, Saskia, 5, 20
De Welde, Kristine, 11–12, 17, 57–58
Ding, Ding, 93–94
Drakulich, Kevin, 90
Dunaway, Gregory, 116

Eijk, Gwen van, 76–77
Ellison, Christopher, 22, 81
Emotion work, 23
Escorts, male, as adaptation precautionary behavior, 71–73

Fathers: precautionary behavior messaging from, 51, 53; safety messaging from, 22, 27–30, 90

Fear of crime: advantages of, 132; disguising, teens, 125–127; fluctuation of, 119–120; gendered, 2, 5–6, 20–22, 132–133; harassment as predictor of, 61; media messaging, 41–43, 53; parental messaging, 19–22, 27–31, 80, 109, 112–115; parenting styles and, 19–22. *See also* Crime myths; Gendered crime and safety beliefs; Parents, crime and safety messaging

Fear of strangers. *See* Stranger danger myth
Fear work transference, 25–28, 72–73
Femininity, 3, 4, 16, 76–77
Ferraro, Kenneth F., 10
Fisher, Bonnie, 65
Fishman, Gideon, 22
Foster, Sarah, 21
Fox, James, 33
Framing: definition, 34; of school safety, 34–36, 38; of school shootings, 104–105; of tracking apps, 99
Francis, Jacinta, 81–82, 98
"Free-range" parenting, 19
Fridel, Emma, 33

Gendered crime and safety beliefs, 4–6, 89–91; media messaging, 39–46; parental messaging, 22–33; school messaging, 33–39. *See also* White woman crime victim myth
Gender-fear paradox, 2, 132–133
Gender gaps: international gender equality rankings, 150; unpaid work and division of labor, 4
Gender Play (Thorne), 2–3
Gender rules, 2–4; childhood play and identity, 2–3; media images, 3; social life, 4; speech patterns, 3; work, 3–4
General Social Survey (GSS), 7
Generation X: definition, 8; kidnapping, fear of, 87–91; negative health consequences, 94; safety lesson locking doors, 86–87; safety lessons, calling home, 85–86; safety lessons, gender differences, 89–91; safety values, learned as children, 84–85; supervision, parental, 86–87, 90–94, 97, 99–100; technology, as new boogieman, 96–99; technology, new fears of, 94–95
Generation Z: childhood, as indoor activity, 83; definition, 9, 83; parental safety messaging, 85–94; parental safety messaging, internet culture, 85, 94–99; stranger-perpetrated kidnapping, fear of, 9; teaching resilience to, 148
Goodey, Jo, 127
Goodrum, Sarah, 60
Grey, Courtney, 32
Guns: in active shooter simulation drills, 38; fear of, 52; ownership/use, as crime prevention behavior, 49–52, 76; ownership/use, gender differences, 51–53; ownership/use, research on, 51. *See also* School shootings

Hagerman, Maggie, 105, 109, 116
Harassment, as predictor of fear of crime, 61
Heath, Courtney, 105, 109, 116
Helicopter parenting, 19, 83–84, 99, 142
Hignite, Lance, 53
Hodes, Martha, 12
Hollander, Jocelyn, 63
Holloway, Natalee, 1
Home security systems, 58–60
Huskey, Michael, 38, 103

Internet. *See* Technology and internet

Kardian, Steve, 15
Katz, Jackson, 146
Keane, Carl, 61–62
Kidnapping: fingerprinting and Child ID kits, 87–88; Generation X, safety values of, 87–91; media coverage, 1, 45–46; "missing children," coining of the phrase, 8; missing white woman syndrome, 11; paranoid parenting, 83; parental over-supervision, 87, 91–92; parental views, generational differences, 8–9; prevention strategies, 1–2; school safety messages, 38; statistics, 8; stranger danger myth, 8–9, 10, 22, 38
Kitchen, Peter, 123
Kleck, Gary, 51
Koskela, Hille, 115
Ku Klux Klan, 12

Lawson, Katie, 90
Lee, Sou, 51–52
Lessne, Deborah, 124
Liebler, Carol, 11
Life360 (tracking app), 99–100
Liska, Allen, 59, 100
Livingston, Sonia, 97–98

Mace/pepper spray, 28, 53–54, 139
Madriz, Esther, 13–14 66–67
Malone, Karen, 83
Malone Gonzalez, Sharon, 31
Marshall, Shantal, 53
Masculinity, 52, 66, 127
Mastro, Dana, 3
May, David, 20–21, 60, 116
McCann, Madeleine, 1
Media: accountability and improvement of, 135; fictional and reality crime shows, 46–48; gendered crime myths learned from, 39–44; gender role attitudes influenced by, 3; gender rules, messaging, 3; industry, how programming is chosen, 135; kidnappings, coverage of, 1, 45–46; magazine articles, 3, 19; news stories, 44–46; *Oprah Winfrey Show, The*, 39–41, 46, 56; perceptions of crime influenced by, 42–44; perceptions of school shootings influenced by, 104; perceptions of victims influenced by, 47, 133
Mesch, Gustavo, 22, 64–65
Miller, Mitchell, 39, 116–117, 124
Missing white woman syndrome, 11, 138
Morrison, Melanie, 73
Morrongiello, Barbara, 89
Mothers: Black mothers, police talk by, 31–32; fear of social media, 98; safety messaging by, 84; safety messaging from, 22–30; safety values learned and passed on by, 85–91; school shootings, framing of, 105; stereotypes, 3–4; tracking app marketing to, 99–100
Mullins, Christopher, 51–52
Muschert, Glenn, 104

Nasar, Jack, 65
National Association for Student Affairs Administrators in Higher Education, campus safety guidance, 73–74
National Child Identification Program (NCIP), 88
Naumann, Laura, 53
Neglectful parenting, 18–19, 20
Neighborliness, youth perceptions of, 113
New Super Power for Women, The (Kardian), 15
Nikolic, Milica, 81
Nostalgia, safety lessons and, 91–94

O'Neal, Elizabeth, 84

Pain, Rachel, 82, 91
Paranoid parenting, 82–83
Parenting styles, 18–20, 24; authoritarian parenting, 18, 20; authoritative parenting, 18, 20; bubble-wrap parenting, 83–84, 87, 96, 142–143; definition, 18; fear of crime, influence on, 19–22; "free-range" parenting, 19; helicopter parenting, 19, 83–84, 99, 142; neglectful parenting, 18–19, 20; paranoid parenting, 82–83; permissive parenting, 18, 19, 20
Parents, crime and safety messaging, 22–33, 112–116, 140–141; of Generation X, 85–94; what youth hear, 109–112. *See also* Fathers; Mothers

Pepper spray/mace, 28, 53–54, 139
Permissive parenting, 18, 19, 20
Play, outdoor: children's views of, 113; gender differences of children's behaviors, 140, 142–143; gender rules, 2–3; of Generation X, as children, 91–94; restricting, negative consequences of, 143; risk-taking, parental gender differences, 89; unsupervised, 90–94, 113, 140
Plumert, Jodie, 84
Police and policing. *See* Criminal justice system
Porter, Jeremy, 15
Precautionary behaviors. *See* Crime prevention, precautionary behaviors
Privilege: avoidance, 67–68, 139; economic, 59, 60; gendered, 10–11; racialized, 10–11, 139
Public spaces, fear of: fear landscapes, 65–66; gender differences in adults, 15–16, 65–66; gender differences in children, 5, 6; parental messages and, 5, 80, 83, 86, 87, 110–111; parental surveillance and, 92; racialized, 58 (*see also* White woman crime victim myth); safety guidelines for children and, 5, 29–30, 84; youth teaching youth, 130
Public spaces, precautionary measures: avoidance, 9, 11, 13, 15–16, 61–63, 66; avoidance privilege, 67–68, 139; buddy system, 73–75; media messages, 44; social control through, 79; teens, risk-management strategies used by, 114–116; weapon, carrying a, 9, 53, 68, 114

Racialization: of fear of public spaces, 58 (*see also* White woman crime victim myth); of fears of rape, 12; of images of crime and, 12; of parental socialization, 31; of privilege, 10–11, 139
Racism: crime myths and, 33; racialized images of crime and, 12; racialized parental socialization and, 31; talking about, 144
Ramsey, JonBenet, 1
Rape Aggression Defense Systems Program (R.A.D.), 55
Rengifo, Andres, 65
Resistance, as adaptation precautionary behavior, 75–77
Rhineberger, Gayle, 47
Rich, John, 32
Ridgeway, Cecilia, 2
Risk perception, crime and, 97–98

Safety values and lessons: calling home, 85–86; gender differences, 89–91; kidnapping, 87–91; locking doors, 86–87; negative health consequences, 94; technology, as new boogieman, 96–99; technology, new fears of, 94–95
Schildkraut, Jaclyn, 104
Schools: bullying prevention programs, 120–121; educational safety campaigns, 34–38; framing school safety, 34–36, 38; improving safety messaging in, 136–138; peer mentor programs, 128–129; safety messaging, what youth hear, 116–121; safety messaging from authority figures, 33–34
School safety drills: active shooter simulation drills, 38; efficacy and negative impacts of, 39, 117–119, 136; Generation Z, commonplace for, 103, 117–118; improvements to, 136; lockdown drills, 38; options-based models, 38–39
School shootings, 103–106; Columbine, Colorado, 103–104; fears of, by Generation X parents, 104–106; framing, 104–105; media coverage, 103–104; prevention programs, 117–120, 136; safety drills, 38, 103, 117–118, 136; Sandy Hook (Newton, Connecticut), 103–106; school safety messages, 103; Uvalde, Texas, 103–104
Schreck, Christopher, 39, 116–117, 124
Scott, Hannah, 9, 61
Self-defense courses, 11, 54–58, 68
Self-talk, as adaptation precautionary behavior, 69–71
Sink, Alexander, 3
Slavery, 12
Smart, Elizabeth, 1
Snedker, Karen, 23
Social control, 58, 78–79
Socialization: fear of crime, role of media, 41–43, 53; fear of crime, role of parents, 19–22, 27–31, 80, 109; gender, 5, 90; police talk, 31; racial, 13–14, 30–31; reverse, 97
Social media: cyberbullying, 101–102, 121, 136; fears of, by parents, 98; fears of, by youth, 147; generational differences, Generation X and Generation Z, 95
Social service agencies, 134
Socio-economic status (SES), crime beliefs and, 81–82
Speech patterns, gendered, 3
STAAR victim prevention campaign, 15
Stanko, Elizabeth, 78
Stereotypes: of criminals and victims, 12–13, 46; gendered, 3–4, 78
Stokes, M. A., 7, 82

Stranger danger myth, 6–10; cyberbullying and, 102–103; educational programs, 7; kidnapping, 8–9; male strangers, 7–8; media messaging, 40, 43, 47, 135; parental safety lessons and, 23, 24, 93–94, 99–100, 109–110; personal characteristics of strangers, 7–8; precautionary behaviors and, 54–55, 58–60, 61, 66, 74, 88; safety values and, 82–84, 86–88, 93–94, 96, 100; school messaging, 37, 38, 39; sexual assault, 9–10; stranger-induced victimization statistics, 6–7; Swedish parents, conversations about, 141–142; victim-centered prevention and, 14–15; youth messaging to other youth, 130

Supervision, parental, 20; gender differences, 5, 21, 86, 87, 90, 140, 142–143; by Generation X, 86–87, 90–94, 97, 99–100; over-supervision, 87, 91–94, 99–100, 106, 140, 143; parenting styles and, 19–21, 24–25, 82, 86, 87; unsupervised play, 90–94, 113, 140

Teachers: as authority figures, 129–130; fear messaging, 38; feeling of safety provided by, 123–125; training on family violence, 137–138; victims of violence, 35

Technology and internet: cyberbullying, 101–103, 147; tracking apps and programs, 99–100, 106–107. *See also* Social media

Teens. *See* Children and teens

Telephone, game of, 108, 110, 121, 131

Television. *See* Media

Thorne, Barrie, 2–3

Tracking apps and programs, 99–100, 106–107

Turner, Jennifer, 31

Turney, Kristin, 32

Valcke, Martin, 97

Van der Burgt, Danielle, 114–115, 120

Victim-centered crime prevention myth, 14–17; cyberbullying and, 103; definition, 14; femininity and, 16, 76–77; literature, 14–15; media messaging and, 14–15, 40, 44, 47; parental safety lessons and, 28–29, 100, 103; "perfect" victim status, 16–17, 43, 77; precautionary behaviors and, 55, 57, 68–69, 78

Victimization: fathers, safety messaging, 27–29; gendered safety myths, 2; media messaging, 43–44, 46–48; online, 96, 102–103; precautionary behaviors and beliefs about, 51, 53, 54–64, 77–78; racial differences and beliefs about, 32–33, 81–82; school statistics, 33; statistics, 2; stranger danger myth and, 6–10; victim-centered crime prevention myth and, 14–17; white woman crime victim myth and, 10–14

Vilalta, Carlos, 58

Vomediano, Laura, 21

Wallace, Lisa, 20–21

Warr, Mark, 22, 81

West, Candace, 4

White woman crime victim myth, 10–14; avoidance privilege and, 67, 139; cyberbullying and, 102; gendered safety lessons and, 2, 17; media messaging, 47; precautionary behaviors and, 55, 57–58, 67; racialized privilege, 10–11; vulnerability, perceived, and, 11

Yanez, Christine, 124

Yavorsky, Jill, 4

Zimmerman, Don, 4

Nicole E. Rader is Professor and Head of the Department of Sociology at Mississippi State University. She is the coauthor of *Fear of Crime in the United States: Causes, Consequences, and Contradictions*.